The Plague in Print

Medieval & Renaissance Literary Studies

IN PRINT

Essential Elizabethan Sources, 1558–1603

Transcribed and edited with critical commentary by

DUQUESNE UNIVERSITY PRESS
PITTSBURGH, PENNSYLVANIA

Published in the United States of America by
Duquesne University Press
600 Forbes Avenue
Pittsburgh, Pennsylvania 15282

Library of Congress Cataloging-in-Publication Data

The plague in print : essential Elizabethan sources, 1558–1603 / transcribed and edited with critical commentary by Rebecca Totaro.
p. cm.—(Medieval & Renaissance literary studies)
Includes bibliographical references and index.
Summary: "This collection of early modern writing related to the bubonic plague includes remedies, literature, orders, prayers, and a bill—each modernized and annotated with two accompanying glossaries, one general and one for medical and herbal terms; the author's commentary highlights the cultural significance of plague references in various early modern literature"—Provided by publisher.
ISBN 978-0-8207-0426-5 (cloth)
1. Plague—England—Literary collections. 2. English literature—Early modern, 1500–1700. 3. Plague—England—History—16th century—Sources. 4. Plague—England—History—17th century—Sources. 5. Plague in literature. I. Totaro, Rebecca Carol Noel, 1968–
PR1125.P53 2009
820.9'3561—dc22

2009037182

∞ Printed on acid-free paper.

Contents

Illustrations

Acknowledgments

The Plague in Print: Elizabethan Essential Sources, 1558–1603 grew out of research conducted for *Suffering in Paradise: The Bubonic Plague in English Literature from More to Milton* (Duquesne University Press, 2005). Augmented by ongoing scholarly exchange with the members of the 2006–07 Folger Institute Colloquium "Vernacular Health and Healing," directed by Mary E. Fissell. Colloquium member Lisa Meloncon acted as a sounding board for chapter 1, bringing her expertise in medieval medical manuscripts to my aid. This research continued during a short-term fellowship at the Folger Shakespeare Library in 2007–08 and the balance of a sabbatical year at Florida Gulf Coast University. I am particularly appreciative of the efforts of university librarians Rachel Cooke and Rebecca Donlan, whose ability to secure access to rare books and manuscripts exceeds my expectations every year. Thanks also to university colleagues Kimberly Jackson, who offered advice on the proposal and introductory material; Patricia Rice, who reviewed the introduction and chapter 6 in full; Joe Wisdom, who as department chair supported my sabbatical and fellowship applications; and S. Gregory Tolley for his review of scientific names in the medical and herbal glossary. Another special debt of gratitude is owed to University of Tennessee, Knoxville, graduate students Deidre Anne Evans and Teresa Hooper for their assistance with the translation of Latin passages. A graduate of Florida Gulf Coast University, Deidre fielded questions over the 2008–09 academic year, and Teresa produced the first translation into English of the letters by William Bullein that are appended to the 1564 edition of *A Dialogue both pleasant and pietyful* (chapter 1). I am also grateful to the editors of and reviewers for Duquesne University Press who joined with me in what quickly became a team effort: thanks especially to the outside reviewer for comments that have made the collection more appealing and useful; to Marketing and Business Manager Lori Crosby for carrying the work forward to readers; to Production Editor Kathy McLaughlin Meyer and freelance editor Ryan M. M. Pfahl, whose reviews of the introductory material, transliterations, and rather daunting notes and appendices have improved the whole, from coherence to punctuation; and to Duquesne University Press Director Susan Wadsworth-Booth, who with professionalism, candor, and patience brought us together and moved the project forward, enhanced at every step.

Introduction

Mention the bubonic plague and the response might very well be, "Bring out your dead!"—a line from the plague scene in *Monty Python and the Holy Grail* that turned the horror of the Black Death into humor for movie audiences of the 1970s and established a quasi-medieval context for the film. However appealing or humorous Camelot appears in film and in legend, life in fourteenth century England was difficult and the bubonic plague pandemic that by some accounts killed as much as half of the world's population made it worse. England's last major outbreak, now known as the "Great Plague" of 1665–66, figures as the subject of Daniel Defoe's *A Journal of the Plague Year* (1722). There were many outbreaks of the plague in the years between 1348 and 1666. *The Plague in Print: Essential Elizabethan Sources, 1558–1603,* performs the important function of revealing in primary documents the power of plague in these years. Well after the Black Death and before the Great Plague, plague writing became a stable, distinct, and popular genre. More specifically, it was in Elizabethan England that plague writing first unfolded fully into recognizable subgenres that addressed religious, medical, civic, social, and individual needs.

The Plague in Print is the only edited collection of this distinct, influential, and provocative writing. The works in this volume merit sustained reading. Each is an engaging product of complex rhetorical strategies intended to alter the thoughts and actions of readers, and each either was widely disseminated and reprinted with little variation in consecutive plague years or is representative of the more ephemeral writing that addressed the needs of a particular plague year. In addition, each work represents a subgenre of plague writing: plague remedy, plague prayer, plague order, plague literature, and plague bill. These categories of plague writing would remain stable through the 1660s and in some cases into and far beyond the eighteenth century, when England feared that the plague that was raging on the continent would again cross the channel.

William Bullein's *A Dialogue both pleasant and pietyful* (1564) is the exemplary piece of plague writing in this collection. Printed in 1564, expanded for publication in 1573, and reprinted in 1578, Bullein's dialogue is an original narrative, written specifically and entirely to address the threat of the bubonic plague. Literary depictions of plague prior to this were limited in scope, like the frame story in Boccaccio's *Decameron* or the appearance of plague in Chaucer's *Pardoner's Tale*, neither of which takes the plague as its primary subject. Bullein crafted a multilayered, lengthy dialogue to bring comfort to readers by offering them a sourcebook of medical and theological advice, replete with a useful index. The opening and closing letters, including another complete and previously untranslated plague remedy in Latin, reinforce these messages, as does its full 1564 title: *A Dialogue both pleasant and pietyful, wherein is a goodly regiment against the fever Pestilence, with a consolation and comfort against death.* Bullein secured a large readership for his plague dialogue not by focusing only on the bleak reality of visitations but by supplying "pleasant" literary entertainment, with morality tales, travel accounts, humorous husband-wife banter, and satire built into the dialogue. This single source exemplifies the interdisciplinary, overlapping approaches early modern men and women took as they attempted to understand, prevent, and recover from the plague.

The 1578 *Orders thought meet* of Queen Elizabeth I is another highlight of the collection, similarly addressing several concerns and serving multiple functions. Intended to manage local government response to the plague throughout England, *Orders* covers everything from charity for the poor who are afflicted to the specific responsibilities of local officials charged to monitor plague and to quarantine those who were found to be infected. Among the orders are statements intended to ensure that local community leaders would find them fair and flexible enough to allow for modification both over time and in the case of special circumstances. In addition, the orders include an extensive plague remedy appended at the end, intended to supply medical information free of charge to the public. The full title of the orders reveals its multiple functions: *Orders, thought meet by her Majesty, and her privy Council, to be executed throughout the Counties of this Realm, in such Towns, Villages, and other places, as are, or may be hereafter infected with the plague, for the stay of further increase of the same. Also, an advice set down upon her Majesty's express commandment by the best learned in Physic within this Realm, containing sundry good rules and easy medicines, without charge to the meaner sort of people, as well for the preservation of her good Subjects from the plague before infection as for the curing and ordering of them after they shall be infected.*

By the end of the sixteenth century, English plague writing had emerged fully formed to endure for generations. Under the Stuarts, it would increase in volume, with changes that were subtle and primarily content-specific, as can be seen in Thomas Dekker's approach to plague literature in *The Wonderful Year* (1603), which concludes this collection. Chronologically, thematically, and structurally, Dekker's prose narrative remains true to Elizabethan efforts to grapple with the plague, and it hints at what would be found during the Stuart years: government instituted corporal punishment for breaking quarantine; hope for relief from the plague ceasing to compensate for the increase in its virulence; and disciplinary specialization increasing and limiting the number of texts that attempted to serve multiple purposes. *The Wonderful Year* is more strictly literary than theological or medical in content and purpose, and it comes already tainted with a tone of bitter resolve, if not outright outrage, which would compete with a qualified hope in the form of Puritan providentialism.

The works in this collection also point up the current void in the emerging canon of popularly known plague writing from Boccaccio's *Decameron* to Camus's *The Plague* and Kushner's *Angels in America*. The most essential English plague writing is often left out of consideration largely due to the interdisciplinarity that gave it viability in the early modern marketplace of print. William Bullein was a physician but his dialogue doubles as a learned Protestant theological treatise, for example. Thomas Moulton was a Dominican friar, but he is known to us because of his popular and influential plague remedy. These authors display knowledge in their professional subject areas but they speak with equal conviction and accuracy from alternative disciplinary vantage points—in all cases, employing an array of period and discipline specific terms that are utterly foreign to most readers now. This collection significantly reduces if not eliminates these difficulties while remaining true to the original words of the authors, from dedicatory materials and indices to closing remarks and printing house identification. By reading a plague entertainment such as Bullein's *A Dialogue both pleasant and pietyful* or Dekker's *The Wonderful Year* in full and side-by-side with plague orders, plague bills, plague prayers, and plague remedies, we gain unique access to the thoughts and practices—literary, religious, medical, social, and civic—of early modern men and women.

These representative writings also cohere around themes that we can now identify as particular to early modern English plague writing: among them, that the plague threatens utter annihilation on a biblical scale; nature is made unnatural as parents abandon their children; the opportunities for selfish gain increase in plague-time; city dwellers may carry the plague with them into the country when they flee, and the country is not always a safe haven; the plague is a shape shifter; mirth is as important to health as bloodletting; one should not only pray but also be careful to avoid bad air; and the harmful effects of the plague are exacerbated by rumor. By reading these collected sources together, we hear the repetition of beliefs and anxieties that bear the marks of prolonged and shared suffering. Furthermore, when these themes emerge in texts with which we are already more familiar, such as Spenser's poetry, Marlowe's plays, Donne's sermons, Milton's epics, Defoe's novels, or Swift's satirical travel account, we are in a better position to engage with them in fresh ways. By attending to plague writing, our ears become more attuned to early modern literature as a repository of cultural meaning wrought in the furnace of crisis and its attendant trauma.

These essential Elizabethan sources grant us unusual access to the lives of early modern men and women, even those we think we know best. Once we realize, for example, that the first encounter that Queen Elizabeth I had with the plague during her reign occurred only months following her nearly fatal battle with smallpox, we are in a better position to understand the forces that shaped her approach to leadership and the degree to which her Privy Council members were motivated to protect her and see that she produce an heir. William Shakespeare was born during an unusually intense plague visitation in Stratford-upon-Avon, and some speculate that were it not for the theater-closings of the 1590s and early 1600s, we would not have Shakespeare's poetry, perhaps not even some of his plays. John Milton and Margaret Cavendish were among the many writers who penned their most famous works while the plague raged in London in 1665–66. Highlighting the complexity of a period that contained the most gruesome of physical afflictions and some of the greatest of human achievements at once, the works in this volume provide what Thomas Dekker might have called a "wonderful" entry point not only into early modern literature but also into English lives, disrupted at their most basic levels and in such a manner as to permit an unusual degree of observation, record-keeping, and new thinking about what it meant to be alive and to die. Through these texts we see a heightened appreciation of the materials and practices of life once taken for granted—those crucial to everyday experience and survival as well as to the creation of individual and cultural memory.

These essential sources also give original voice to current thoughts about the relationship between disease and human populations, as the world braces for the next pandemic, and even as the revival of the Monty Python film in musical format suggests. Now on tour throughout England, Canada, and the United States, *Spamalot* won the Tony Award for Best Musical in 2005, and it is no surprise that one of its most celebrated new song and dance numbers is an expansion of the popular plague scene from the 1975 film. In "He's Not Dead Yet," plague victims sing,

> Oh we're off to war
> Because we're not yet dead
> We will all enlist
> As the Knights that Arthur led.

Thumbing their noses both at the plague and at those who would tell them that the best thing they can do in plague-time is stay in bed, the plague victims form not only a chorus but a chorus line, celebrating life in Pythonesque style. They comment on history and on current politics in order to elicit from the audience a cathartic laugh. To elicit this change from suffering to relief, from despair to hope, and from complacency to action is the fundamental purpose of plague writing—a genre that is clearly "not dead yet."

Editorial Notes

My goal has been to make these six early modern texts accessible without compromising their character. In each case, I have reproduced the full printed text of the earliest available and complete edition listed in the English Short Title Catalog, noting for easy identification corresponding Short Title Catalog (STC) numbers, always from the second edition of the STC. I have included in all cases relevant dedicatory remarks, letters, and appended materials. For accuracy, I have compared available copies from research libraries, including the Folger, Huntington, Bodleian, Cambridge, and British libraries. Spelling has been modernized, except in the case of archaic verb endings and obsolete words. Unusual, archaic, and field-specific terms appear in the glossaries: one for general terminology and one for medical and herbal terminology, including weights, measures, tools, and practices. I have regularized the spelling of terms that occur frequently in various texts with various spellings; for example, "herb-of-grace," "HerbGrace," and "herb of grace" become "herb of grace," just as "saith," "sayeth," and "sayth" become "sayeth" in every case. Standardization and definition of terms in the glossaries are based on cross referencing the texts collected here with Oxford English Dictionary entries, early modern herbals—including *The Great Herbal* (1526; STC 13176); *A book of the properties of herbs* (1552; STC 13175.15); and Nicholas Culpeper, *The English Physician* (1652; Wing C7501)—and with the notes and glossaries provided by Hobby, Hibbard, Pendry, and Wilson (editors of other early modern texts noted in "Suggestions for Further Reading"). Identification of proper names listed in the Glossary of Names derives primarily from cross-referencing entries in the Oxford *Dictionary of National Biography* with those in other sources, including dictionaries edited by McKerrow and by Plomer.

I have altered punctuation judiciously when necessary for clarity; this includes the addition of apostrophes for possessives and a modern management of comma, colon, and semicolon usage as well as the addition of quotation and question marks where appropriate. I silently expanded all abbreviations and wrote out Roman numerals, in the case of biblical references turning Roman into Arabic numerals. I have retained the original capitalization and italics in all texts, except when a change of punctuation made it necessary or when consistency within a text or across later editions of the same text recommends it. For example, I have italicized the titles of all medical works, and when in a single work, "God" appeared as "God," "god," and "GOD," I have standardized the capitalization so that all occurrences of the word in that text appear as "God." Notes included in the margins of the original text now appear in the endnotes (always preceded by "[Marginal note]"), as does the occasional clarification of context-specific meaning. In the case of marginal numbering of paragraphs, as in *Orders thought meet,* I have left the numbers in the body of the text, and in the case of exceptionally long paragraphs, as in the homily in *A Form to be used in Common Prayer,* I have divided those in which a shift in content is suggested. Endnotes referring to biblical passages, other than those provided in the original texts as marginal notes, correspond to the Geneva Bible and in some cases are cross-referenced with corresponding passages in the Great Bible to confirm meaning or spellings. For ease of identification, in all texts I have standardized names of books of the Bible; in addition, I have abbreviated them in all notes.

Whenever I have adopted an editorial change, the effort has been to apply it consistently throughout the text in question and across texts as useful. This does not mean that I have provided a flawless execution of transliteration, the task cumbersome and complicated. I expect the reader will discover areas that are less than clear, but it is my hope that these places will be few and that they will be still easier to access than they would be in their original form. As a rule, I have restricted my own speculations on the texts and on the terms within them, leaving analysis to the reader.

1

Plague Remedies

Thomas Moulton: Plague remedy (1531)

As an infusion of classical and continental medical knowledge coincided with an increase in the population and the number of licensed and unlicensed practitioners contributing to the medical marketplace in early modern London, printed health regimens became popular in England, and the majority of them included remedies for plague. In fact, some believe that the first medical book printed in English was the unusual stand-alone plague remedy, *Here beginneth a little book,* dating to 1485 (STC 4589). Authors of these early remedy books were often not physicians but clergy members who borrowed heavily from the medieval plague remedy manuscripts developed in the wake of the 1348 pandemic. In these works, the plague did not appear as a scientifically defined organism that one could track through animal and to human populations but rather as a set of symptoms brought on by a combination of astrological influences, imbalances of bodily humors, and vaporous air—a diagnosis based on humoral theory originating in the writings of Hippocrates and distilled by Galen.

The best known of these medieval plague remedies was written by fourteenth century physician and citizen of Liège, John of

Burgundy. It is this remedy that Dominican friar Thomas Moulton (fl. 1530?) translated into English and revised as a guide for non-specialists desiring practices and recipes they could manage for themselves in their own homes. Moulton's remedy began as a manuscript, a copy of which is housed in the British Library as part of Sloane 3489, a medical miscellany. Highly popular in print form as the first chapter of the anonymous *The Mirror or Glass of Health,* it was reprinted nearly two dozen times in the sixteenth century. Of the editions that have survived largely intact, the first is from 1531, which you will find in this collection (STC 18214a.3). It lacks only the title page, which is here reproduced from a similar copy at the Glasgow University Library (STC 18214a.7). The last edition is from 1580 (STC 18225). In 1657, Moulton's plague remedy was revived as part of another compendium of medical knowledge entitled *The Complete Bone-Setter Enlarged,* and this larger work was reprinted twice more in London's last plague years, 1665 and 1666 (Wing [CD-ROM, 1996] M2967; M2968; and M2968A, respectively). The plague remedy is the only text in this collection that was initially published prior to 1558 and that was predominantly issued in print form as one part of a larger whole. It was republished five times in Elizabeth's reign, and in this case its inclusion in the larger regimen confirms its value as indispensable medical knowledge.

It is likely that for well over 100 years, Moulton's English version of the Burgundy remedy circulated autonomously to some degree as well, perhaps printed on its own but more certainly rebound by owners with various complementary materials, including hand-written remedies. One indication of the autonomy of the plague remedy is in the text itself: namely, the opening introduction by the author which includes an explanation of his purpose for writing. This work set the standard for plague remedy books in the period, and by its discussion of theology, astrology, herbal remedies, and bloodletting practices it reminds us of the complexity of early plague writing. Compare this directly with the plague remedy offered by Medicus in Bullein's *A Dialogue,* with Bullein's

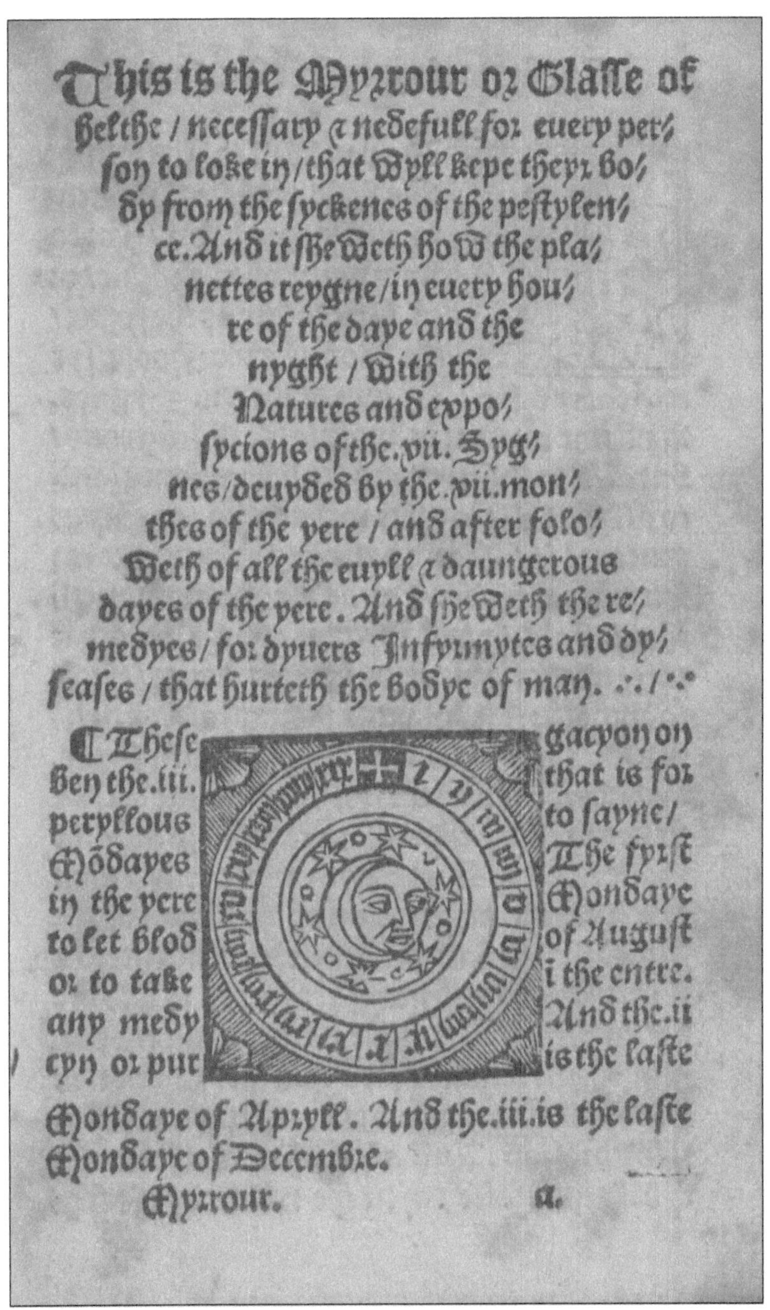

This is the Myrrour or Glasse of
helthe / necessary & nedefull for euery per-
son to loke in / that wyll kepe theyr bo-
dy from the syckenes of the pestylen-
ce. And it sheweth how the pla-
nettes reygne / in euery hou-
re of the daye and the
nyght / with the
Natures and expo-
sycions of the .vii. Syg-
nes / deuyded by the .xii. mon-
thes of the yere / and after folo-
weth of all the euyll & daungerous
dayes of the yere. And sheweth the re-
medyes / for dyuers Infyrmytes and dy-
seases / that hurteth the body of man. .·./·.·

¶ These ben the .iii. perylous Mōdayes in the yere to let blod or to take any medycyn or purgacyon on that is for to sayne / The fyrst Mondaye of August i the entre. And the .ii is the laste Mondaye of Apryll. And the .iii. is the laste Mondaye of Decembre.

Myrrour. a.

Fig. 1. *This is the Mirror or Glass of Health,* title page, STC 18214a.7. Reproduced by permission of the Glasgow University Library.

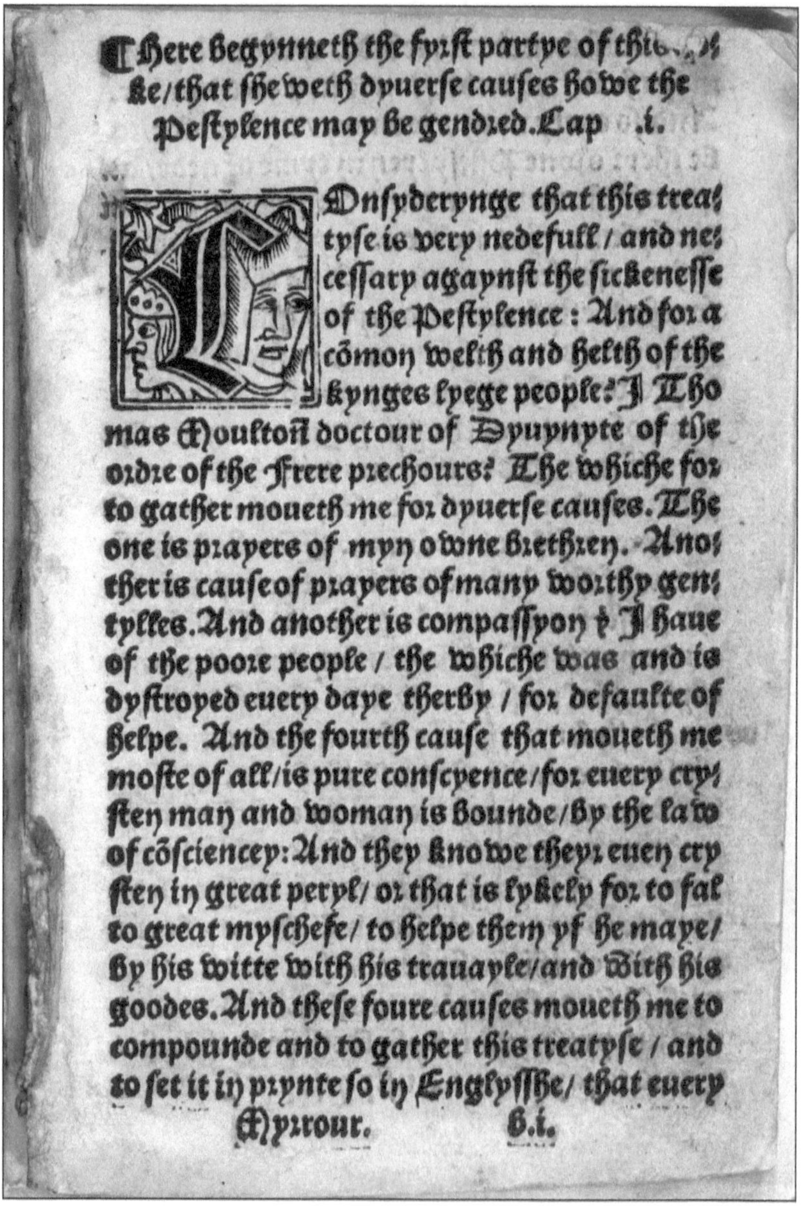

¶ Here begynneth the fyrst partye of this bo=
ke/that sheweth dyuerse causes howe the
Pestylence may be gendred. Cap .i.

Consyderynge that this trea= tyse is very nedefull/ and ne= cessary agaynst the sickenesse of the Pestylence: And for a cōmon welth and helth of the kynges lyege people: I Tho mas Moultoñ doctour of Dyuynyte of the ordre of the Frere prechours: The whiche for to gather moueth me for dyuerse causes. The one is prayers of myn owne brethren. Ano= ther is cause of prayers of many worthy gen= tylles. And another is compassyon ỳ I haue of the poore people / the whiche was and is dystroyed euery daye therby / for defaulte of helpe. And the fourth cause that moueth me moste of all/is pure conscyence/for euery cry= sten man and woman is bounde/by the law of cōsciencey: And they knowe theyr euen cry sten in great peryl/ or that is lykely for to fal to great myschefe/ to helpe them yf he maye/ by his witte with his trauayle/and with his goodes. And these foure causes moueth me to compounde and to gather this treatyse / and to set it in prynte so in Englysshe/ that euery

Myrrour. b.i.

Fig. 2. Plague remedy in *This is the Mirror or Glass of Health,* chapter 1, first page (fol. B1r), STC 18214a.3. Reproduced by permission of the Folger Shakespeare Library.

letter to Richard Turner, and with the plague remedy appended to Queen Elizabeth I's *Orders thought meet.*

Here beginneth the first part of this book that showeth diverse causes how the pestilence may be gendered.

Capitulo one.

Considering that this treatise is very needful and necessary against the sickness of the Pestilence, and for a commonwealth and health of the King's liege people, I, Thomas Moulton doctor of Divinity, of the order of the Frere preachers,[1] the which for to gather moveth me for diverse causes. The one is prayers of mine own brethren. Another is cause of prayers of many worthy gentles. And another is compassion that I have of the poor people that was and is destroyed every day thereby, for default of help. And the fourth cause that moveth the most of all, pure conscience, for every Christian man and woman is bound by the law of conscience, and they know their even Christian[2] in great peril, or that is likely for to fall to great mischief, to help them if he may by his wit, with his travail, and with his goods. And these four causes moveth me to compound and to gather this treatise and to set it in print so in English that every man both learned and lewd, rich and poor, may the better understand it and do thereafter. And so every man, woman, and child to be their own Physician in time of need against the vengeance and corruption of the Pestilence that now is reigning with other diseases many more. And this treatise for the Pestilence is divided and parted in three parts, and consequently ensueth the seven days with the Planets, with the natures and expositions of the twelve Signs, divided by the twelve months of the year, with the remedies for many diverse other diseases that hurteth and grieveth the body of man.

And the first part of this book telleth diverse causes how the Pestilence may be gendered.

The second part telleth how man, woman, and child, shall preserve and keep themself from the Pestilence, if so be that man, woman, or child be curable, that falleth therein.

The third part telleth the remedy, help, and medicine against the Pestilence.

The first part I say of this treatise, as I telled, be showed diverse causes, which may be the ground of this Pestilence that now reigneth. I find by the treating of four doctors, the four Pillars that upholdeth holy church—that is to say Saint Augustine, Saint Jerome, Saint Gregory, and Saint Ambrose—where they speak of this matter, they say that sin that reigneth among the people and namely that sin that reigneth among head men and the governors of the church and of the law is cause of the Pestilence: vengeance, taken for sin. Hereof I find example and figure in holy writ, in the second book of Kings in the 24 Chapter. There showeth holy writ openly that for the sin of king David, God sent unto him his Prophet and gave him choice of three things, whether that he had leuer that God should send upon him, for his sin and of his people, hunger seven year; or else he had leuer that he should send upon him pursuit of Enemies and to be overcome of them three months; or yet that he had leuer that he should send upon him Pestilence three days and three nights. And then king David truly chose Pestilence, so that from that time that he had chosen thus Pestilence, or[3] it were noon of the day, there was dead twenty-seven thousand of his people. And then king David saw that vengeance was taken for his sin by Pestilence. Mourningly with great sorrow and great compassion of heart, he cried, "God almighty. Mercy." And when he had done, anon the Pestilence ceased.

Also for sin that reigned in the people, hideous Pestilence hath been taken, as was showed of Jerusalem, as telleth Vincent in *speculo historiali,* and Eusebius telleth the same.[4] Therefore, every man in what degree or what state he be, put away sin through heartily sorrow and very contrition, asking of God meekly, mercy and forgiveness entirely with shrift of mouth and satisfaction doing and penance for his sins.[5] Then he putteth away the cause of Pestilence, that in case is vengeance taken for sin. And soothly (saving we ought not to deem lightly of God's privates)[6] this may be well one cause of this hideous Pestilence that now is reigning.

Also they say generally in this realm, and sooth it is that many tokens are showed, that men likely deem that this sin is cause in part of this Pestilence as the corrupt air and the venom thereof, the which was caused by a conjunction of Saturn and Jovis. The which planets their working within a few years and the malice of the conjunction and of other sin, this left in the air and beneath. The which malice and venom hath his respect and his influence more in the complexion of man than of beast, in as much as the working of that conjunction and of other sin was more principally in the sin of mankind than in the sin of another manner of beast. But the working of other conjunctions diverse are beforehand, had their working in the signs of other beasts and their influence in the complexions of them. And therefore the malice of the Conjunctions was cause why that the more fell of such beast, more than of other that time. But this Conjunction aforesaid, the which was wrought more principally in the sin of mankind, more than of any other, whose venom and malice yet reigning, is the cause of the corruption of the air, the which air corrupt is cause of the Pestilence that now is reigning. But nevertheless if all so be that it be impossible by all Philosophers that the Element of the air should in his own kind and in his own substance be corrupt or else infect, sithen it is simple and clean is his substance, wrought without any venom or corruption, nevertheless, yet by the way of vaporous humosities and humors the which that are corrupt and drawen from the earth beneath, by virtue Attractive of the bodies that been above, and mingled with the air, so by Accidental cause is the air corrupt and in part cause of this Pestilence.

But then thou mayst mew against me and say that if so were that the venomous air, and the corruption thereof, should be cause of Pestilence (or else man, woman, and child should be infect thereby) that it seemeth every man, woman, and child should be infect and corrupt by the Pestilence in that country the that air corrupt is reigning, sithen the air in such a place is common to all manner of man. To this answereth Avicenna in his *Canon*, in the part there he treateth *De cura Februm*,[7] that if all the Pestilence air be reigning in a country and if it be common to all Inhabitants of that country, yet there shall none be infect therewith but they that be replete and full of corrupt humors, the which corrupt humors hath their respect and, according to, receive the corruption and the venom of that air. Else, in what country or city that such air were corrupt or venomed, in all manner of men that receiveth that air in the same country, or in the same city, should be venomed and dead thereby. Ye see well and know well that the element of the fire hath no predomination nor will not burn but matter that is combustible and according to receive fire. On the same wise, the element of the air that is Pestilence corrupt infect neither man, woman, nor child, but such as hath such venomed and corrupt humors within themself disposed to the same (the Pestilence thereof in such time that such Pestilence air reigneth in). After, diversity of venomous humors and corruption in men reigning, and through the working of that venomous Pestilence air of diverse sickness and perilous, gendered in man, woman, and child. And this alteration in kind is wrought by the malice and influence of the Conjunction aforesaid, the which malice of Conjunction is likely to be cause of many other wonderful Alterations betwixt king and king, lord and lord, man and man, woman and woman, father and son, brother and brother, and many other. Also it is likely to be cause of deposing of lords out of lordships, and enhancing and inhighing of knaves, and emperies of mighty men spoiling and destroying of kingdoms and lordships, and also it is like to be cause of great fires, great mists, and great water by land, and cause of many great perils by the sea. Also it is likely to be cause of many wonderful tokenings of great winds and many other wonderful things. Also destroying of many sects and principally of the Saracen's sect, and of many other wonderful sickness. Also the schism of holy church is likely to cease and diverse states to end, and therewith many things is likely to fall by the judgment of Astronomy, the which I will not write for diverse causes.

But know it well, all manner of men, that these things I rehearse not as things told by prophesy but as conclusions following and showed by Astronomy and also by Astrology for as declareth Hippocrates in his Book that he made (*De Epidemia*) there shall never physician be true in working, no sure practicer of physic, but he work and practice by rules of Astronomy, for Hippocrates sayeth that it is impossible that a man shall cure a sickness but if he know the cause of his sickness. There is some sickness that is caused by moving and working of the bodies above, the which a man may not know without astronomy and astrology. Then it seemeth well that it is impossible to a man to cure sickness generally, but he can of Astronomy and Astrology. For as I find in *Libro interpretationem,*[8] all the four Elements and all other things beneath that been compound of them are gendered by the course of the planets above, and all the lively bodies beneath hath in part, their being, their health, and their sickness by the moving and the sickness of the bodies above.

Thus endeth the first part of this Pestilence treatise.

And followeth the second part that showeth how man should preserve and keep him from the Pestilence.

Capitulo two.

The second part of this treatise is how thou shalt keep, govern, and preserve thyself from the malice of the Pestilence air and from the venom and corruption that is gendered thereby, the which part is principal cause of this Pestilence that now is reigning.

The first and the principal preservation there against is this, to govern thee well and wisely and for to fly all that may gender any fever or ague. First, thou needeth to keep thee severally from all manner of excess and outrage of meat and drink, and namely from all manner of fenors[9] meats as goose, dovebirds, mallards, venison, lamprey, skates, and eels, and also other fenors meats. Eat no great meat, no onions, nor leeks, nor garlic, nor no fruit, for all these gathereth and engendereth unkindly heats and so bringeth a man to an ague, and he be in any wise of nigh disposition thereto. And use no baths nor stews, nor sweat not too much, for all openeth the pores of a man's body and maketh the venomous air to enter and for to infect the blood and the spiritual members of man and for to destroy all lively spirits in man. Also keep thee from haunting of Lechery, for that both openeth the pores and destroyeth the kind natural and also enfeebleth the spiritual members and the lively spirits of man.

Also in the time of Pestilence in no wise suffer too great thirst and if thou thirst, look thou drink but measurably and not but for to slacken thy thirst, and namely such drinks as will abate thy heat, as is Tisane water mingled with vinegar, or water of Borage, water of Endive, water of Lettuce, water of Violets, water of Roses, water of Scabious, water of Tormentil, water of Dittany mingled in even proportion or else by themself. For these drinks, if the Pestilence reign in the heat of the Summer, been profitable and sovereign to them that been Choleric of complexion, for they be hotter and drier than other.

Also to sleep on afternoons and when thou shalt go to bed, shut thy doors and thy windows close, and in an earthen pan full of Charcoal fire, cast this powder made of these things: of Laurel leaves, dried Rosemary, and dried Frankincense, of each of them alike much, and cast half a spoonful of this powder in the fire.

Also use fire in thy chamber all the times of the day and of the night of these things, as fire of Juniper, and if you may not get this Juniper, make the fire of clean dry Ash Wood. And use to cast in the fire always Frankincense, Storax, Calamint, Ladanum, and the fumosities of these, and the smoke. If the air be corrupt of the virtue Attractive, of the lively spirits, and the spiritual members overthwart by the veins of the heart and so envenoms it—and these hasteth a man to his death. But if the matter of the Pestilence be gendered betwixt the thigh and the body, it is a tokening that it commeth from infection of the liver, and then if the matter appear in the share beside the privy members, bleed on the foot in the same side, on the vein that is betwixt thy great toe and the next toe, for if the botch be drawing thither and thou bleed on the arm, the matter then will draw up again to the liver and so to the heart, and that is perilous. And if the botch be more outward to the side and farther from the privy members, bleed then on the vein between the ankle and the foot and the heal or else on the vein that is under the ankle that is called the Saphena, or else look that thou be soon ventosed with a ventosing best beneath the botch, but that is very painful. Nevertheless in case that the vein may not be taken or else that the vein may not bleed, it must needs be suffered in such peril may thou be. If the matter appear in the cleansing part of the head, consider well on what side it appeareth, and bleed on the vein under the tongue on the same side or else on the head vein or on the arm, the which vein lieth next the Cardiacle, the which Cardiacle lieth in the middes of the arm, right in the bought of the arm, or else bleed on the vein that is on the hand, that is betwixt the thumb and the next finger, or else be ventosed betwixt the shoulders. But take good heed that when soever thou hast bled of any of these veins that thou sleep not after thy blood letting of thirteen hours.

If thou be rich and may well spend, then it were good to have this Pomander evermore in thy hand and hold it to thy nose that thou may receive the savor and small thereof. For comforting of the brain and of all other Spiritual members, the which thou shalt make thus: take Ladanum pured, an ounce; storax Calamint, dissolved Roses, Cloves, Maces, of each one three halfpenny weight; of chosen Ambre, and of chosen musk of either of them an halfpenny weight; and make them in powder that ought to be made in powder, and five spoonful of oil of bay, an ounce of virgin wax, and dissolve them. And when they be dissolved, put all together and mingle them well unto they be cold, and make thereof a ball the quantity of a walnut, and that is called the Pomander. The scent or smell thereof will comfort the lively spirits in man, and if thou rule thee thus as I have taught thee, thou may by the grace of God and by this governance preserve thyself from the Pestilence.

Thus endeth the second part of the Pestilence treatise.

And followeth the third part that showeth and a man be taken with the Pestilence, what remedy and medicine is best therefore.

Capitulo three.

Here the third part of this treatise telleth what is against this sickness of the Pestilence that reigneth among the people and what medicine is best therefore. Avicenna in his Canon on that part there he treateth *De cura Februm*, there is no sickness that falleth in kind but there is medicine in kind for it. Therefore if so be it be taken in due time, then if thou shalt fall into this sickness, look that thou be letten blood, as I have told. And if there be any fever or any ague annexed thereto and the corrupt blood be drawen away, on this bleeding as I have told (and the principal members ventosed), the heart ought then to be comforted with good Letwares,[10] or with cold water stilled. The which Letwares be these that will withdraw unkindly heats, as conserve of Violets, conserve of Borage, conserve of Bugloss drawn with Sugar decoct with water of Tormentil, water of Endive, water of Roses, water of Borage, mingled by even proportions. And then take these every day and every hour of the day with water of Tormentil, water of Scabious, water of Violets, or else water of Endive. Also it were needful to have this water distilled of these herbs, of Dittany, of Scabious, of Tormentil, of Violets, of Endive, and Lettuce, and for to drink these mingled in white wine of Gascon, or else of Rochelle wine, and namely the whiles the unkindly heat reigneth.

And it were needful to have water of Roses and Betony to wash thy temples, and thy pulse withal, of thy arms and thy hands. And also it were needful to take of the last, that is to say of Rose, and of Betony, and put thereof in a saucer of pewter or in a silver piece and chafe it a little, and lap a linen cloth fourfold and wet it therein. And that while thou are in thy great heat of the ague, lay the linen cloth wet in the water upon thy temples and upon thy forehead and another upon thy liver. Take also two other cloths lapped and wet on the same wise and lay in every Armhole one. And this practicing shall do thee great ease, whether thou be curable and shall live or incurable and shall die.

But the most needful thing of all, if so be that this appear in any wise foresaid, is for to draw the botch by craft away from the cleansing place, a great space from the heart. And that shall I tell thee how. And in all my practicing in Physic this eighteen year, I wist it never fail but twice and that was not long of the Medicine. And one other time but of other defaults, the which I will not write at this time, though it will expel and void it. And look in the time of Pestilence that thy codwares be always freshly washen, and after the washing look that they be dipped in the fine water of Roses, and on the same wise the kerchief that thou lappest thy head in on nights, and let it dry by the fire, and not by the Pestilence air. And when thou layest thee down to sleep, lay under thy head and under the end of the pillow that is toward thy visage Rosemary, Hyssop, sovereign Mints, Perial rial,[11] Laurel leaves. Put in thy mouth Maces and Cloves, or else Nutmegs. Look every day that thou take of fine Treacle proved the quantity of a bean and a half. Also bear in thy purse these manner of spices: Maces, Cloves, Cubebs, Canel, or else Cinnamon, and chew thereof, and eat thereof all the times of the day.

And if thou be a poor man and may not attend to the costs of these things, take then every day fasting, nine sops in fine vinegar of white wine or else of red wine, and drink to them a saucer full of vinegar or thou pass out of thy house or place.

Also one of the best governance of all is in bloodletting, for thou shalt understand that a man is in spiritual members principal—that is for to say the heart, the liver, and the brain—and every one of these hath his place given him by kind, by the which he may void all such superfluities and cleanse himself.

The heart hath his cleansing place in the armhole.

The cleansing place of the liver is betwixt the thigh and the body.

The cleansing place of the Brain is under the ears at the ear roots and in the throat.

Then this sickness of the Pestilence commeth thus: when the pores of a man are open, then first entereth the venomous and corrupt air and as soon as it hath mastery and mingled with man's blood. Then runneth it to the heart, that is root and ground of man's life, for to destroy mankind and for to infect and destroy all living spirits in a man, and so finally for to kill and slay him. But the heart and the clean blood flyeth all that is noyous and contrarious unto kind. And in as much as in him is expelled all such manner of corruption and venoms, from him to his cleansing place to the armhole. But then, for that place is sometime stopped, that it may not out, and it passeth then all to the principal member next, that is the liver, for to infect and for to destroy it.

And then it doth as the heart doth in his kind and expelleth it from him to his cleansing place betwixt the thigh and the body; for it is also sparred in case, and stopped, it may not out but passeth the meats and the veins unto the third principal member, that is the brain. But then he would expel it to his cleansing place that is under the Ears. And it may not in case out; therefore the stopping and the sparring of the meats and pores and for thickness of the foul and corrupt blood and the venomous matter is moving that is mingled therewith, and thus long time the matter is moving or it resteth in any place, sometime twelve hours and sometime twenty-four hours, and sometime more and sometime less, after the degree and the gentleness and the greatness of the sickness's corruptions and venoms that be gendered. But then at the last sometime within twenty-four hours, it pass not out of the cleansing place, nor at none other place through bleeding; then it festers in some place and cast a man into an ague and maketh a botch in some of the three cleansing places, or else next to them on some vein, for ye shall well wit that a botch groundeth him evermore and setteth on a vein and letteth the blood and letteth the blood then, that it may not have his kindly course by the vein as he should have, but it is infect thereby. And so all the principal and spiritual members are infect, and thus slayeth men.

Finis.

Thus endeth the third part of this Pestilence treatise.

2

Plague Prayers

The Church of England:
A Form to be used in Common prayer (1563)

Between the punctuations of flight and return, people waited out plague visitations, and they did what they could to prepare and defend themselves by turning not only to medical practitioners but also to their Bibles and prayer books, which were indispensable sources of consolation in plague-time. Plague was always construed as a divinely instituted punishment for sin, and the favorable "cures" were prayer and fasting. Psalm 91, for example, promises to those who put their faith in the Lord, "Thou shalt not be afraid... of the pestilence that walketh in the darkness; nor of the plague that destroyeth at noon day." For centuries the church had prescribed not the making of poultices but the organization of special services, not avoidance of vaporous air but the avoidance of sin, not bloodletting but prayer. Prior to the Reformation, the most commonly employed weapon against plague was saintly intercession. After the Reformation, and with the growth of and competition in the medical marketplace, the church stepped up its efforts to comfort and cure during plague-time. Church-directed prayer schedules, public fasts, and communal acts of thanksgiving accompanied each visitation. Individual preachers delivered sermons that were later published, and in 1563, under the direction of the Elizabethan government, the church in England created a nationwide schedule of prayer and fasting. In that year, the first serious plague-year of her reign, Elizabeth I worked with William Cecil (1520–98), Archbishop Matthew Parker of Canterbury (1504–75), and Bishop Edmund Grindal of London (c. 1519–83) to formulate this religious program. Doing so, the government and the church together broke with the past to prescribe actions to be taken against plague by all people in England at once. The schedule of prayer for times of plague included special services on Sundays, Wednesdays, and Fridays in addition to fasting every Wednesday—a practice justified at length with respect to its place in the newly reconstituted Protestant Church of England. They followed this form of common prayer with *A short form of thanksgiving to God for ceasing the contagious sickness of the plague* (STC 16507). *A Form to be used in Common prayer* is the single source in this collection that does not give voice to multiple beliefs about and practices for preventing the plague. It proclaims in providentialist terms that God alone brings plague to the sinful and God alone can heal the faithful. Compare this text with the theology and prayers presented by Theologus in Bullein's *A Dialogue both pleasant and pietyful,* which was printed within the year.

In future plague years, Elizabeth I and her successors reissued *A Form to be used in Common prayer* (STC 16506.3) largely unchanged: see, for example, the versions from 1593 (STC 16524); 1640 (STC 16557); and 1665 (Wing [2nd ed.] C4119A). This form would serve as a model for all alternative schedules of common prayer created in response to crisis, such as that for the great earthquake of 1580 (STC 16512) and to prevent Spanish victory in 1588 (STC 16519).

By the Queen.

Most Reverend father in God, right trusty and right well-beloved, we greet you well. Like as Almighty God hath of his mere

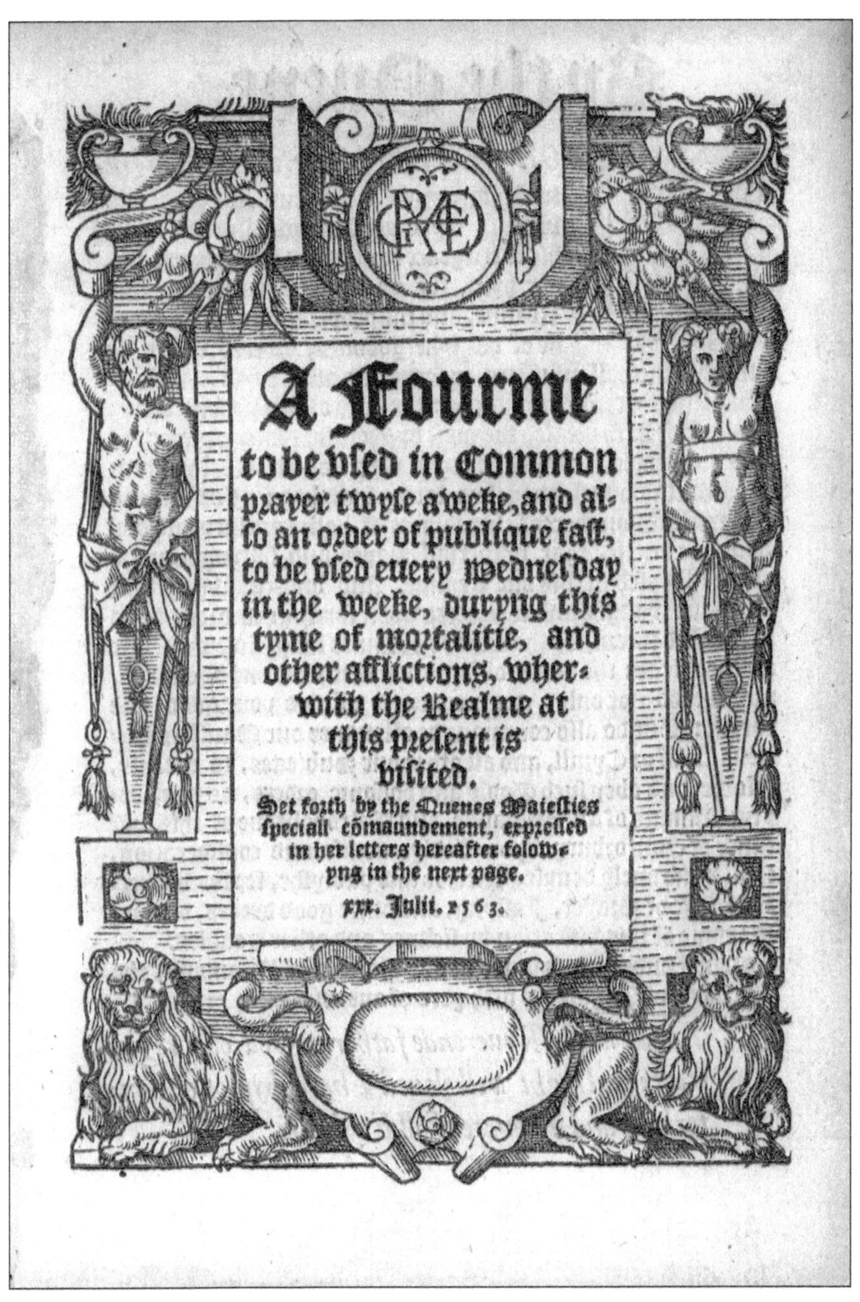

A Fourme
to be vsed in Common
prayer twyse a weke, and al-
so an order of publique fast,
to be vsed euery Wednesday
in the weeke, duryng this
tyme of mortalitie, and
other afflictions, wher-
with the Realme at
this present is
visited.

Set forth by the Quenes Maiesties
speciall cōmaundement, expressed
in her letters hereafter folow-
yng in the next page.

xxx. Iulii. 1563.

Fig. 3. *A Form to be used in Common prayer,* title page, STC 16506.3. Reproduced by permission of the Folger Shakespeare Library.

grace committed to us, next under him, the chief government of this Realm, and the people therein, so hath he of his like goodness ordered under us sundry principal ministers to serve and assist us in this burden. And therefore considering the state of this present time, wherein it hath pleased the most highest, for the amendment of us and our people, to visit certain places of our Realm with more contagious sickness than lately hath been, for remedy and mitigation thereof, we think it both necessary and our bounden duty that universal prayer and fasting be more effectually used in this our Realm. And understanding that you have thought and considered upon some good order to be preserved therein, for the which ye require the application of our authority for the better observation thereof amongst our people, we do not only commend and allow your good zeal therein, but do also command all manner of our Ministers Ecclesiastical or Civil and all other our Subjects to execute, follow and obey such Godly and wholesome orders as you, being Primate of England and Metropolitan of that province of York, upon Godly advice and consideration, shall uniformly devise, prescribe, and publish for the universal usage of Prayer, Fasting, and other good deeds during the time of this visitation by sickness and other troubles.

Given under our Signet, at our Manor of Richmond, the first day of August the fifth year of our reign.

To the most Reverend father in God our right trusty and right well-beloved Archbishop of York and Primate of England.

The Preface.

We be taught by many and sundry examples of holy Scriptures that upon occasion of particular punishments, afflictions, and perils, which God of his most just judgment hath sometimes sent among his people to show his wrath against sin and to call his people to reverence and to the redress of their lives, the godly have been provoked and stirred up to more fervency and diligence in prayer, fasting, and alms deed, to a more deep consideration of their consciences, to ponder their unthankfulness and forgetfulness of God's merciful benefits towards them, with craving of pardon for the time past, and to ask his assistance for the time to come, to live more Godly, and to be defended and delivered from all further perils and dangers. So king David in the time of plague and pestilence which ensued upon his vain numbering of the peopled, prayed unto God with wonderful fervency, confessing his fault, desiring God to spare the people and rather to turn his ire to hymwarde,[1] who had chiefly offended in that transgression. The like was done by the virtuous king Jehosaphat and Ezechias in their distress of wars and foreign invasions. So did Judith and Hester fall to humble prayers in like perils of their people. So did Daniel in his captivity, and many other more in their troubles. Now, therefore, calling to mind that God hath been provoked by us to visit us at this present with the plague and other grievous diseases, and partly also with trouble of wars, it hath been thought meet to set forth by public order some occasion to excite and stir up all godly people within this Realm, to pray earnestly and heartily to God to turn away his deserved wrath from us, and to restore us as well to the health of our bodies by the wholesomeness of the air, as also to Godly and profitable peace and quietness. And although it is every Christian man's duty of his own devotion to pray at all times, yet for that the corrupt nature of man is so slothful and negligent in this his duty, he hath need by often and sundry means to be stirred up and put in remembrance of his duty. For the effectual accomplishment whereof it is ordered and appointed as followeth.

First, that all Curates and Pastors shall exhort their Parishioners to endeavor themselves to come unto the Church with so many of their families as may be spared from their necessary business (having yet a prudent respect in such assemblies to keep the sick from the whole in places where the plague reigneth), and they to resort not only on Sundays and holidays but also on Wednesdays and Fridays during the time of these present afflictions, exhorting them there reverently and Godly to behave themselves and with penitent hearts to pray unto God to turn these plagues from us, which we through our unthankfulness and sinful life have deserved.

Secondly, that the said Curates shall then distinctly and plainly read the general confession appointed in the book of Service, with the residue of the Morning prayer, using for both the Lessons the Chapters hereafter following, that is to say,

For the first Lesson, one of these Chapters, out of the old Testament.

The 2 Kings, Chapter 24; Leviticus 26; Deuteronomy 28; Jeremy 18, unto these words, "Let us, etc." and 22; 2 Paralipomenon,[2] Chapter 34; Isaiah 1; Ezekiel 18 and 19; Joel 2; 2 Esdras 9; Jonas, the 2 and 3 Chapter together. Which Chapters would be read orderly on Sundays, Wednesdays, and Fridays.

And for the second Lesson, one of these Chapters out of the new Testament.

Matthew 3, 6, 7, 24, 25; Luke 13; Acts 2, beginning at these words, "Ye men of Israel hear these words," to the end of the Chapter, etc.; Romans 2, 6, 12, 13; Galatians 5; Ephesians 4, 5; 1 Timothy 2; Apocalypse 2.

The order for the Wednesdays.

On Wednesdays (which be the days appointed for general fast, in such form as shall hereafter be declared), after the Morning prayer ended, as is aforesaid, the said Curates and Ministers shall exhort the people assembled to give themselves to their private prayers and meditations, for which purpose, a pause shall be made of one quarter of an hour and more, by the discretion of the said Curate, during which time, as good silence shall be kept as may be.

That done, the Litany is to be read in the middest of the people, with the additions of prayer hereafter mentioned.

Then shall follow the ministration of the Communion, so oft as a just number of Communicants shall be thereto disposed, with a Sermon, if it can be, to be made by such as be authorized by the Metropolitan or Bishop of the Diocese, and they to entreat of such matters especially as be meet for this cause of public prayer, or else, for want of such Preacher, to read one of the Homilies hereafter appointed, after the reading of the Gospel, as hath been accustomed. And so the Minister, commending the people to God with the accustomed benediction, shall dismiss them.

If there be no Communion, then on every of the said Wednesdays after the Litany, the ten Commandments, the Epistle, Gospel, the Sermon or Homily done, the general usual prayer for the state of the whole Church shall be read, as is set forth in the book of Common prayer. After which shall follow these two prayers: "Almighty God, the fountain of wisdom," etc., and "Almighty God which hath promised," etc., with the accustomed benediction.

The Order for Fridays.

On Fridays shall be only the Morning prayer and the Litany, with the prayers now appointed to be annexed to the same.

Homilies to be read in order on Wednesdays.

1. First, an Homily entitled, "An Homily concerning the Justice of God in punishing of impenitent sinners," etc. newly now set forth for that purpose.
2. The eighth Homily of the first Tome of Homilies,[3] entitled, "Of the declining from God."
3. The ninth Homily of the same Tome, entitled, "An exhortation against the fear of death."
4. The Homily of Fasting, in the second Tome of Homilies.
5. The Homily of Prayer, in the same Tome.
6. The Homily of Alms deeds, in the same Tome.
7. The Homily of repentance, in the same Tome also.

When these Homilies are once read over, then to begin again, and so to continue them in order.

After the end of the Collect in the Litany, which beginneth with these words, "We humbly beseech thee O father," etc., shall follow this Psalm, to be said of the Minister, with the answer of the people.

The Psalm to be said in the Litany before one of the prayers newly appointed, whereof one verse to be said of the Minister, and another by the people, clerk, or clerks.

1. Come let us humble ourselves and fall down before the Lord with reverence and fear (Ps. 95).
2. For he is the Lord our God and we are the people of his pasture and the sheep of his hands.
3. Come therefore, let us turn again unto our Lord, for he hath smitten us and he shall heal us (Hosea 6a).
4. Let us repent and turn from our wickedness, and our sins shall be forgiven us (Acts 3).
5. Let us turn, and the Lord will turn from his heavy wrath and will pardon us, and we shall not perish (Jonas 3).
6. For we acknowledge our faults, and our sins be ever before us (Ps. 51).
7. We have sore provoked thine anger, O Lord. Thy wrath is waxed hot, and thy heavy displeasure is sore kindled against us (Lam. 3).
8. Thou hast in thine indignation stricken us with grievous sickness and by and by we have fallen as leaves beaten down with a vehement wind (Isa. 64).
9. Indeed we acknowledge that all punishments are less than our deservings. But yet of thy mercy, Lord, correct us to amendment and plague us not to our destruction (Jth. 8; Job 11; Wisd. 11).
10. For thy hand is not shortened that thou canst not help; neither is thy goodness abated that thou wilt not hear.

11. Thou hast promised, O Lord, that afore we cry thou wilt hear us; whilest we yet speak thou wilt have mercy upon us (Isa. 65).
12. For none that trust in thee shall be confounded: neither any that call upon thee shall be despised
13. For thou art the only Lord who woundest and dost heal again, who killest and revivest, bringest even to hell and bringest back again (Tob. 3; Job 5; Hosea 6).
14. Our fathers hoped in thee; they trusted in thee and thou diddest deliver them (Ps. 22).
15. They called upon thee and were helped; they put their trust in thee and were not confounded.
16. O Lord, rebuke us not in thine indignation; neither chasten us in thy heavy displeasure (Ps. 6).
17. O remember not the sins and offences of our youth, but according to thy mercy think thou upon us, O Lord, for thy goodness (Ps. 25).
18. Have mercy upon us, O Lord, for we are weak. O Lord, heal us, for our bones are vexed.
19. And now in the vexation of our spirits and the anguish of our souls, we remember thee and we cry unto thee: hear, Lord, and have mercy (Bar. 3; Jonas 2).
20. For thine own sake and for thy holy namesake incline thine ear and hear, O merciful Lord (Dan. 9).
21. For we do not pour out our prayers before thy face, trusting in our own righteousness, but in thy great and manifold mercies.
22. Wash us thoroughly from our wickedness and cleanse us from our sins.
23. Turn thy face from our sins and put out all our misdeeds.
24. Make us clean hearts, O God, and renew a right spirit within us.
25. Help us, O God of our salvation, for the glory of thy name. O deliver us and be merciful unto our sins for thy namesake (Ps. 79).

26. So we that be thy people and sheep of thy pasture shall give thee thanks for ever and will always be showing forth thy praise from generation to generation.
27. Glory be to the father and to the son, etc. As it was in the beginning, is now, and ever shall be, etc.

After this Psalm shall be said by the Curate or Minister openly and with a high voice, one of these three prayers following. And after that, orderly the rest of the Collects appointed in the Litany. At which time, the people shall devoutly give ear and shall both with mind and speech to themselves assent to the same prayers.

A Prayer, containing also a Confession of Sins, which is to be said after the Litany as well upon Sundays as Wednesdays and Fridays.

Almighty, most just and merciful God, we here acknowledge ourselves most unworthy to lift up our eyes unto heaven, for our conscience doth accuse us and our sins do reprove us. We know also that thou Lord, being a just judge, must needs punish the sins of them which transgress thy law. And when we consider and examine all our whole life, we find nothing in ourselves that deserveth any other thing but eternal damnation. But because thou, O Lord, of thy unspeakable mercy, hast commanded us in all our necessities to call only upon thee and hast also promised that thou wilt hear our prayers, not for any our desert (which is none) but for the merits of thy son our only Savior Jesus Christ, whom thou hast ordained to be our only mediator and intercessor. We lay away all confidence in man and do flee to the throne of thy only mercy, by the intercession of thy only son, our Savior Jesus Christ.

And first of all, we do most lament and bewail from the bottom of our hearts our unkindness and unthankfulness towards thee our Lord, considering that besides those thy benefits which we enjoy as thy creatures common with all mankind, thou has bestowed many and singular special benefits upon us, which we are not able in heart to conceive, much less in words worthily to express. Thou hast called us to the knowledge of thy Gospel. Thou hast released us from the hard servitude of Satan. Thou hast delivered us from all horrible and execrable Idolatry, wherein we were utterly drowned and hast brought us into the most clear and comfortable light of thy blessed word, by the which we are taught how to serve and honor thee and to live orderly with our neighbors in truth and verity. But we, most unmindful in times of prosperity of these thy great benefits, have neglected thy commandments, have abused the knowledge of thy Gospel, and have followed our carnal liberty, and served our own lusts, and through our sinful life have not worshipped and honored thee as we ought to have done. And now, O Lord, being even compelled with thy correction, we do most humbly confess that we have sinned and have most grievously offended thee by many and sundry ways. And if thou, O Lord, wouldest now, being provoked with our disobedience, so deal with us as thou might and as we have deserved, there remaineth nothing else to be looked for but universal and continual plagues in this world, and hereafter eternal death and damnation, both of our bodies and of our souls. For if we should excuse ourselves, our own consciences would accuse us before thee and our own disobedience and wickedness would bear witness against us. Yea, even thy plagues and punishments which thou dost now lay upon us in sundry places do teach us to acknowledge our sins. For seeing, O Lord, that thou art just, yea even justice itself, thou punishest no people without desert. Yea, even at this present O Lord, we see thy hand terribly stretched out to plague us and punish us. But although thou shouldest punish us more grievously than thou hast done and for one plague send an hundred, if thou shouldest pour upon us all those the testimonies of thy most just wrath, which in times past thou pourest on thy own chosen people of Israel, yet shouldest thou do us no wrong, neither could we deny but we had justly deserved the same. But yet, O merciful Lord, thou art our God, and we nothing but dust and ashes. Thou art our creator, and we the work of thy hands. Thou art our pastor; we are thy flock. Thou art our redeemer, and we thy people redeemed. Thou art our heavenly father; we are thy children. Wherefore punish us not, O Lord, in thine anger, but chasten us in thy mercy. Regard not the horror of our sins but the repentance thereof. Perfect that work which thou hast begun in us, that the whole world may know that thou art our God and merciful deliverer.

Thy people of Israel often times offended thee and thou most justly afflicted them, but as oft as they returned to thee, thou didst receive them to mercy. And though their sins were never so great, yet thou always turned away thy wrath from them and the punishment prepared for them, and that for thy covenant sake, which thou made with thy servants Abraham, Isaac, and Jacob. Thou hast made the same covenant with us (O heavenly father) or rather a covenant of more excellency and efficacy and that namely through the mediation of thy dear son Jesus Christ our Savoir, with whose most precious blood it pleased thee that this covenant would be as it were, written, sealed, and confirmed. Wherefore, O heavenly father, we, now casting away all confidence in ourselves or in any other creature, do flee to this most holy covenant and Testament wherein our Lord and Savior Jesus Christ once offering himself a sacrifice for us on the cross, hath reconciled us to thee for ever. Look therefore O merciful God, not upon the sins which we continually commit but upon our mediator and peacemaker Jesus Christ, that by his intercession thy wrath may be pacified and we again by thy fatherly countenance relieved and comforted. Receive us also into thy heavenly defense and govern us by thy holy spirit to frame in us a newness of life, therein to laud and magnify thy blessed name for ever and to live every of us according to the several state of life whereunto thou Lord hast ordained us.

And although we are unworthy (O heavenly father) by means of our former foul life, to crave any thing of thee, yet because thou hast commanded us to pray for all men, we most humbly here upon our knees beseech thee, save and defend thy holy Church; be merciful, O Lord, to all commonweals, Countries, Princes, and Magistrates, and especially to this our Realm and to our most gracious Queen and governor Queen Elizabeth. Increase the number of Godly Ministers. Endue them with thy grace to be found faithful and prudent in their office. Defend the Queen's Majesty's Council and all that be in authority under her or that serve in any place by her commandment for this Realm. We commend also to thy fatherly mercy all those that be in poverty, exile, imprisonment, sickness, or any other kind of adversity and namely those whom thy hand now hath touched with any contagious and dangerous sickness, which we beseech thee, O Lord, of thy mercy (when thy blessed will is) to remove from us and in the meantime grant us grace and true repentance, steadfast faith, and constant patience, that whether we live or die, we may always continue thine, and ever praise thy holy name and be brought to the fruition of thy Godhead. Grant us these and all other our humble petitions (O merciful father) for thy dear son's sake, Jesus Christ our Lord. Amen.

Or else in the stead of the other, this Prayer may be used, and so to use the one one day, the other an other.

Eternal and ever living God, most merciful father, which of thy great long suffering and patience has hitherto suffered and borne with us most miserable offenders who have so long strayed out of thy way and broken all thy laws and commandments, and have, neither by thy manifold benefits bestowed upon us unworthy and unthankful sinners nor by the voice of thy servants and preachers by continual threatening out of the holy word, hitherto been moved, either as thy children of love to return unto thee our most gracious father, either for fear of thy judgments or as humble and lowly servants to turn from our wickedness. And therefore, most righteous judge, thy patience being (as it were) overcome at the last with our obstinate unrepentance, thou hast most justly executed those of thy terrible threats now partly upon us, by plaguing us so (with most dreadful and deadly sickness, with troubles of wars, with penury and scarceness of food and vittal) whereby great multitudes of us are daily afflicted and consumed, we beseech thee O most merciful father, that in thy wrath thou wilt remember thy old great mercies, and to correct us in thy judgments, and not in thy just anger, lest we be all consumed and brought to naught. Look not so much upon us as upon our deservings, O most righteous judge, to take just vengeance on our sins, but rather remember thy infinite mercies, O most merciful father, promised to us by thy dearly beloved son our Savior Jesus Christ, for whose sake, and in whose name, we do earnestly and humbly crave mercy and forgiveness of our sins and deliverance from this horrible sickness, being thy just punishment and plague for the same. And as thy holy word doth testify that thy people of all ages, being justly plagued for their sins, and yet in their distress unfeignedly turning unto thee and suing for thy mercy, obtained the same. So likewise we, most worthily now afflicted with grievous and dreadful plagues for our iniquities, pray thee, O most merciful father, to grant us thy heavenly grace, that we may likewise both truly and unfeignedly repent and obtain thy mercy and deliverance from the same which we beseech thee, O father of all mercies and God of all consolation, to grant us for the same Jesus Christ's sake, our only Savior, mediator and advocate. Amen.

This prayer may be said every third day.

It had been the best for us, O most righteous Judge, and our most merciful father, that in our wealths and quietness, and in the middest of thy manifold benefits continually bestowed upon us most unworthy sinners, we had of love harkened to thy voice and turned unto thee our most loving and gracious father. For in so doing, we had done the parts of good and obedient, loving children. It had also been well if at thy dreadful threats out of thy holy word continually pronounced unto us by thy servants our preachers, we had of fear, as corrigible servants, turned from our wickedness. But alas, we have showed hitherto ourselves towards thee neither as loving children (O most merciful father), neither as tolerable servants,

O Lord most mighty. Wherefore now we feel thy heavy wrath, O most righteous Judge, justly punishing us with grievous and deadly sickness and plagues. We do now confess and acknowledge, and to our most just punishment do find indeed to be most true, which we have so often heard threatened to us out of thy holy scriptures, the word of thy eternal verity that thou art the same unchangeable God of the same justice that thou wilt, and of the same power that thou canst, punish the like wickedness and obstinacy of us impenitent sinners in these days as thou has done in all ages heretofore. But the same thy holy Scriptures, the word of thy truth, do also testify that thy strength is not shortened but that thou canst, neither thy goodness abated, but that thou wilt, help those that in their distress do flee unto thy mercies, and that thou art the same God of all, rich in mercy, towards all that call upon thy name and that thou dost not intend to destroy us utterly but fatherly to correct us, who hast pity upon us, even when thou dost scourge us, as by thy said holy word, thy gracious promises, and the examples of thy saints in thy holy Scriptures expressed for our comfort, thou hast assured us. Grant us, O most merciful father, that we fall not into uttermost of all mischiefs to become worse under thy scourge but that this thy rod may by thy heavenly grace speedily work in us the fruit and effect of true repentance, unfeigned turning, and converting unto thee—a perfect amendment of our whole lives that, as we through our impenitency do now most worthily feel thy justice punishing us, so by this thy correction, we may also feel the sweet comfort of thy mercies graciously pardoning our sins and pitifully releasing these grievous punishments and dreadful plagues. This we crave at thy hand, O most merciful father, for thy dear son our Savior Jesus Christ's sake. Amen.

A short meditation to be said of such as be touched in affliction.

O father, doubtless our own wickedness do reward us, but do thou, O Lord, according to thy name. Our oft transgressions and sins be many. Against thee have we sinned, yet art thou the comforter and helper of thy humble subjects in the time of their trouble. For thou O Lord art in the middes of us, and thy name is called upon us. Forsake us not, O God. Forsake us not for the merits of thy only son our Savior Jesus Christ, to whom with thee and the holy ghost be all honor and glory. Amen.

Psalms which may be sung or said before the beginning, or after the ending of Public Prayer.

1, 2, 3, 4, 5, 6, 13, 15, 25, 26, 30, 32, 46, 51, 67, 79, 84, 91, 102, 103, 107, 123, 130, 143, 147.

The Order for the general Fast.

It is most evident to them that read the Scriptures that both in the old Church under the law and in the Primitive Church under the Gospel, the people of God hath always used general fasting both in times of common calamities as War, Famine, Pestilence, etc., and also when any weighty matter touching the estate of the Church or the commonwealth was begun or intendeth. And it can not be denied but that in this our time, wherein many things have been reformed according to the doctrine and examples of God's word and the Primitive Church, this part for fasting and abstinence, being always in the Scripture as a necessary companion joined to fervent prayer, hath been too much neglected.

Wherefore, for some beginning of redress herein, it hath been thought meet to the Queen's Majesty, that in this contagious time of sickness and other troubles and unquietness, according to the examples of the Godly king Jehosaphat, and the king of Ninive, with others, a general Fast should be joined with general Prayer throughout her whole Realm and to be observed of all her godly Subjects, in manner and form following.[4]

1. First, it is ordained that the Wednesday of every week shall be the day appointed for this general Fast.

2. Secondly, all persons between the age of sixteen years and

sixty (sickly folks and laborers in harvest or other great labors, only, expected) shall eat but one only competent and moderate meal upon every Wednesday. In which said meal shall be used very sober and spare diet, without variety of kinds of meat, dishes, spices, confections, or wines, but only such as may serve for necessity, comeliness, and health.

3. Item, in that meal it shall be indifferent to eat flesh or fish, so that the quantity be small and no variety or delicacy be sought. Wherein every man hath to answer to God if he in such Godly exercises either contemn Public order or dissemble with God, pretending abstinence and doing nothing less.

4. Item, those that be of wealth and ability ought that day to abate and diminish the costliness and variety of their fare and increase therewith their liberality and alms towards the poor that the same poor, which either indeed lack food or else that which they have is unseasonable and cause of sickness, may thereby be relieved and charitably succored to be maintained in health.

5. Last of all, this day being in this manner appointed for a day of general Prayer and Fasting ought to be bestowed by them which may forbear from bodily labor in Prayer, study, reading, or hearing of the Scriptures, or good exhortations, etc., and when any dullness or weariness shall arise, then to be occupied in other godly exercises. But no part thereof to be spent in plays, pastimes, or idleness, much less in lewd, wicked, or wanton behavior.

When there is a Sermon, or other just occasion, one of the Lessons may be omitted, and the shortest of the three prayers appointed in the Litany by this order may be said, and the longest left off.

Forasmuch as diverse Homilies, appointed before to be read in this form of Common prayer, are contained in the second Tome of Homilies now lately set forth by the Queen's Majesty's authority, therefore it is ordered that the Churchwardens of every Parish shall provide the same second Tome or book of Homilies with all speed, at the charges of the Parish.

An Homily concerning the Justice of God in punishing of impenitent sinners and of his mercies towards all such as in their afflictions unfeignedly turn unto him. Appointed to be read in the time of sickness.

The most righteous God, and the same our most merciful father, abhorring all wickedness and impiety, and delighting in all righteousness and innocency, and willing that we his people and children should herein be conformed and become like to our God and heavenly father, that we might be also partakers of his inheritance and everlasting kingdom, in his holy Scriptures containing the perfect rule of righteousness and written for our learning and direction towards his said kingdom, both by great threatenings doth continually fear us from all impiety and wickedness so displeasant to him and also by most large and gentle promises like a loving father, doth provoke and incite us to righteousness and holiness so acceptable unto him, and so leaveth nothing unassayed, no ways unproved, whereby he might save us from perpetual destruction and bring us to life everlasting. To this end, all those threatenings of temporal punishments and plagues whereof the Scriptures be so full, are to be referred [to], that we for fear of temporal punishments, refraining from all unrighteousness, might also escape eternal pain and damnation. Whereunto it would finally bring us, if we should not by repentance turn from the same and return unto our God and most merciful father, who would not the destruction and death of sinners but rather that they should convert and be saved.[5]

But when he perceiveth that neither gentleness can win us as his loving children, neither fear and threatenings can amend us, as being most stubborn and rebellious servants, at the last he performeth indeed that which he hath so oft threatened, and of fatherly sufferance and mercy so long, upon hope of amendment deferred his longanimity and patience being now overcome with our stony hardness and obstinate impenitency. After this sort, we shall find by the holy Scriptures and histories Ecclesiastical that he hath dealt with his people of all ages, namely the Israelites, whom in sundry other places but especially in the 26 of Leviticus and 28 of Deuteronomy, as well by fair promises as by menaces, he laboreth to bring to due obedience of his law, which is perfect righteousness. "If" (sayeth he) "thou hear the voice of the Lord thy God and keep his commandments, all these blessings shall come upon thee. Thou shalt be blessed in the City and in the field. The seed of thy body, the fruit of thy earth, the increase of thy cattle, shall be blessed, etc. Thou shalt have seasonable weather, fruitful ground, victory of thy enemies, and after, quiet peace in thy costs and I will be thy loving Lord and God, thy aid and defender, and thou shalt be my beloved people.

But if thou wilt not hear the voice of the Lord thy God, nor keep his commandments, but despise his laws, etc., all these curses shall come upon thee. Thou shalt be cursed in the City and in the field. Thy Barn, all thy storehouses shall be cursed. The fruit of thy body, of thy cattle, and of thy ground shall be cursed. Thou shalt be cursed going out and coming in. The Lord shall send thee famine and necessity. He shall strike thee with agues, heats, and colds, with pestilences, and all other evil diseases, yea, and with all the botches and plagues of Egypt. He shall make heaven over thee as it were of brass, and the earth which thou treadest on as it were Iron. He shall send thee unseasonable weather, etc., wars, and overthrow thee at thine enemy's hands, and thy carrion shall be a pray to the birds of the air and the beasts of the earth, and there shall be no man to drive them away," and so forth: many more most horrible evils and mischiefs, written at large in those two Chapters, where ye may see how lovingly on the one part he promiseth to the obedient and how terribly on the other part he threateneth the disobedient and how largely and at length he prosecuteth the matter, specially in the threatenings and the menaces, most meet for the Jews, a people ever stiff necked and rebellious.

And indeed the whole writings of the prophets and universally of all the Scriptures be nothing else but like callings to true obedience and to repentance from our transgressions by like promises and threatenings, yea, and greater also, as by promise of life everlasting to the faithful obedient and penitent, and contrarily of everlasting damnation and death to the stubborn, rebellious, and impenitent sinners. And to prosecute this matter, when the Jews were monished, remonished, prayed, threatened, so oft by so many prophets, and all in vain, did not the Lord at the last bring upon them all those evils which he had threatened—namely famine, war, and pestilence, as ye may read at large in the books of Judges, Kings, and Chronicles, in the lamentations of Jeremy, namely the 2, 4, and 5 Chapters and in other places of the Prophets and the old Testament, containing the descriptions of extreme famines, horrible wars and captivities, and dreadful plagues, whereby God punished and afflicted his people for their sins and rebellion against him most sharply?[6] Yea, and when all this could not amend them but that they waxed worse under the rod and correction, did he not at the last, which is most horrible, utterly destroy them with famine, war, and pestilence, and carried the rest into captivity and destroyed utterly their Cities and countries, according to the prophecy of Isaiah, and as our savoir Christ likewise in the Gospel foreshoweth of the miserable destruction and ruin of their Cities and temple, so horrible that one stone should not be left upon other?[7] In like manner, the same immutable God proceeded aforetime with the Christians of Asia, Africa, and Greece. He sent them like Prophets, learned doctors, and holy saints—Saint Clement, Ignatius, Tertullian, Cyprian, Origin, Gregorius, Basil, Chrysostom, Augustine, and many more—who out of holy Scriptures likewise warned and warned them again to turn from their sins and to return to God, unto whom after, when they would not be warned with words, he sent them the swords of the Goths, Huns, Vandals, Saracens, and Turks.[8] He sent them likewise famines and pestilences, and finally when neither threats nor punishments could amend them by those nations and especially the Saracens and Turks, he hath either utterly destroyed them or else made them most miserable captives of the miscreants Turks, under them to be in all unspeakable slavery and misery, and that which is most horrible of all, where their forefathers worshipped Christ the Savior of the world, to serve in his stead filthy and damned Mahomet, the deceiver of the world.

Now to come to our times (most dearly beloved in our savior Christ), hath not God likewise begun this order of proceeding with us Christians of this age? Hath he not sent amongst us his Prophets and preachers who out of God's holy word have continually called us to repentance, continually denounced unto us that he is the same immutable God, of the same justice that he will and of the same power that he can persecute the same wickedness and impenitency with like punishments and plagues? In the which also he hath used his wonted clemency in denouncing evils before he bring them upon us, that by speedy repentance we might avoid and escape them. And hath he not, I pray you, prosecuted the same his proceedings with us, also continuing in impenitence, by sending us sundry plagues at sundry times, wars, famines, exiles, horrible fires? And hath he not now at the last, after almost twenty years patience and forbearing of us, sent us the pestilence, which of all sicknesses we most fear and abhor, as indeed it is to be feared? Seeing we have so long despised his justice, requiring our innocency, he cannot but visit with his justice punishing our iniquity, and that he doth the more justly execute upon us than he did upon his people of any time before us, for that we, besides the warning of his Scriptures and preachers of his word, by so many examples of the punishments of all former ages for like vices, have not been amended or moved to any repentance.

Wherefore now at the last, he hath sent to us, that could never in health by any means be brought to the obedience of him, horrible sickness and the dreadful fear of death present at our doors and before our eyes. We that could never skill of compassion towards the misery of others are now ourselves by his just judgments fallen into extreme misery. We that have not visited and comforted the sick, according to God's will, are now fallen into such sickness that the nearest of our friends refuse to visit us. We that could never be brought from the love of this world are now most justly brought in fear suddenly to leave and depart out of this work. We that loved our wicked mammon so much that we could not find in our hearts to bestow any part thereof upon the relief of our poor brethren and sisters are now brought in fear suddenly to lose it altogether, and ourselves also with it, by sudden and dreadful death of our bodies and for the abusing of it, in danger and dread to lose our souls also everlastingly. We that set all our delight in gathering together a heaping of worldly muck, in building of fair houses and purchasing of lands, as though we should live forever, are now justly put in fear of loss of life, and all with it, as the short warning of two or three days and often not many more hours.

All those doctrines of the vanity of this transitory life and world set out in the scriptures in so many places, preached unto us in so many sermons, which we yet could never hitherto by hearing believe, are now put in practice indeed and set before our eyes and our sense to see and perceive most certainly. Wherefore unless we now at the last repent, I see not what time is left for repentance. It had been the best indeed, as we have been oft forewarned, to have turned to our heavenly father in time of quietness for love of our father rather than fear of the rod, for that had been indeed the part of loving and good children, but not to be mended with stripes, is now the part not of servants that be corrigible but of indurate and desperate slaves. Let us not (O dearly beloved) fall into the uttermost of all mischiefs, that we should be incorrigible with punishment also and worse under the scourge, as were those stiff-necked Jews, who when first after threatening and then after plagues of war, famine, and pestilence, they remained indurate and incorrigible.[9] Lastly, as he by his holy Prophets had threatened them, he overthrew them as a high wall down to the ground and dashed them all to pieces, as an earthen vessel, that their ruin might be without help and their destruction remediless. Which most horrible mischief that we may avoid, let us avoid the cause thereof: contempt, obstinacy, and hardness of heart, in God's most just wrath and scourge now used for our correction.

There is yet no cause for all this why we should despair or distrust but rather that we should turn from our sins and return to our merciful father, craving pardon and deliverance at his hand. For the declaration whereof it shall be showed out of the Scriptures,[10] first, that God doth not punish us in this world and send us these miseries and sickness of hatred to destroy us but of love, mercifully to correct us. And out of infinite places, it shall suffice to rehearse a few notable, serving for this purpose. And here the testimony of Job, a man both sore punished and most favored of God, hath a worthy place, who well understanding God's goodness and mercy, even in his grievous punishments: "Blessed or happy" (sayeth he) "is the man whom God punisheth. Therefore refuse not thou the chastening of the almighty. For though he make a wound, he giveth a plaster; though he smite, his hand maketh whole again. He shall deliver thee in six troubles and in the seventh there shall no evil come unto thee. In hunger, he shall feed thee from death, and in the wars, he shall deliver thee from the power of the sword," and so forth, how God in dearth and destruction will help and save and how that such correction keepeth us from sinning. And again in the 36 Chapter, God by punishing and nurturing of men roundeth them (as it were) in the ears,[11] warneth them to lean off[12] their wickedness and to amend. If they now take heed and serve him, they shall wear out their days in prosperity and their years in prosperity and joy.

And Tobit, a man likewise exercised in afflictions, sayeth, "Blessed is thy name, O God of our fathers, who when thou art angry, showest mercy, and in time of trouble, forgiveth the sins of them that call upon thee."[13] And by and by after, "This may every one that worshippeth thee look for of a certainty, that if his life be put to trial, he shall be crowned. If he be in trouble, he shall be delivered. If he be under correction, he shall come to thy mercy. For thou delightest not in our destruction, for after tempest, thou sendest calm, and after mourning and weeping, thou bringest joy and rejoicing. Thy name O God of Israel be blessed for ever." And in the 6 Chapter of Hosea God sayeth, "In their adversity they shall seek me and say, 'Come, let us turn again unto the Lord, for he hath smitten and he shall heal us. He hath wounded us and he shall bind us up again. After two days shall he quicken us, and the third day shall he raise us up so that we shall live in his sight. Then shall we have understanding and endeavor ourselves to know God.'"[14]

And in the third chapter of the Proverbs, "My son" (sayeth Solomon) "despise not the chastening of the Lord; neither faint when thou art rebuked of him, for whom the Lord loveth, him he chasteneth, yea, and delighteth in him even as a father in his own son." The Apostle to the Hebrews hath the like most comfortable doctrine, which he yet amplifieth more, saying, "Ye have forgotten the exhortation which speaketh unto you as unto children: 'My son despise not thou the chastening of the Lord; neither faint when thou art rebuked of him, for whom the Lord loveth, him he chasteneth, yea, and scourgeth every son that he receiveth."[15] If ye endure chastening, God offereth himself unto you as unto sons. What son is he whom the father chasteneth not? If ye be not under correction, whereof all are partakers, then are ye bastards and not sons. Therefore, seeing we have had fathers of our flesh, which corrected us, and we gave them reverence, shall we not much rather be in subjection unto the father of spirits, and live? And they verily for a few days nurtured us after their own pleasure, but he nurtureth us for our profit, to the intent that he may minister of his holiness unto us. No manner chastening for the present time seemeth to be joyous but grievous; nevertheless, afterward it bringeth the quiet fruit of righteousness unto them which are exercised thereby. And in the third of the Revelation, Christ sayeth, "As many as I love, I rebuke and chasten. Be zealous therefore and repent." And Saint Paul declareth that neither trouble nor peril, neither life nor death, nor any other thing can separate us from the love of God, if we through Christ trust in his mercy. And the first to the Corinthians, he teacheth that God doth punish and correct us in this wretched world, that we should not be condemned with the wicked world.[16]

Secondly, it is most comfortable to call to remembrance such places of the Scriptures as contain God's merciful promises made to all such as in their trouble unfeignedly call unto him for help, whereof certain be hereunder noted for the more readiness to have them before our eyes. In the 4 of Deuteronomy, as God threateneth to bring the Jews into all miseries if they do disobey him, so sayeth he, "if thou then in thy greatest distress do turn unto the Lord thy God and hear his voice and seek him, thou shalt find him, if thou seek him with all thy heart and soul. For the Lord thy God is a merciful God. He will not forsake thee, nor destroy thee." And in the 30 Chapter of the same book, "If" (sayeth the Lord) "for thy sins, the curses written in this book do light upon thee and thou moved with repentance of thy heart turn unto the Lord and obey his commandments with all thy heart and with all thy soul, the Lord thy God shall bring thee again out of captivity and will have compassion upon thee and will turn and set thee again from all the nations among which the Lord thy God shall have scattered thee. Though thou were cast to the extreme parts of heaven, even from thence will the Lord thy God gather thee and from thence will he set thee. And the Lord thy God will bring thee into the land which thy fathers possessed, and thou shalt enjoy it. And he will show thee kindness and multiply thee above thy fathers. And the Lord thy God will circumcise thine heart and the heart of thy seed that thou mayest love the Lord thy God with all thy heart and with all thy soul that thou mayest live. And the Lord thy God will put all these curses upon thine enemies and on them that hate thee and that persecute thee. But thou shalt turn and hearken unto the voice of the Lord and do all his commandments which I command thee this day. And the Lord thy God will make thee plenteous in all the works of thy hands in the fruit of thy body and in the fruit of thy cattle and in the fruit of thy land, for thy wealth. For the Lord will turn again and rejoice over thee to do thee all good as he rejoiced over thy fathers."

The book of Psalms is very plentiful of such comfortable promises. Psalm 50, "Call upon me in the time of thy trouble and I will deliver thee" (sayeth the Lord) "and thou shalt honor me." Psalm 86, "Thou Lord art good and gracious, and of great mercy unto all them that call upon thee." And by and by, "In the time of my trouble, I will call upon thee, for thou hearest me." In the 91 Psalm be large promises of God's help and deliverance; yea, and that expressly from the plague and pestilence and all other evils. Psalm 145, "The Lord is nigh to all them that call upon him; yea, all such as call upon him faithfully." And Solomon in dedicating of his Temple testifyeth that if either in war or famine or pestilence or any other plague for our sins we do convert unto God and ask mercy that we obtain it.[17] And God appearing to him doth promise and assure the same, which promise of God, the good king Jehosaphat doth repeat in 2 of the Paralipomenon and the 20 Chapter, and according to the same in his distress obtained God's mercy and help. And the Lord by his prophet Jeremy sayeth, "If that people again whom I have thus devised convert from their wickedness, I will repent of the plague that I devised to bring upon them. Again, when I take in hand to build or to plant a people or a kingdom, if the same people do evil before me and hear not my voice, I will repent of the good that I devised to do for them." And in another place, "Ye shall cry unto me. Ye shall go and call upon me, and I shall hear you. Ye shall seek me and find me. Yea, if so be that you seek me with your whole heart, I will be found of you" (sayeth the Lord) "and will deliver you." And again in another place, "I heard Ephraim that was led away captive complain on this manner: 'O Lord, thou hast corrected me and the chastening have I received as an untamed calf. Convert thou me and I shall be converted, for thou art my Lord God; yea, as soon as thou turneth me, I shall reform myself, and when I understand, I shall smite upon my thigh."[18] And by his Prophet Ezekiel he sayeth, "If the ungodly will turn away from all his sins that he hath done and keep all my commandments and do the thing that is equal and right, doubtless he shall live and not die. As for all his sins that he did before, they shall not be thought upon but in his righteousness that he hath done he shall live. For, have I any pleasure in the death of a sinner" (sayeth the Lord God) "but rather that he convert and live?" And shortly after again, "When the wicked man turneth away from his wickedness that he hath done and doth the thing which is equal and right, he shall save his soul alive. For in so much as he remembreth himself and turneth him from all the ungodliness that he hath used, he shall live and not die." And again, "Wherefore be converted and turn you clean from all your wickedness so shall there no sin do thee harm. Cast away from you all your ungodliness that ye have done. Make you new hearts, and a new spirit. Wherefore will ye die, O ye house of Israel? Seeing I have no pleasure in the death of him that dieth" (sayeth the Lord God) "turn you then, and ye shall live."[19] And likewise by his Prophet Joel, "Although an horrible destruction be threatened to be at hand, yet" (sayeth the Lord) "turn unto me with all your hearts, with fasting, weeping, and mourning. Rent your hearts and not your clothes. Turn you unto the Lord your God, for he is gracious and merciful and of great compassion and ready to pardon wickedness." And anon, "Every one that calleth upon the name of the Lord shall be saved." And the Lord himself testifyeth that he hath performed these his promises accordingly saying, "Thou calledst upon me in troubles, and I delivered thee and heard thee what time as the storm fell upon thee."[20] Yea, and it is so accustomed unto God to help those that in their troubles fly unto him for succor, that he is as it were by a special name called in the Scriptures the helper and refuge in the day of trouble, the father of mercies, the God of all comfort, that thereby we might in our distress be the more encouraged to sue to the throne of his heavenly grace, whereunto our Savior most lovingly calleth all such as feel the burden of adversity and their sins withal.[21]

Now it remaineth for the third part. Rehearsal be made of certain examples of such as being in trouble and trusting to God's merciful promises called upon him and were delivered. And first of David, a man wonderfully exercised in worldly troubles to his eternal health and salvation, who confesseth that God was ever his helper and deliverer when he called upon him in trouble, sickness, or any other adversity, and that in very many places of the Psalter, a number whereof are noted in the margins. Yea, when he was in desperate state concerning all worldly help, crying out that the snares and sorrows of death had compassed him round about and that the pangs of hell had come upon him and taken hold of him and that he would yet call upon the name of the Lord, beseeching him to deliver his soul and that God out of his holy temple would not fail to hear and speedily to help and save him,[22] and notably and directly to this purpose, the same king David, as is testified in 2 book of Kings, and 24 Chapter, when 70 thousand were in three days slain with the plague, for his and their sins, making most humble confession of his offences and earnest prayer for mercy and pardon, obtained the same, and the plague at God's commandment suddenly ceased. Ezekias and the people with him, in their great distress whereunto they were brought for their sins, called upon the merciful Lord, and he heard and holpe them, not remembering their sins. Jonas, when by disobedience he had offended God and was swallowed up of the Whale, yet by prayer he was delivered even out of the belly of hell, as he himself speaketh, that none, even in most desperate state should distrust in God's mercy and help.[23] The Jews also, ever most stubborn and rebellious against God, yet when they being afflicted most worthily did in their distress call upon the Lord for mercy and help, he heard and relieved them, as appeareth by all the scriptures of the old testament, but especially and notably the 107 Psalm, which rehearseth the manifold rebellions of that nation against their Lord and God and the sundry afflictions that he therefore sent upon them. But ever this verse, as it were the burden of the Psalm or song, is often times among rehearsed: "But they cried to the Lord in their trouble, and he delivered them from their distress." And in the end of the Psalm is added that they that be wise will consider these examples and thereby understand the mercies of the Lord in the like distress to fly thereunto.

The like rehearsal of God's mercies, showed unto them when they in their troubles called upon him, is in the book of Nehemiah, or 2 of Esdras, and the 9 Chapter. How mercifully relieved God Ishmael and his mother in their great distress? What mercy was showed to wicked Manasses, truly repenting? Likewise to

Nebuchadnezzar, turning unto the lord in his trouble? How graciously is the prodigal son received of his father in his extreme misery procured by his own wickedness? How mercifully is the thief pardoned even in the miserable end of his most wicked life? Yea, all those diseases which the Gospel recordeth to be so miraculously cured by our Savoir Christ, in such as sued to him for health and by faith trusted to obtain the same, what be they else but testimonies to us of our like relief in our grievous sickness if with like faith we call to him for help?[24] For it is the same Lord of all, rich in mercy towards all that call upon him. Neither is his hand shortened or weakened that he can not, nor his goodness abated or diminished that he will not, now help his servants that in their distress do fly to his mercy and goodness. For it is now also true as it was then when it was written of the sheep and penny lost and found again, and that there is more joy in heaven upon one sinner repenting than upon ninety righteous.

I have more largely prosecuted this part, for that I thought it necessary that we should be instructed by the doctrine of God's word, his merciful promises, and the comfortable examples of his Saints in their troubles that God doth punish us in this wretched world that we be not damned with the wicked world and that he will not refuse nor reject such as being punished for their sins do unfeignedly in their distress return unto him.[25] For where our negligence in coming to him heretofore in the time of our quietness might now in the day of our trouble come into our minds to the great disfiguring of our fearful consciences, I thought it expedient to stir up and erect our good hope in his mercies in the time of our troubles by the manifold, most sweet, and assured comforts of the holy Scriptures, written for our doctrine and consolation, both at all times and specially in the time of affliction, for then is that heavenly medicine most necessary, when our disease doth most grieve and fear us, which we should undoubtedly receive at God's merciful hand, to our eternal health, if we according to the above written doctrines, promises, and examples, do unfeignedly turn to the Lord our God in these days of our affliction. "Unfeignedly,"

I say, not for the time of affliction only, as Mariner in the tempest, neither as dogs returning again to their vomit, but to remain such in health and security as in sickness and danger we promised to be, and all the days of our life hereafter, being delivered from fear of all plagues to serve the Lord our God sincerely and continually in all holiness and righteousness acceptable to him.[26] Wherefore I thought good to admonish us that we do not by dissembling with God, who can not be deceived, deceive ourselves. But, that as the Lord would have this plague not to be an utter destruction unto us but to be our fruitful correction as by the doctrine and examples above rehearsed appeareth, so we of this cross might win that gain and gather that fruit, which may be healthful unto us, as it was to those godly Saints which were before under like correction and chastisement of the Lord. Therefore let us learn by this affliction to mourn for our sins, to hate and forsake sin, for the which God doth thus show his anger and displeasure against us. For when shall we mourn for our sins, if not now in the time of mourning? When shall we hate them, if not now when they so grievously wound us and bring us to present danger of double death both of body and soul, if we fly not from them? When shall we forsake sin in our life, if we cleave to it now when life forsaketh or is most like to forsake us? And if we shall enter into particularities, when will we forsake our pride, if not now when all glory is falling into the dust? When will we leave our envy, malice, hatred, and wrath, if not now when we are going to the grave where all these things take an end? When will we give over our gluttony, if not now when we must forgo the belly and whole body also? When will we leave our fleshly lusts, if not now when our flesh shall turn to dust? When will we give over the cares of this life, if not now when we shall cease to live? When will we cease from our usury, if not now when we must lose both the increase and the stock wholly? When shall we willingly give over the love of wicked mammon, if not now when we can not hold nor use it but will we, nil we, we must part from it? Wherefore, either now let us make us friends of it who may receive us into the heavenly tabernacles, or else there is no hope that we ever will. When shall we relieve the poor in their need, if not now thereby to provoke the Lord to succor us in this our great distress? When will we awake, that we sleep not in death, if not now at the point of death? When shall we ever truly remember the last times, thereby to avoid sin, if not now in the last times themselves?

And as we ought now in affliction to fly all wickedness, so ought we to learn the love of righteousness, whereunto, of long, by gentleness, God hath drawn us and now by his just punishment meaneth to drive us. Let us learn the fear of God now punishing us, which by his long sufferance and patience heretofore was almost clean gone out of our hearts. For there be special promises that he will hear them that fear him. And when will we fear him, if not now when he punisheth us? Let us learn patience, knowing that affliction in the children of salvation worketh patience, patience bringeth trial, trial hope, and hope shall not suffer us to be confounded.[27] For the short evil of our troubles in this world, patiently taken, worketh in us an exceeding high and everlasting weight of glory in the world to come. Let us learn the contempt of this wretched life and wicked world with all her trifling and uncertain joys and manifold and horrible evils. For when shall we understand that this life is as a vapor, as a shadow passing and fleeing away, as a fading flower, as a bull rising on the water, if not now in the decaying, passing, and vanishing away of it? When shall we forsake this wicked world, if not now when it so forsaketh us?[28] Let us learn the desire of heaven and the life to come where be both many and most great and certain joys, mingled with no evils, no plagues of famine, war, pestilence, or other sicknesses and miseries, whereof this wretched life is full, as we now by experience prove.

To conclude, let us, giving over all wickedness, now at the last when we are in most greatest danger to give over ourselves, and helping the needy and poor that the Lord in our necessities may relieve us—let us, I say, now at the last, turn unto the Lord our God and call for help and mercy, and we shall be heard and relieved according to the doctrine of God's word and his merciful promises made unto us and after the examples foreshowed to us out of the holy scriptures afore declared and in infinite other places to our great comfort.[29] For if, as God by affliction goeth about as our heavenly schoolmaster, to teach us thus to fly from sin and to follow righteousness to contemn this world and do desire the life to come, with such other Godly lessons, so we, like his good disciples, do well learn the same. We shall not need much to fear this plague as dreadful and horrible but with the blessed man of God, Job, to trust in him, yea, though he should kill us bodily, and patiently to take our sickness as God's good visitation and fatherly correction and in it quietly and constantly to commit ourselves wholly to the holy will of our most merciful father, by our Savior Christ, whether it be to life or death, knowing that he is the Lord of life and death and that whether or not we live or die, we be the Lord's, for it can not perish which is committed unto him.[30] In whom, they that believe, though they die, shall live, and in whom, all that live and trust faithfully in his mercy shall not die eternally, and by whom, through our Savoir Christ, all that die in him have life everlasting, which I beseech the same our most merciful heavenly father, for the death of our Savior Jesus Christ, to grant unto us all, unto whom, with the father and the holy ghost, one eternal majesty of the most glorious God, be all honor, glory, and dominion, world without end. Amen.

Imprinted at London
in Paul's Churchyard, by Richard
Jugge, and John Cawood Printers
to the Queen's Majesty.
Cum Privilegio Regiae Majestatis.

3

Plague Literature

William Bullein: A Dialogue both pleasant and pietyful (1564)

William Bullein (c. 1515–76) was a practicing physician, first in Northumberland and Durham and later in London. He was also the first English writer to pen a sustained work of literature in English that took the bubonic plague as its exclusive focus. By the time he wrote *A Dialogue both pleasant and pietyful,* Bullein had already written a remedy book on pleurisy and two medical regimens in which he used dialogue and included discussion of the plague. *A new book entitled the government of health* (1558; STC 4039) contains a full plague remedy, and in *Bullein's bulwark of defense against all sickness, soreness, and wounds* (1562; STC 4033), the character Health explains to Sickness that the origin of the plague is Adam's fall. Bullein was not the first to make this claim; nor was he the first to depict the plague as an agent of God, justly taking the life of sinners. Chaucer's *Pardoner's Tale* contains the quintessential fourteenth century example of this portrait of plague. In the sixteenth century morality play *A comedy or interlude entitled, Enough is as good as a feast* (1570?; STC 24933), William Wager similarly incarnates death in the form of God's Plague who comes to claim the life of the avaricious Worldly Man. William Bullein's tragic-comic prose work, *A Dialogue both pleasant and pietyful,* reinforces this message, as the character *Mors* explains to *Civis* that he comes with a pestilent dart to bring his life to an end and collect his soul for God. Bullein's dialogue differs from its English predecessors by its full attention to the plague, its length, and its interdisciplinary, dialogue form: it includes within it medical remedies, animal fables, lessons in Aristotelian meteorology and physiology, humorous husband-wife banter, the interpretation of allegorical tableaux, tall tales told by a self-proclaimed world traveler, a theological interpretation of the plague, and prayers. Bullein presents each of these layers of his narrative in dialogue form that encourages a reader's active participation and lightens an otherwise potentially sermon-like reading experience with sardonic humor and variety. Bullein has also given his *Dialogue* a decidedly Protestant, reforming agenda—a trend observed in much of the English plague writing that follows it.

Because of the complexities of the narrative, with its many parts (some of them more overtly related to the plague than others), this dialogue often proves difficult for current readers. It may be helpful to consider each section separately at first, comparing each to one of the other texts in this collection: the remedies presented by Bullein's Medicus speak to those in Moulton's plague treatise (1531) and Elizabeth I's *Orders thought meet* (1578); the beliefs conveyed in the words of Bullein's Theologus have much in common with those in *A Form to be used in Common prayer* (1563); and the comic relief is an early, jovial version of what will be expressed in a much darker humor in Dekker's *The Wonderful Year* (1603). As a whole, the work represents the complex system of beliefs about and practices for managing the plague in early modern Protestant England; it gives us insight into sixteenth century printed plague texts, which had not yet crystallized into the discrete subgenres; and it paints a vivid picture of England's growing population concerns, with London the epicenter both of commerce and of plague. The dialogue form is an apt vehicle to bear the burden of multiple approaches to this difficult subject.

The first printed edition of Bullein's *A Dialogue both pleasant and pietyful against the fever pestilence* dates to 1564 (STC 4036 and 4036.5, the latter a complete copy used in this collection). It was reissued by Bullein in 1573 (STC 4037) and in 1578 (STC 4038) with expanded sections of dialogue, primarily that for characters Medicus, Roger, and Mendax. In the expanded dialogue of Mendax, for example, Bullein created what some consider to be the first depiction of a utopian society written in English: the city of Nodnol (London, spelled backwards) in the country of Taerg Natrib (a close approximation of Great Britain). In all editions, Mendax's description is foreshadowed by that of Medicus, who speaks of the appealing and yet troubling discovery of Terra Florida: with their ideal climate and abundant natural medicines, Floridians would never need physicians. The appearance of these utopian visions in a plague text speaks to the special Elizabethan hope that the future might be a golden one—healthier and wealthier.

Missing from the 1573 and 1578 editions but appearing in the original reproduced here are two letters in Latin appended at the end, after the letter to Frances Barlowe. In the notes to this section are full translations for each letter, supplied by Teresa Hooper. The first letter to Richard Turner, an influential Protestant reformer, includes a remedy for the plague that Bullein says comes from the famous Italian humanist physician Johannes Baptista Montanus; the second is a letter to well-known London surgeon Thomas Gale, thanking him for the gift of a book (likely Gale's *Certain Works of Surgery* [1563/64?]). This translation makes possible for the first time an easy comparison of this plague remedy with others from the period, including those offered in Bullein's *A Dialogue* as well as those by Thomas Moulton (chapter 1) and in the 1578 plague orders (chapter 4).

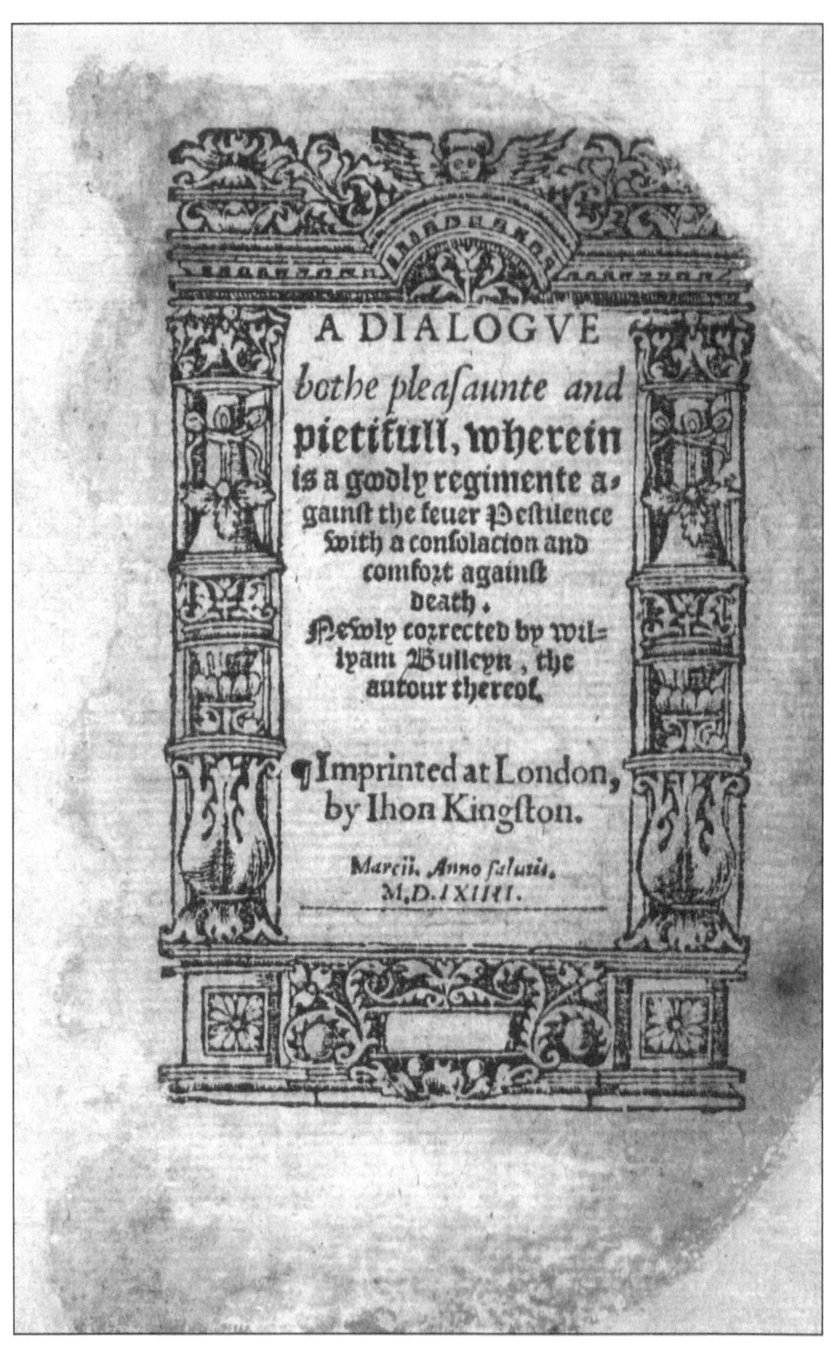

A DIALOGVE
bothe pleaſaunte and
pietifull, wherein
is a goodly regimente a-
gainſt the feuer Peſtilence
with a conſolacion and
comfort againſt
death.
Newly corrected by wil-
lyam Bulleyn, the
autour thereof.

¶ Imprinted at London,
by Ihon Kingſton.

Marcii. Anno ſalutis.
M.D.LXIIII.

Fig. 4. *A Dialogue both pleasant and pietyful,* title page, STC 4036.5. Reproduced by permission of the Huntington Library, San Marino, California.

To the Right Worshipful and his singular good friend, master Edward Barrett of Bellhouse of Essex, Esquire. William Bullein sendeth salutations.

Right worshipful sir, if any chamber, hall, gallery, or any new decked house were appareled or hanged all in one mourning dark color, it would rather move sorrow than gladness but no pleasure to the beholders of the same. Therefore, the diversity or variety of pleasant colors do grace and beautify the same through the setting forth of sundry shapes and, as it were, to compel the comers in to behold the whole work. Even so I do commend unto you this little book (wherein I write part thereof in your own house), which do entreat of sundry things, to you I do hope not unprofitable, wherein I have shortly described our poor needy brother his poverty, calling upon the merciless rich, whose whole trust is in the vain riches of this world, entangled as it were among Briars, so that in the hour of death, God is farthest from his mind, and the goods evil gotten are worse spent and come to nothing, at what time no Physic can prevail. I have also not forgotten the shameful sin, which reigneth in this world called ingratitude, which lineally came from the loins of that false villain Judas: neither the Sycophants, Gnatos, Liars and Flatterers of this world, the very poison of the soul. "Oh better," sayeth Solomon, "is the wounds of the friend than the kisses of the flatterer." Further, how many means may be used against the Pestilence as good air, diet, medicines accordingly, the which if it do not prevail, then commeth on the merciless power of death over all flesh, fearing no King, Queen, Lord, Lady, bond or slave, but rather maketh all creatures alike to him. Then do I conclude with the divine, God's chief and most best instrument in the church, etc. And as I do well consider, a gentleman of your good nature can but take your friend's simple token in good part. Even so I am sorry that it is no better to pleasure you, yet giving God most humble thanks for the same, who keep you in good health and worship.
This 12 of March. 1564.
Yours ever William Bullein.
Nullus unquam hominem mortalem beatumindicet, antequam bene defunctum viderit.[1]

To The Reader.

Good reader, when adversity draweth near to any city or town and the vengeance of God appeareth, either by hunger, sickness or the sword, then man's nature is most fearful, but yet worldly providence to help themselves, which in the time of prosperity or quietness is careless and forgetful, neither mindful to fear God nor pitiful to help their neighbor in adversity, and when they are touched by the fearful stroke of the Pestilence of their next neighbor, or else in their own family, then they use medicines, fly the air, etc., which indeed are very good means, and not against God's word so to do. Then other some falleth into sudden devotion, in giving alms to the poor and needy, which before have done nothing else but oppressed them, and have done them wrong. Other do look [away] from their hearts, God's lively word, and refuse grace offered by Christ's spirit, thinking there is no God. Some other are prevented by death in their flourishing years, which in the Cross of death, have their only consolation in Jesus Christ. All this is described here in this plain Dialogue, praying you patiently to take it in good part. From him that is yours to command. W. Bullein.

A Dialogue.

The interlocutors are twelve persons.

Mendicus
Civis
Uxor
Medicus
Antonius
Roger
Crispine
Avarus
Ambodexter
Mendax
Mors
Theologus

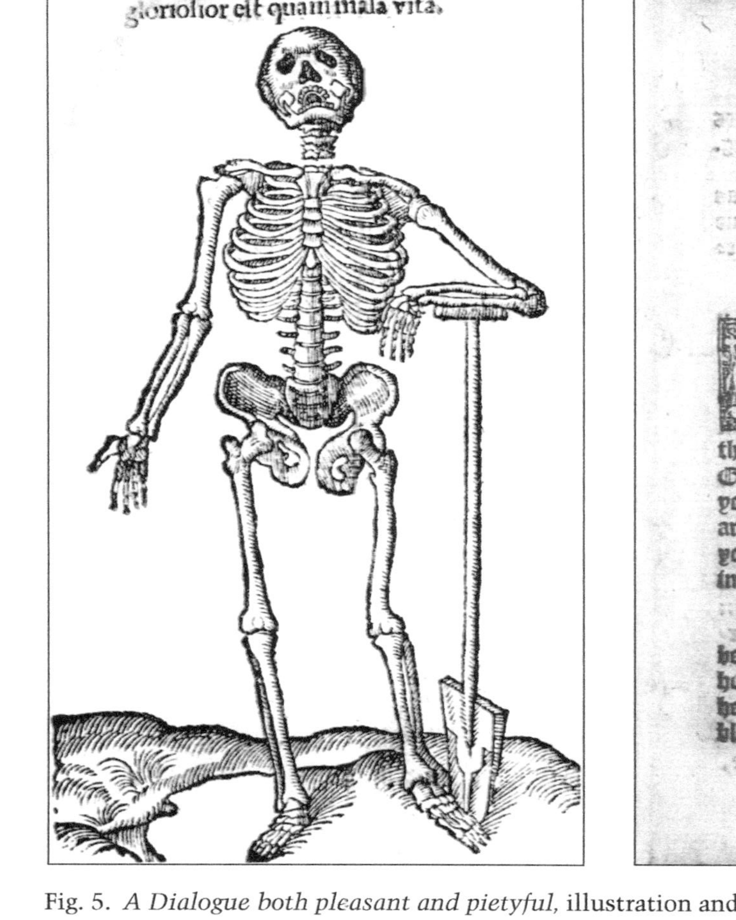

gloriosior est quam mala vita.

A DIALOGVE FOL.1.

¶ *The interlocutours are* twelue persones.

Mendicus.	Chrispinus.
Ciuis.	Auarus.
Vxor.	Ambo dexter.
Medicus.	Mendax.
Antonius.	Mors.
Roger.	Theologus.

Mendicus.

God saue my gud Maister and Maistres, the barnes, and all this haly houshade, and shilde you from all doolle and them, and sende you comforte of all thynges that you waud haue good of: and God and our dere leddie, shilde and defend you from this Peste. Our father whiche art in heauen, hallowed bee your name, your kyngdome come, your will bee doen in yearth as it is in heauen. &c.

Ciuis.

Me thinke I doe heare a good manerlie begger at the doore, and well brought vp, how reuerently he saieth his Pater noster, he thoues not GOD, but you hym, Gods blessing on his hart. I praie you wife, giue

A.v. the

Fig. 5. *A Dialogue both pleasant and pietyful,* illustration and first page (A4v, A5r), STC 4036.5. Reproduced by permission of the Huntington Library, San Marino, California.

MENDICUS:

God save my good Master and Mistress, the Barneses, and all this holy household, and shield you from all dole and shame, and send you comfort of all things that you would have good of. And God and our dear lady, shield and defend you from this Pest. Our father which art in heaven, hallowed be your name, your kingdom come, your will be done in earth as it is in heaven, etc.

CIVIS:

Me think I do hear a good mannerly beggar at the door, and well brought up. How reverently he sayeth his Pater noster. He "thou"s not God, but "you" him. God's blessing on his heart. I pray you wife, give the poor man something to his dinner.

UXOR:

Sir, I will hear him say the Lord's prayer better before I give him anything.

CIVIS:

What a reckoning is this? Dame, do as I command you. He is poor; we have plenty. He is very poor and hungry; therefore, dispatch him a God's name, and let him go.

UXOR:

Soft fire maketh sweet Malt. He shall tarry my leisure.

MENDICUS:

Mistress, if you be angry with the saying of my *Pater noster* in English, I will say it in Latin, and also my *De Profundis*.[2] But so God help me, I do not ken none of them both.

UXOR:

I think the same. Such Carpenter, such chips; your curate is some honest man I warrant you, and taketh much pain in feeding his flock, as seemeth by your learning. I pray you, what country may be you?

Mendicus:

Saving your honor good Mistress, I was born in Redesdale in Northumberland and came of a wight riding, surname called the Robsons, good honest men and true, saving a little shifting for their living. God help them, silly poor men.

Uxor:

What doest thou here in this country? Me think thou art a Scot by thy tongue.

Mendicus:

Trowe me never more, then, good dame. I had better be hanged in a Withie of a Cowtail,[3] than be a rowfooted Scot, for they are ever fair and false. I have been a felon, sharp man on my hands[4] in my young days, and brought many of the Scots to ground in the North Marches, and gave them many grisly wounds no man for man durst abide me luke, I was so fell.[5] Then the limmer Scots hared me, burnt my goods, and made deadly feed with me and my barns, that now I have nothing but this sorry bag and this staff and the charity of such good people as you are, good mistress. Also, I have many of my surname here in the city that would think no shame on me: yea, honest handcrafty men.

Civis:

How got you in at the gates, my good friend?

Mendicus:

Dear sir, I have many countrymen in this fair city that came of honest stock in our land, and some a little beyond us twenty or thirty miles that can make pure shift in the city and in the country also. I came in no place but either the parson, Bailey, Constable, or chief of the parish is of our country born, and some pure men as mine own self, God ken, among whom the Beadle of the beggars being a Redesdale man born, a good man and a true, which for ill will in his youth did flee the Country. It was laid to his charge, the driving of kine home to his father's byre, but Christ knoweth he was sackless and live as honestly in his age as his sire did when he was young, good master.

Civis:

I was born in the North my fellow, and do live here in this city. I came hither when I was young and when I was very poor, but now I am in good case to live among the rest of my neighbors.

Mendicus:

God's benison on you, and our dear lady's. I come hither purely in mine age. I have nothing but wisdom.

Uxor:

Give God only thanks, for so is his holy will and commandments that we should call upon him in the days of trouble and only honor him. We have no commandment to honor our lady.

Mendicus:

I think one woman would take another woman's part. Do as it shall please you. I am no clerk but an ingram man, of small consideration in such arrogant buke farles.[6]

Civis:

What news in the Country, as you come by the way, Country man?

Mendicus:

None but old manners, fair sayings, false hearts, and no devotion. God amend the Market. Much toiling for the purse, deceiving of each other. In the Country, strife, debate, running for every trifle to the Lawyers. Having nothing but the nutshells, the Lawyers eat the Kernels. Also much raising of rents, causing great dearth, much poverty. God help, God help, the world is sore changed: extortioners, covetous men, and hypocrites do muckle prevail. God cut them shorter, for they do make a black world, even hell upon earth. I think the great fiend or his dam will weary them all. None other news I ken, but that I did see mickle providence made in the country for you in the city which do fear the Pestilence. I met with wagons, carts, and horses, full laden with young bairns for fear of the black Pestilence, with their boxes of medicines and sweet perfumes. O God, how fast did they run by hundreds and were afraid of each other, for fear of smiting.

Civis:

I have some of my children forth. God send them well to speed.

Mendicus:

Master, why go you not with them yourself?

Civis:

No, youth are apt to take the Plague, and further, parents are more natural to their children than children to their fathers and mothers: nature doeth descend but not ascend. Also, if the citizen should depart when as the Plague do come, then there should not only be no plague in the city, but also the city should be void and empty for lack of the inhabitors therein. Therefore God's will be done among his people. I do not intend to flee; notwithstanding, I pray God of his mercy, deliver us from this Plague, for if it do continue, God knoweth, it will not only take away a number of poor people but many wealthy and lusty merchants also.

Mendicus:

If such plague do ensue, it is no great loss. For, first it shall not only deliver the miserable poor man, woman, and bairns from hurt and carefulness into a better world but also cut off many covetous usurers, which be like fat, unclean swine, which do never good until they come to the dish but root out every plant that they can come by. And like unto great stinking muckle medin-hills, which never do pleasure unto the land or ground until their heaps are cast abroad to the profits of many, which are kept neither to their own comforts, nor others, but only in beheading them: like unto cruel dogs, living in a Manger, neither eating the Hay themselves, nor suffering the horse to feed thereof himself. And in sick Plagues, we poor people have mickle good. Their loss is our gain. When they do become naked, we then are clothed against their wills; with their doles and alms, we are relieved. Their sickness is our health, their death our life. Besides us Beggars, many me men have good luck, as the Curate, Parish clerk, and the bell man. Often times the executors be ne losers by this game. And *in fine,* in my fantasy it is happy to the huntman when he have nothing of the Cat but the silly skin. We beggars covet not for the carcass of the dead body, but do defy it. We look for auld cast coats, doublets, hose, caps, belts, and shoes by their deaths, which in their lives they would not depart from, and this is our hap.

Civis:

Go thy ways to *Antonius Mantuanus'* gates, for thither, even within this two hours, I did see Master *Antonius Capistranus* solemnly riding upon his Mule, with a side gown, a great chain of gold about his neck, his Apothecary Senior Crispine a neighbor's child, born hereby in Barbary, and his little Lackey, a proper young applesquier, called *Pandarus,* which carrieth the key of the chamber with him. These are all gone in at the gates to that noble Italian. His almner this day, because his master was very sick, applied the poor men with the purse, with much devotion for the time, being without hope of his Master's recovery.

MENDICUS:

I pray God send us many such prayers, for it is merry with us when any man's hurt do turn to many men's gains. I will go thither. Fare you well good Master. I will draw near and harken what master doctor will say, if I might be in place.

CIVIS:

Farewell, for thou doest not care which end do go forward, so that thy turn may be served.

[scene change to the house of the ailing Master *Antonius*]

MEDICUS:

How do you good Master *Antonius?* Lord God, how are you changed? How chanceth this? What is the matter that you look so pale? You did send for me by your servant *Johannes de Corsica,* a gentle young man which lamented much for you, and when I heard it, with all speed I came from my other patients, of whom I think I have taken mine *ultimum vale*.

ANTONIUS:

You are welcome Master doctor, with all my heart. Now, help at a pinch or else never, for I do fear myself very much. Oh, my heart.

MEDICUS:

I warrant you man, let me feel your pulse, and then shall I proceed to the cure, with Medicine and diet accordingly.

ANTONIUS:

Take your pleasure good Master Doctor. Here is my hand. Feel my pulse, and then you shall see mine urine and know the time of my sickness.

Medicus:

These are no very good tokens, neither in your urine, pulse, stool, etc., but I will do the best for you that I can do by art.

Antonius:

And then you shall want no gold, for though I lack help, yet I want no gold of every coin, and silver also. My warehouses are well filled with wares of sundry kinds, which I do sell unto the retailers. Further, I have wares of most ancient service, which owe me nothing, both in packs, vessels, and chests, etc., which are not fit for the retailers. Them do I keep for shifts, when any gentleman or long suitor in the law are behindhand and know not what to do. Then by good sureties or assured lands by statute merchant, etc., I do sometime make thirty or fifty in the hundred by year. I have diverse such honest ways to live upon through the witty and secret handling of my brokers here in the city and my factors, which are at Antwerp, etc., by whom I do understand the state and what commodity is best. Further I have extended upon ancient lands in the country for the breach of covenants that, to conclude with you master doctor, I could never have died in a worse time, my business is such. I would of all things live still, for here I do know what I have and how I am used, but when I am gone, I do not know what shall happen unto me, nor whom to trust with that which I have gotten with travel and obtained by fortune.

Medicus:

You do speak like a wise man as ever I heard, and most things that you have taken in hand have great profit with you. Of my part, I would be loath to lose you, both for an unfeigned love that I do bear unto you for your wisdom and also for your liberality and gifts given to me many a time. Lo, here is the Damask gown yet in store.[7] Here is also a Flagon-chain of the hundred Angels[8] that you did give me in your last great Fever.

Antonius:

Who is able to resist such a multitude of Angels? I think few Doctors of Physic. But rather than I would die, I will let fly a thousand more.

Medicus:

That is the way, I assure you, to perfect health, and for that cause the Physician was ordained, as it is written: "Honor the Physician with the honor that is due unto him, because of necessity, for the Lord have created him, and he shall receive gifts of the king."[9]

Antonius:

That is a good sweet text for Physicians, but why do you leave out these words in the middes of the matter? Which is, "of the most highest cometh learning," and so I do remember, I heard our curate read in the church, as by chance I came in with a Sergeant to arrest two Bankrupts.

Medicus:

What your curate pleased him to read, I care not, for I meddle with no Scripture matters but to serve my turn. But I know that which I have said is written in the Bible.

Antonius:

Be all things written in the Bible true? I pray you, tell me.

Medicus:

God forbid Master *Antonius*, then it would make a fray among Merchants, for it is written, "None shall enter into God's dwelling or rest with him upon his Mountain that lendeth his money upon usury or to usury, whereby to hinder his neighbor."[10] And this is now become the greatest trade. And many be undone by borrowing, and few do lose by lending, specially men of your worshipful experience. And how like you this text?

ANTONIUS:

Text how they will text. I will trust none of them all, say what they will. There be many such sayings against men, as the ten commandments, etc. Well, for my part, I have little to do in these matters. Marie, I would be glad to live orderly and Civilly, so that the world should not wonder at my doings, but if damnation should arise, when the Scripture do threaten it to men, then should witty words in bargaining, with facing oaths, and pleasant venerous table talk, with reviling of our enemies, etc., be accompted damnation. Then I warrant you, hell is well furnished with courtiers, merchants, soldiers, husbandmen, and some of the clergy, I warrant you also—among whom there are many more spiteful than Spiritual, even as there are among the Physicians many more covetous than kindhearted. I mean not you, master doctor.

MEDICUS:

Sir, I do know you do not. But so God help me, one thing doeth much rejoice my heart in your communication.

ANTONIUS:

What is that?

MEDICUS:

I think that we two are of one religion.

ANTONIUS:

What is that, I pray you? For I know not mine own religion.

MEDICUS:

Command your folks to depart out of the chamber, and your young scapes also which you have gotten by chance medley for want of marriage, for the old proverb is, small Pitchers have wide ears, and the field have eyes, and the wood have ears; therefore, we must common closely, and beware of blabs.

ANTONIUS:

Well, now the doors are sparred. Say on your mind of what Religion are you? Be plain with me, man.

MEDICUS:

Hark in your ear sir, I am neither catholic, Papist, Protestant, nor Anabaptist. I assure you.

ANTONIUS:

What then? You have rehearsed choice and plenty of religions. What do you honor? The Sun, the Moon, or the Stars, Beast, Stone, or Fowl, Fish or Tree?

MEDICUS:

No forsooth. I do none of them all. To be plain, I am a *Nullafidian*, and there are many of our sect.

ANTONIUS:

Oh. *Qui dixit in corde suo non est deus.*[11] Well, we differ very little in this point, but if I do live, we shall draw near to an unity. In the meantime, let your Apothecary provide some good things for the body. I pray you open the door.

MEDICUS:

Master, I pray you, call *Crispine* hither into the Gallery, and *Leonardus de Montano* with him.

CRISPINE:

What is your pleasure master doctor?

Medicus:

How do you like this Garden?

Crispine:

There are plenty of goodly herbs, both cleansing, healing, losing, binding, and restoring. I never did see more choice of sundry kinds of strange flowers, most pleasant to the eye and sweet also. The fine knots are done by good art, geometrically figured: a sweet conduit in the middest, made of fine stone, plentifully casting forth water like fine silver streams many ways, in which conduit, I did behold by the space of one hour a marvelous thing, the meaning thereof I know not.

Medicus:

What was it *Crispine*?

Crispine:

The pillar was eight foot square and eighteen foot high, with compartments of cunning Masonry, curiously covered with fine gold. Upon the top, a Tiger fearfully having a young child in his arms ready to kill it, the child had a crown of gold upon his head and in his left hand a Globe, figuring the whole world and was called *Microcosmos,* about which was written *Globus conversus est.*

Medicus:

This gentleman came of a great house. This is the crest of his arms, for he descended of the most ancient Romans, I warrant you; he is no upstart, assure yourself.

Crispine:

I had thought it had rather signified the conditions of a cruel tyrant or some bloody conqueror, which by usurpation, getting the victory of any commonwealth, as Lands, Countries or Cities, eftsoons do spoil the true heirs and owners of the land which do wear the crown, change the state of the Commons to the worser part, spoiling them with sword and bondage, which appeared by these words: *Globus conversus est;* the world is changed or turned.

MEDICUS:

A good observation. What did you see then?

CRISPINE:

I did behold on the one side the nine Muses, with strange instruments of Music sitting under the hill *Parnassus,* and the Poets sitting under the green trees, with Laurel garlands beset with Roses about their heads, having golden pens in their hands, as *Homer, Hesiod, Ennius,* etc., writing verses of sundry kinds. And *Lucan* sat there very high, near unto the Clouds, appareled in Purple, saying,

Quantum sermotus Ego:
Cardine Pernasus gemino petit ethera colle.
Motis Phoebo Bromioque sacer.[12]

And near them sat old Moral Gower, with pleasant pen in hand, commending honest love without lust and pleasure without pride, holiness in the Clergy, no tyranny in rulers, no falsehood in Lawyers, no Usury in Merchants, no rebellion in the Commons, and unity among kingdoms, etc.

Skelton sat in the corner of a Pillar, with a frostbitten face, frowning, and is scant yet clean cooled of the hot burning choler kindled against the cankered Cardinal Wolsey, writing many a sharp *distichons* with bloody pen against him, and sent them by the infernal rivers *Styx, Phlegethon,* and *Acheron* by the Ferryman of hell called *Charon,* to the said Cardinal.

How the Cardinal came of naught
And his prelacy sold and bought;
And where such Prelates be,
Sprung of low degree,

And spiritual dignity,
Farewell benignity,
Farewell simplicity,
Farewell humanity,
Farewell good charity.
Thus parvum literatus,[13]
Came from Rome gatus,
Doctor dawpatus,
Scant a bachelaratus.
And thus Skelton did end,
with Wolsey his friend.

Witty *Chaucer* sat in a chair of gold covered with Roses, writing Prose and Rhyme, accompanied with the spirits of many Kings, Knights, and fair ladies, whom he pleasantly besprinkled with the sweet water of the well consecrated unto the Muses, called *Aganippe.* And as his heavenly spirit commended his dear Brigham for the worthy entombing of his bones, worthy of memory in the long sleeping chamber of most famous kings. Even so in tragedy, he bewailed the sudden resurrection of many a nobleman before their time in spoiling of Epitaphs, whereby many have lost their inheritance, etc. And further thus he said, lamenting,

Covetous men do catch all that they may have,
The field and the flock, the tomb and the grave:
And as they abuse riches, and their graves that are gone,
The same measure they shall have every one.
Yet no burial hurteth holy men, though beasts them devour;
Nor rich grave prevaileth the wicked, for all earthly power.

Lamenting Lydgate, lurking among the Lilies, with a bald sconce, with a garland of Willows about his pate, booted he was after Saint Benedict's guise, and a black Stamell robe, with a loathly monsterous hood hanging backward, his stooping forward bewailing every estate with the spirit of providence, foreseeing the falls of wicked men, and the slippery seats of Princes, the ebbing and flowing, the rising and falling of men in authority, and how virtue do advance the simple and vice overthrow the most noble of the world. And thus he said,

Oh noble Princes conceive and do learn,
The fall of kings for misgovern,
And prudently piecing this matter,
Virtue is stronger than either plate or mail;
Therefore consider when wisdom do counsel,
Chief preservative of Princely magnificence,
Is to almighty God to do due reverence.

Then Bartley with an hooping Russet long coat, with a pretty hood in his neck, and five knots upon his girdle, after Francis's tricks. He was born beyond the cold River of Tweed. He lodged upon a sweet bed of Camomile, under the Cinnamon tree. About him many Shepherds and sheep, with pleasant pipes, greatly abhorring the life of Courtiers, Citizens, Usurers, and Bankrupts, etc., whose old days are miserable. And the estate of shepherds and country people, he compted most happiest and sure, etc., saying,

Who entreth the Court in young and tender age
Are lightly blinded with folly and outrage,
But such as enter with wit and gravity
Bow not so soon to such enormity.
But or they enter, if they have learned naught,
Afterward is virtue the least of their thought.

Next them, in a black chair of Jet stone, in a coat of arms, sat an ancient knight in Orange Tawny, as one forsaken, bearing upon his breast a white Lion, with a Crown of rich gold on his head. His name was sir Davie Linse, upon the mount, with a hammer of strong steel in his hand, breaking asunder the counterfeit crosskeys of Rome forged by Antichrist. And thus this good knight of Scotland said to England the elder brother and Scotland the younger,

Habitare fratres in unum,
Is a blessful thing.[14]
One God, one faith, one baptism pure
One law, one land, and one king.
Clap hands together brethren dear,
Unfeigned truce together make,
And like friends do ever accord,
But French and Roman do first forsake.

You are without the continent,
A sole land of ancient fame,
Ab origine a people old,
Bold Britons ecleped by name,
Sicut erat in principio.[15]
Grant, oh God, it may be,
In saecula saeculorum,[16]
That we may have peace in thee.
Then we shall fear no foreign power,
That against us shall advance
The Tartar cruel, the curse of Rome,
Ne yet the power of France, etc.

On the second square was a fair dial for this Orison, unto which was added the hours of the planets. Upon the same was written in large letters of fine gold, *Tempora labuntur.*

MEDICUS:

There stop and lay a Straw.[17] For *Tempora labuntur* is to say, "by little and little, time do slip away." I will hear the rest of the matter at leisure. What is it a clock?

CRISPINE:

But early day, scant eight of the clock.

MEDICUS:

Well I pray you, dispense all things in order *Contra Pestem,* in the same sort, both number of the Simples, Dose and quantity, even as you did it yesterday, which was given to *Paul.*

CRISPINE:

Sir, I have spent all my fine Myrrh. What shall I do?

MEDICUS:

You are a wise man, put in *Quid pro quo,* called *αντιβαλλόμενα.*[18] *Hoc est simplicia que aliorum facultati similium penuria subponi possunt medici consilio. Intelligis?*[19]

CRISPINE:

Etiam domine,[20] *Doctor.*

MEDICUS:

Move te otius, and quicquid agas prudenter agas.[21]

CRISPINE:

By God, he shall pay for the malt grinding. He have enough; he know none end of his pelf. It will come to an evil end. God send me more such cheats. What, me think I see two men in long gowns with short beards at the gates. What are they, a God's name?

MEDICUS:

I know them very well; they are two pettifoggers in the Law. The one is called master *Avarus,* a good gentleman and of a great house, a man of good conscience. Indeed he is my cousin germane on my mother's side. Surely he can give good counsel and is fit to be with such a man as master *Antonius* is. Indeed they have been long acquainted and will never give over unto the end.

CRISPINE:

Who is the other on the left hand? He seemeth to be a proper gentleman and a studious. He is lean, an handsome cleanly man. Me think he have on each side of his gown a bag and his hand in them.

MEDICUS:

Every man have his grace and gesture. I promise you, I durst commit a great secret unto him. Oh, he is a paragon.

CRISPINE:

What meaneth he by winking like a Goose in the rain and biting of his lip?

MEDICUS:

Do you note that? It is a good sign of a constant man. Mark it when you will. He is a witty fellow, and one that is in great estimation, fit for Master *Antonius*. His name is *Ambodexter.* Go down with speed, and say you have given master *Antonius* his purgation, and this day he have no leisure to speak with any man, and also how that he is amended, for, if the curate were here for the soul, we for the body, and *Avarus* for the purse, here were but a mad company. We should never agree together but fall into discords.[22] Dispatch them with speed. Fare thee well. I will go and cause him to be letten blood and keep him from sleep; then shall he be purged tomorrow in the morning. Bring the powder against the plague with you.

CRISPINE:

God give you good morrow, gentle master *Avarus*. What, master *Ambodexter*? How fare you both? Master *Antonius* did much desire to have spoken with you eight hours past. Indeed within this two hours, saving your worships, he hath taken a purgation, which have cast such air abroad that I was not able to abide in the chamber. I had forgotten my perfumes to make all well.

AVARUS:

What think you of him? Shall he escape or no? Who is with him? I pray you tell me.

CRISPINE:

None but Doctor *Capistrane,* which also desire your absence, because he have him in cure and trust to make him sleep after his lack of rest, and tomorrow take your pleasure with him.

AVARUS:

Fare thee well. We have drawen and engrossed his books.[23] Commend us to master Doctor.

[CRISPINE departs.]

It were a good pastime to take the footcloth from his Mule, for two or three hours in pastime.

Ambodexter:

I had rather have the Mule.

Avarus:

What the devil doeth this doctor here? If this purging were not, we would cleanse and expulse with our resets that which should serve our turn well enough.

Ambodexter:

I warrant you, the Doctor do make work for us both. We shall bring our matters to pass in good time. Take no care man for the matter. We will prevent the doctor tomorrow, when he cometh hither, with a present, and bring him some pretty things wherein he delighteth. We shall find such means to persuade with him by little and little to be executors of his will, according to his old promise. Further, he will take it kindly that we do claim kindred on him by his mother's side, which was a kind-heartd woman and full of meritrix, ha, ha, ha. She was indeed of those qualities. Her son is like the mother, as seemeth by one in the house.

Avarus:

I fear that damosel will mar all together. She doeth rule the roost; she ware the keys. He can never have her out of his sight, yet Reinold his man thinketh himself in more estimation with her than his master.

Ambodexter:

The last year, I counterfeited a sickness of purpose, as I can when I lust. I framed my Physician to my fantasy. No man thought that I should have lived two days. When I was alone, I laughed. You remember whom I made mine executor, even *Antonius Mantuanus*. I then providently by three things did foresee this time and cause. The first was his great surfeits in banqueting; the second, his watching at Chess and Cards; the third, you know what.

Avarus:

Well, well, be as be may is no banning.[24] I do fear many things. First, the medicines may chance recover him; then we shall have nothing. Well, Reinold and the damosel be ever in presence and watch him. She cheers her master with a loving countenance. Reinold says that he hath done true service a long time, etc. Well, I smell another pad in the straw.[25] When all this is done, the curate is a crafty Rhetorician. Well can he persuade and rehearse God's vengeance, threats and plagues, by examples most fearful, like thunderbolts, describing the scalding house of hell, *ve, ve, ve,* with the story of *Dives* and *Pauper,*[26] and the day of judgment, reading the Homily of death, crying out all is but vanity, vanity, and vexation of mind, damnation, except repentance and true confession from the heart, restitution of wrongs. He will keep astir, and bring our cousin into a fool's paradise. It is he that will raise up all the beggars in the town. He will cry, "Give with your own hand, for today you are a man, tomorrow earth and ashes."

Ambodexter:

First, let us be sober and seem to be sorrowful for him, desiring nothing but only his life.[27] If he stand in great danger, the doctor shall have his leave and tarry no longer with him, in whom I think he have no hope to recover. Let him be well rewarded. Secondly, let Reinold be sent into the country to the debtors for money. Tell him it shall turn to his great profit and how his master doeth intend to take him as his son and will trust none but only him to fetch the money in the country. Thirdly, I will seem to fantasy the minion, wishing her to be my wife, alleging what broken sleep she hath caused me to have, and the cause of my coming hither only for her stay.[28] Then I will practice for the keys of the great black chest and of the steel casket. Fourthly, master Curate shall be gently saluted with a Barnard's blow: we will commend him, we will pray with him, and also receive the Communion with our cousin, that he may have a good opinion in us, and deliver him a bag with five pound in pence to give to the poor, in whose absence, peradventure, our Scribe and we shall frame the will. How like you this practice? If this will not serve, I have a shift of descant in store that I learned in Bosom's Inn.

Avarus:

The Devil take altogether. So that we had the gold, practice this I pray you. You have a good wit; by my troth I could not sleep all this night for this matter. If you were not, I could do nothing, but stand like a sheep.

Ambodexter:

I warrant you, I have had long experience in this trade everywhere within this Realm.[29] I can do the like with the help of *Avarus*, which is a very good pen man, close and honest. He writeth sundry hands and is a lively graver of Seals himself, also is a kindhearted fellow, for he will not stick to lend his friend an oath if need do require.

Avarus:

The world is full of starting holes. Men may scant know how to trust men now a days, but for the good report that I do hear of this honest fellow, I will be glad to have his acquaintance. I knew diverse of his kinsmen twenty years ago. God have mercy of all Christian souls. It was then a merry world, and will never be so good again, until these Gospeling Preachers[30] have a sweating sickness in Smithfield and their Bible burnt. Well, would some were at liberty for their sakes. Well, well.

Ambodexter:

Oh I do remember that reverent mortified father, that holy man Bishop Boner, that blessed Catholic confessor of Rome. If he were again at liberty, he would not dally to mock them but trimly would roast these fellows,[31] and after burn them. You know his workmanship very well.

Avarus:

He is my cousin germane, and *Perjurus*, that honest fellow, was his boy and brought up with him in his youth. And your grandfather did pen his prologue, in the book called *De vera obedientia*, when as they laughed merrily, saying they had rather put to their hands[32] than either their heads or hearts. Wise men, wise men.

Ambodexter:

Yea, such wise men will serve the time, *Prudenter agere*,[33] and be as wise as Serpents, and simple as Doves.

Avarus:

To have the nature of a serpent, I will stand with them, but beshrew my heart if I would be as simple as a Dove, either so simple, fearful, or doltish, but rather as my good lord Boner, *Quasi Leo rugiens querens quein devoret*.[34] And thus he would expound that text, which must have such a gloss upon it.

Ambodexter:

I am alone upon glosses. I have art in store to sophist. I was brought up three years with a Friar of *Montpellier*.[35] He taught me how to handle *prosa, obscurum, inordinatum*, and *barbarum*, with *genus* and *species*. Full well I can handle the matter, both *pro* and *contra*. Commonly these are my figures and serve well to my purpose, as *Enigma, proaemiae, ironiae, sarcasimus, antiphrasis*, and *charientismus*. I have many rotten rules which do serve for the purse. I learned them at Paris. They are written in an old Barbarous French book. When we are at more leisure, I will show thee all my cunning, my gains and profits. Now let us confer both together this afternoon about our matters.

AVARUS:

Contented in that case; as for terms and tricks in Logic, I force not of them. They will pay for no horse-bread. It is gold that maketh a glad heart. He deserveth reverence and rule that hath it and kept it. Go let us dine together, and send for our friends *Rapax, Capax,* and *Tenax*[36] to keep us company an hour or two, for they are good fellows.

AMBODEXTER:

Agreed. I like their company very well. They are my friends, and kindhearted men.

AVARUS:

And mine also. Go, let us depart and not be seen much together abroad standing in counsel, because our matters are not current.

MEDICUS:

Crispine, where have you been so long? I thought it a year since your departure, but I have shorted the time in beholding this pitiful picture of *Lucretia,* and this fearful siege of *Pavia,* but this Map of the description of *Terra Florida* in *America* have rejoiced me. There the gold and precious stones and Balms are so plentiful. Silver and spice are nothing with them. No labor is in that land. Long life they have. One thing there is which liketh me not among them.

CRISPINE:

What is that master Doctor?

MEDICUS:

They have never sickness until death do come; therefore, there is no good dwelling for us in such a land. Further, it is said that they have no debate nor strife in their commonwealths.

CRISPINE:

Marie, then it is as unprofitable for Lawyers as for Physicians. I trust we shall never be in that case in this our country.

MEDICUS:

God defend us from such a Commonwealth. It would mar altogether. Now let us go to the chamber door and see how the world goeth with master *Antonius* and take our *Phlebotomer* with us, to let him blood.

CRISPINE:

I will wait on your mastership.

MEDICUS:

How do you, good master *Antonius?* Have you taken any rest since I was with you?

ANTONIUS:

No more, Master Doctor, than if I had been laid on hot coals. Oh sir, there was never man in such a case as I am in. I have had most fearful dreams of thieves to rob me. Me thought I was in the top of a high tower, telling of money, and suddenly there came an earthquake, and shook the tower in pieces, and cast me down upon weapons all bloody, which a great number of Morians had in their hands. From them I fell in the fire, which was like high mountains about me, whereas was much noise and a cruel battle. I did see there many of mine old acquaintance which sometime were of great honor, both men Spiritual and Temporal, and the Pope himself, with many of his friends. They were in extreme wretchedness and sore handled of fearful Monsters and worms gnawing upon their breasts, upon whom was written, "Conscience hath accused me, and hell devoured me." *Ve, ve, ve!* And thus I am tossed to and fro. Alas, what shall I do? Also, I did hear many ragged and sick people cry vengeance on me, and men in prison also that said I had undone them to enrich myself. Oh good God!

Crispine:

Sir, I pray you let me harken in your ear.

Medicus:

What is the matter?

Crispine:

I will depart. His talk doeth so much trouble me. Me think he doeth wound my conscience. Also, I will home and cast away a great number of rotten drugs wherewith I have gotten much money in deceiving the people. God forgive me.

Medicus:

The vicar of saint fool's be your ghostly father. Are you so wise? Tarry still with me. Let him pay for your rotten drugs, for I may say to you that he is almost rotten already himself. Methink your conscience is too much spiced with sudden devotion.

Antonius:

What mean you Master Doctor, to whisper in the Apothecary's ear?

Medicus:

Nothing sir, but I have appointed at what time that you should receive your Clyster and how your Tisane should be made, and in what order that your frontary should be applied to your forehead, to cause you to sleep quietly. These dreams are nothing, but proceeding of the abundance of choler; you are hot and dry. Also the time is very hot. The Sun is now twenty degrees in *Leo*. The Dog days are to be observed. Notwithstanding, fear nothing. I warrant you, life for life, discomfort not yourself, a man or a Mouse.

ANTONIUS:

You are a merry gentleman. Do your pleasure with me. I will put myself into your hands, I tell you. Hold. Here are twenty old Angels that did see no Sun this ten year. Your Apothecary shall be well considered. He seemeth to be an honest man, and a cunning fellow. Let him set up all the boxes and glasses in the window and put on his bonnet.

MEDICUS:

What mean you sir? I pray you remember yourself. So God help me, you are to blame. Well, I will not contrary you. My chief desire is to help you, without the respect of money or gold, or other of your commodity. *Crispine,* set the boxes in the window, and you, Surgeon,[37] prepare your lace, staff and lance, with your ounce vessels, that I may consider his blood in order and due quantity, for hither unto he is but in the augmenting of his fever. Further, he had no fit this ten hours. Let him blood by little and little, and although he do fall into *Lipothymion,* it is no matter. Let him blood until it partly do change into a good color. Oh Lord, how might you live if this blood should have remained any longer? Did you ever see the like? What a good heart he hath. The worst is past. This would have been a great sore or apostemacion. Stop up the vein a God's name.

CRISPINE:

I did never see the like but once whereas your Mastership did a great cure upon a noble man.

MEDICUS:

Oh, are you advised of that *Crispine?* He is a good friend of mine. I have twenty pound yearly of him. He sent me a fat Buck upon Monday last and gave me my Mule also, with a Velvet footcloth.

Crispine:

Sir, when you sent me home, I left your mule standing at the door, but as I returned, I met a lackey clothed in Orange Tawny and white, with a pair of bare, tanned legs and a blue nightcap with a plume of feathers, riding on him as fast as he might gallop.

Medicus:

Oh, the passion of Christ! My mule is stolen! I will hence. I had rather lose twenty pound. I will tarry no longer. My Mule! I will teach him to ride on my Mule, I warrant him.

Crispine:

Sir, he needeth no teaching. He can ride well, I warrant you. I heard him say to a young man with a long cloak lined with yellow that his master sent him to carry a letter to a merchant adventurer that was cross-sailed into *Terra Florida*.

Medicus:

Give me my gown. Fare thee well, Master *Antonius*. As evil luck as ever I had in all my life.

Antonius:

I had thought the loss of your friend and of your Mule had not been both alike to you. What, for twenty pound? I will pay it double. The knave shall not escape. *Crispine* hath taken good marks upon him. I will send to every Ward, blind lane, Inns, Woods, and fields after the villain. I will take the matter on me, because you come to me so gently. Quiet yourself. Sit down again in the chair. I were cast away if you were gone, good master doctor.

Medicus:

I care not so much for the mule but that my lord will take much unkindness and think I should set light by his gift, and the Ruffians will laugh me to scorn when they know how I am handled of the knave boy. Well, I am contented with your offer. I pray you, beware you sleep not. You shall sup the thin broth of a chicken by and by, made with the four great cold seeds and cordial Herbs. *Crispine,* I pray you make the broth in some stone or silver vessel. Copper or Brass is not good for Master *Antonius.* Such vessels are Leprous.

ANTONIUS:

If you will have it made of gold, you shall.

MEDICUS:

We shall make shift with other things. Gold shall serve to deaurate or gild your lozenges, electuaries, and *manus christi* withal.

ANTONIUS:

Contented, so that it maketh on my side whatsoever it be. But me think I feel sleep approaching. What shall I do?

MEDICUS:

Draw the Curtains. Open the lukette of the Window. Set Sallows about the bed, besprinkled with vinegar and rose water. Take off that hot mantle. Let his head and shoulders be bolstered up. Lie not on your back. Lean towards this side. Let us talk together like friends why are you so heavy and earthlike.

ANTONIUS:

I must needs: I was made of earth. But where is the earth placed, of which I was made, and of what fashion is it? Although I walk upon the same, yet do I stand in doubt of the matter.

MEDICUS:

The earth is most heavy and can be in no place but in the middest of heaven, not moveable, but round and hangeth continually, about the which are the lands and countries of the world fixed, which *Aristotle* doeth call *Medium terrae, medium mundi.*[38]

ANTONIUS:

Are there not bodies which are called simple?

MEDICUS:

Yes forsooth, those are the four: the fire hot and dry, the air hot and moist, the water cold and moist, the earth cold and dry, and these are called the Elements.

ANTONIUS:

Are there not bodies called mixed? What are they?

MEDICUS:

Animalia, as man, beast, fish, fowl and Worms; *Vegetabilia,* as Herb, Grass and Trees; and *mineralia,* things under the earth, as metals.

ANTONIUS:

Lord, how is this world stayed?

MEDICUS:

The two Poles *Articus* and *Artarticus,* South and North, are the extreme limits about whom the whole frame of heaven is wrapped and is called *Axis coeli.*[39]

ANTONIUS:

Men sayeth that certain stars do govern the things beneath, here in earth.

MEDICUS:

They do so indeed, as it is well proved when as the Sun and Moon do enter into any of their circles, in those great bodies, then our little bodies in earth do feel the goodness or evilness of them, as *Aries*, *Leo*, and *Sagittarius*, are hot, dry and bitter, choleric, and are governing hot and dry things, and this is called the fiery triplicity. The second triplicity is of air, hot and moist, sanguine, sweet, and do govern Sanguine people. And other triplicity is of water, cold and moist, phlegmatic, having the government of cold raw bodies. The last is the earth, the mother of all things, cold and dry, melancholy.

ANTONIUS:

What do the knowledge of these things profit to Physic? I pray you tell me.

MEDICUS:

Most chiefly, for whereas the Philosopher do leave, there the Physician do begin. That is, he must be first a good natural Philosopher. He must have the knowledge of times and seasons and be acquainted with complexions of men, observing the nature of things, and the climates under heaven, with the course of the Sun, Moon, and Stars, Air and diet, etc.

ANTONIUS:

I pray you, is there a soul in man?

MEDICUS:

Yes, forsooth.

ANTONIUS:

Why then, there must needs be a greater thing, as the cause of every living soul, which I take to be God, which hath made all things, and when you and I talked together, you seemed that *Non est deus.*

Medicus:

I professed to follow *Aristotle,* but my meaning was that I credit not the Bible matters. I am no Divine. I find no reasons there for my turn. They are too hard things for me. I commend them to *Darbel* and *Duns,* etc.

Antonius:

Why? Doeth *Aristotle* show any better reasons than is in the Bible? Then I pray you, what is the power of the soul?

Medicus:

In the soul, sayeth *Aristotle* in his book of *Ethic,* it hath three sundry powers. The one is named vegetable, in which every man taketh part with herbs, trees, and plants. The second part of the soul is named sensible. In this part, man and beast are both alike in moving, etc. The third part is more, which is rational, or having reason. And this part of reason hath both act to do well and power to do evil. And these two are called *Intellective,* which learneth, descerneth, and judgeth in everything that may be seen, felt, heard, or understanded, but the power unreasonable, as sudden raging, crying, etc., is ascribed unto the Lion, Horse, Hog, etc. How like you this manner of talk? Yet here is no scripture but *Aristotle,* I assure you.

Antonius:

Then it should appear that the soul hath virtues. How many I pray you?

Medicus:

The first virtue is called *Intellectual,* from which springeth wisdom, science, and prudence. And the second is called moral, which is the mother of many good things, as chastity, liberality, humanity, and good manners.

Antonius:

What is the cause of these two virtues in the soul?

Medicus:

The virtue *Intellectual* engendereth and is nourished by learning of good tutors and men of experience or reading of good books of Philosophy, which is a secret virtue in the soul. And also the moral cometh by good custom, and not by nature, as if one man had two sons, the one brought up in keeping cattle, the other in daily learning good lessons. Although nature did frame their bodies like in shape, yet they should not be like in conditions. Moral provideth that natural things in them both can not be moved by contrary custom. For stones naturally, though they be cast never so high by art, yet must they naturally fall down again. Even so of fire being driven down, yet it will cast his flames upward. So, virtue is not in us by nature but only by power to receive them, for every thing that is in us by nature, first it is in us by powers, and after commeth to act, as it commeth to the senses of mankind. For none can deny but first man hath power to hear, see, feel, etc., so the power doeth prevent and cometh before the act in nature.

Antonius:

Then if power goeth before the act, then a man is called honest, good, or chaste before either honesty, goodness, or chastity appeareth in him.

Medicus:

In things moral, evermore the act goeth before the power. An example: a Schoolmaster is called a Teacher, because of his learning, which is the work going before the power. And the cause of a good man is his good works, and so of the evil, whose work is either drunkenness, adultery, theft, etc. They make him evil.

Antonius:

Then it should appear that this thing called *Actus*, or work, bringeth virtue and vice in man.

Medicus:

What else? Doeth not every man that liveth eat? But if he eat too much or too little, doeth it not bring sickness? Even so of too much labor or idleness, of too much boldness or cowardness. Are not these acts vicious and evil? And doeth not one mean moderate them both? Extremes are ever hurtful.

Antonius:

What remedy then, I pray you?

Medicus:

Nothing is better than a mean, called temperance, which is governed by prudence, which is ever content between both and rejoiceth in it.

Antonius:

So then, if a man fell into extreme adversity and sustain it patiently in his sickness, poverty, or cause of grief, call you this a mean, or no?

Medicus:

In every work or suffering, there is pleasure or displeasure. If a man do rejoice in trouble, in chastity, in bearing of cruel words or slander, the same is a prudent man, and his suffering maketh it a mean to him, but other men that are chastised and will suffer outwardly, and it grieveth them in so doing, the same is vicious and lacketh mean or prudence.

Antonius:

Hath the soul any delights in her or no?

Medicus:

Yes truly, in three things. The first profitable, whereof springeth husbandry to nourish the earth, as also Physic to help the body, knighthood to go to battle, etc. The second is delectable, as taking pleasure in things done, which is chiefly nourished of the soul, in which consisteth all the pleasures of the world. The third is called good, that is to be virtuous, loving, sober, patient, and also to the soul or mind are enjoined, habit, power and passion.

Antonius:

Have young children the soul in all points as women have or no, in operation or election?

Medicus:

Aristotle sayeth, that operation of the will of the soul is common to children, but the election or choice be not in them to will.

Antonius:

What is will in the soul?

Medicus:

The will is the intent, but election is the antecedent to the intent, for election goeth before operation or work, and the work doeth follow the same, as doing of things, buying, selling, and all the arts and sciences are so to be considered. First, by election, then by operation: as by art I do prove you to have the pestilence, experience hath taught me, which young children can not know—as or begun with their principles.

Antonius:

Now I will stop and lay a straw, and comment as yet no more of the matters of the soul but only of the body, and namely in this point of the pestilence. What is the cause of the same, good Master doctor?

Medicus:

That which we do see, we do testify, and that which we do testify is true. Therefore, no man ought in matters which appertaineth to the estate of life to write fables or lies but that which is of great authority and of good experience. This pestilent fever, sayeth *Hippocrates,* is in two parts considered: the first is common to every man by the corruption of air. The second is private or particular to some men through evil diet, repletion, which bringeth putrefaction, and finally mortification. And *Galen* in the *Differences of Fevers* doth affirm the same, saying, *Unam aerem viciatum ac putridum, alteram homoree corporis virioso victu colectos, et ad putrescendum paratos.*[40] *Avicenna* also, *Tractus quartus de febrius pestilentialibus, chapter 1:*[41] when there doeth come a sudden alteration or change in the quality of water from cold to heat or transmutation from sweetness to stink, as it chanceth in waters through corrupted mixture of putrefied vapor infecting both air and water, which of their own simplicity are clean, but through evil mixture are poisoned,[42] or when strong winds do carry pestilent fume or vapors from stinking places to the clean parts, as bodies dead of the plague, unburied, or mortality in battle, death of cattle, rotten fens, coming suddenly by the impression of air, creeping to the heart, corrupting the spirits—this is a dispersed pestilence by the inspiration of air.[43] Also by repletion, Venus, bathing, or opening the pores, rotten food, fruit, much Wine, or immoderate labor, or the time being hot and moist. These are great causes.

Antonius:

At what time of the year doeth the Pestilence cast forth her poison?[44]

Medicus:

In the time of Harvest, sayeth *Hippocrates*, are most sharp and deadly sicknesses (but less danger in the Springtime), and in the time of sundry change of Winds, when the weather is hot and moist.[45]

Antonius:

To what persons, I pray you, doeth the Pestilence come?

Medicus:

Most chiefly to them under the place infected; then to sluttish, beastly people that keep their houses and lodgings unclean, their meat, drink, and clothing most noisome, their labor and travel immoderate; or to them which lack provident wisdom to prevent the same by good diet, air Medicine, etc.; or to the bodies hot and moist. And these bodies do infect other clean bodies, and whereas many people do dwell on heaps together, as *Avicenna* sayeth: *Et communicat multitudine hominum, etc.*[46] (*Febrius chapter 1, tract 4*).

Antonius:

By what sign or token is this perilous plague or stripe of the Pestilence best knowen among the Physicians? Go not about the bush with subtle words, but plainly speak the truth to me, being in this fearful danger, as you do well know that I am in.

Medicus:

The signs are most manifest, which are the stars running course or race after their causes. Oh, the most fearful eclipses of the Sun and Moon, those heavenly bodies, are manifest signs of the pestilence among men; and the stars cadente in the beginning of Harvest, or in the month of September; or much South wind or East wind in the *Canicular* days, with storms and clouds, and very cold nights and extreme hot days, and much change of weather in a little time; or when birds do forsake their eggs, flies or things breeding under the ground do fly high by swarms into the air; or death of fish or cattle, or any dearth going before. These are the signs of the pestilence and evident presages of the same.

ANTONIUS:

These are good signs general, but particular, what manifest tokens do signify the Plague or Pestilence in a man's own proper body?

MEDICUS:

They which are smitten with this stroke or plague are not so open in the spirits as in other sickness as are but strait-winded. They do swoon and vomit yellow choler, swelled in the stomach with much pain, breaking forth with stinking sweat. The extreme parts very cold, but the internal parts boiling with heat and burning. No rest; blood distilling from the nose; urine somewhat watery, and sometimes thick with stink, sometimes of color yellow, sometimes black; scalding of the tongue; ordure most stinking. With red eyes, corrupted mouth with blackness, quick pulse and deep but weak, headache, altered voice, loss of memory, sometimes with raging in strong people.[47] These and such like are the manifest signs, how the heart hath drawen the venom to it by attraction of the air, by the inspiration of the arteries to the heart, and so confirming it to be the perilous fever Pestilential. This is most true: of this cometh foul buboes, *anthraxes* and carbuncles, sores, through putrefaction, as *Galen* sayeth (*Libri 3 De presage; Avicenna, Febrium 1, tract 4; Galen, libri 1 De differentia, chapter 4; and Rasis de constitutione pestilentiae, ad almansorem*).[48] Also, this fever is scant to be recovered and almost past help when these *Symptomatas* do appear, as *Galen* sayeth ([*Libri*] *3, De presage: ex pul. qua propter neque hos curare tentandum erit*).[49]

Antonius:

You have declared unto me a fearful tale of the Plague, whereof thousands have and shall die—a pitiful case how it cometh among people suddenly, even as you have showed, the cause primitive in the air. The antecedent, when the same air is drawn into the heart by attraction of the arteries; the conjunct, when it with boiling heat doeth change, by putrefaction, nature into the worse part, and almost past cure of any Physician when it is come to this point, as I gather by your late talk, which doth put me in great fear of my life. But I will common with you for others, which are not infected: how may they be most safely defended, master Doctor?

Medicus:

Would you fain know? Surely I will declare thee the best defense that I can. I will hide nothing. First of all, let all men, women, and children avoid out of the ill air into a good soil, and then, according to their age, strength of nature, and complexion, let every one of them with some good Medicine draw from the body superfluous moisture and diminish humor hot and dry, and use the regimen of diet to drying, sharpened with vinegar or tart things, and lesser meats: not so much wine as they have used in custom, neither Potage, Milk, unripe fruits.[50] Hot spices, dates or Honey, or sweet meats, wine with Sugar are not tolerable. No anger or perturbations of the mind, specially the passion called fear, for that do draw the spirits and blood inwards to the heart, and is a very mean to receive this plague. Neither use acts venerous, nor bathing, either with fume, Stove, or warm water: (for this cause) they all do open the pores of the body. Neither quaffing or much drinking. Even so, thirst or dryness is not tolerable, or immoderate exercise or labor, specially after meat. Music is good in this case, and pleasant tales, and to have the meats well sauced with clean sharp vinegar. Forget not to keep the chamber and clothing clean; no privies at hand; a soft fire with perfumes in the morning.[51] Shift the lodging often time, and close in the South East winds, specially in the time of mists, Clouds, and winds. And use to smell upon some pleasant perfume and to be letten blood, a little at once, and to take Pills *contra Pestem* that is a good preservative against the plague.

Antonius:

These are good rules, and happy are they that do wisely observe them in time, place, and manner accordingly, but if one be newly infected, what remedy then, as when a man is sick and the sore appeareth not?

Medicus:

A coming forth like a buboes are signs of those parts from which they do swell, as example in the left side, head, neck, flanks, etc., but often times the plague sore will not appear.[52] The very cause is this: nature is too weak and the poison of the infection too strong that it cannot be expelled, and this is most perilous of all, when such a cruel conqueror doeth reign within the heart, the principal part of life, now possessed with death. The causes of this I have declared before with signs to the same. Notwithstanding, consider two things: first whether it is in bodies sanguine and choleric or them which are phlegmatic or melancholy or not. The first two, blood is the cause. The second two, abundance of evil humors. Therefore let blood whereas it hath the victory, and purge whereas other humors have predomination or chief rule. In some men that have very strong bodies, first purge, then let blood.[53] Note this, that what side be infected, let blood on that side. If it be about the head, open *Cephalica.* If it be under the arms, *Basilica* or heart vein. If it be about the throat, then open *Malleola.* About the flanks, belly, legs, etc., open *Jecorary.*[54] If they are very weak or young, then boxing is good to the neck, shoulders, back and thighs. If the stomach be full, then with speed vomit, and these things draw the venom from the heart, and remove the poison.

Antonius:

This is good in the cure of the Pestilence, for I do praise this blood-letting very well, in the beginning of the sickness.

Medicus:

Blood must be letten in the beginning of the sickness. For example, like as a pot is cleansed of the scum or foam in the beginning when it playeth on the fire and thereby the liquor is cleansed within the pot, even so, blood letting and pills do help and cleanse the Pestilence when it beginneth first to boil within the body. Howbe it, certain people may not bleed, as women which have their times abundantly or men having flux of the Hemorrhoids, children very young, or people weak and aged.

Antonius:

I pray you, what quantity of blood must be letten?

Medicus:

Forsooth four ounces, or little more, and must be done every month, sometime in the *Median,* sometime in the *Basilica,* etc. And not to sleep after the same, during six, seven, or eight hours.

Antonius:

What Pills do you use against the Plague?

Medicus:

The best Pills generally under heaven, and is thus made: take the best Yellow Aloes, two ounces; Myrrh and Saffron, of each one ounce. Beat them together in a Mortar a good while. Put in a little sweet Wine. Then roll it up, and of this make five Pills, or seven of one dram; whereof, take every day next your heart, a scruple or more. It will expulse the Pestilence that day, etc.[55]

Antonius:

Have you any good potion in store for the Pestilence, to be drunk a Mornings, when the Pills are not taken?

Medicus:

None better than this: take *Theriaca*, of the making of *Andromachus*, two scruples, which is a Treacle incomparable passing against both poison and Pestilence,[56] and the *Antidotari* of *Mithridatum*, one scruple; bole Armeniac prepared, half a scruple; and the waters of distilled Roses, Scabious, and Bugloss, of each one ounce mingled together.[57] But this Medicine must be had of *Crispine*, or one of his companions, which use no rotten ware.

Antonius:

Have you any good powder?

Medicus:

One better, I assure you, than a king's ransom, and thus it must be made: take the leaves of *Dictamnus*, and the roots of Tormentil, of Pimpernel, of Setwall, of Gentian, of Betony, of each half an ounce; bole Armeniac, prepared, an ounce; *Terra sigillata*, three drams; fine Aloes and Myrrh, of each half an ounce; Saffron, a dram; Mastic, two drams. Beat them together finely and searsed. This is the powder. Of this must a dram be drunk in four or six spoonful of Rose or Sorrel water when danger approacheth or in the time of danger.

Antonius:

These are strong things for many weak stomachs. Is there any other wholesome things?

Medicus:

The syrups of Violets, of Sorrel, of Endive, of sour Limondes, of each like, mingled with Borage water, and a Tisane made of Barley, mingled together, is very wholesome to drink. Put in the powder of bole Armeniac, which is of a singular virtue to cool, for *Galen* did help thousands at Rome with the same Bole and the *Theriaca* mingled together, in a great pestilence. But in the pestilence time, one being infected therewith, let him sweat by warm things, as hot tiles, etc., and let not the patient eat, sleep, nor drink, and eat light meats, as Hen, Capon, Chicken, Partridge, eating often, and little at once, with sauce, made sharp of vinegar, Oranges, sharp Limondes, or Sorrel. And in the first day of the sickness that the patient be kept from sleep by talking, sprinkling of sweet water, rubbing of the body, as nose, ears, or soft pulling of the hairs, as they may be suffered, or a sponge dipped in vinegar, applied to the nose. And if vehement dryness or heat doeth approach, then drink the Syrups last rehearsed, and have the Chamber clean kept and also perfumed four times of the day. Beware of stink. Let the perfumes be made with *Olibanum*, Mastic, wood of Aloes, Benjamin, *Storax*, *Ladanum*, Cloves, Juniper, or suchlike, and sprinkle all the chamber about with vinegar. Roses in the windows, or green branches of Sallow or of Quinces are good, sprinkled with Rose water and Vinegar.[58]

Antonius:

I have heard say that Garlic and new Ale should be good for the Plague.

Medicus:

You do say truth. Garlic is good for to bring it, but not against it. It is so hot and hath power attractive, and that is very evil and a mean to bring the plague. So are Onions, Leeks, Rocket, Radish, and such baggage, which are sold about in every street in Plaguey time as means for to bring the same. It is pity to suffer such things. Further, the multitudes of infected people among the whole, infecting them, or wearing the apparel of the dead bodies of the

Pestilence, which should be burned, for it is like a fire, when it have gotten the victory and cannot be quenched. Privies, filthy houses, gutters, channels, unclean kept, also the people sick, going abroad with the plague sore running, stinking and infecting the whole, or unwise rash passing with an empty stomach out of the house. Neither to sit tippling and drinking all the day long, nor use running, wrestling, Dancing, or immoderate labor, which do not only open the pores but also cause the wind to be short and the pulses to quick and the Arteries draw to the heart when it panteth the pestilential air and poison. And what is worse than fear of mind when one doeth hear ill tidings, the death of father, mother, child, etc.? By it the spirits and blood are drawen inwards to the heart. Also of care, anger, wrath, etc., these are all perilous. Mirth must be used, specially in this case.[59] Cats, Dogs, Swine, Ducks, Doves, Hens, or Geese are very unwholesome near unto the place or mansion of dwelling, or lie dead in ditches near the town. Or many people lying together in one bed, or long watching in the night, costiveness of the belly, shut up the hothouse doors, and tennis play, which are most venomous. Be never without the electuary of nuts, thus made:[60] cleave walnuts; twenty fat figs; thirteen herb of Grace; two handful Wormwood; Feverfew, or rather *Cotula Foetida,* called *Buphthalmos,* called Ox-eye, and *Scabious,* of each one handful; the roots of *Aristolochia longa,* half an ounce; *Aristolochia rotunda,* an ounce and a half. The roots of Tormentil, and of the lesser Bur called *Petasites,* Pimpernel, of each two ounces and a half; the leaves of the very *Dictamnus*[61] one handful; Bayberries three drams; the powder of Heart's horn two drams and a half; Maces, Myrrh, Bole Armeniac, and the earth of Limodes,[62] of each drams three; Salt of the Sea a dram and a half; *Nux vomica,* drams two; Bugloss flowers, one handful, stamped together by art; and with clarified honey make it. This is good to be eaten a dram every morning. Forget not the Pill of *Rufus;* of them may be taken one at once.

Antonius:

After, or with this Pestilence, there will a fearful sore appear, as we have that knowledge Universal, by painful experience, which we do call the plague sore. What do you say to the same sore?

Medicus:

This sore is called *Carbunculus,* of *Carbo* a Cole,[63] or *Anthrax.* They are both one, and not two, and is engendered of most sharp, hot and gross blood, which nature doeth cast forth through the skin to one particular part, with extreme pain and peril to the body, whose Primative cause was the corruption of air or diet, drawn to the heart, of which pestiferous smoke or poisoned fume this sore hath his cause, and the same sore is the effect following.

Antonius:

What are the signs when it commeth near hand?

Medicus:

A fever going before, noisome and loathsomeness of stomach, wambling of the heart, pulse not equal, urine stinking, desirous of sleep, perilous dreams with starting through the sharpness of hot and burning humors, and then a little push will creep forth like a scab, sometime more than one. Then it will increase and shine like pitch or *Bitumen,* with passing pain, and then it will have a crust like unto the squams or flakes of Iron when they fall off when the Smith doeth work. And in color like ashes is this crust, wrought by extreme heat and burning; therefore it may be called the burning coal or *Ignem persicum.* Further, there are four colors to be observed in the sore besides the crust: yellow, red, green, and black. The first two are not so dangerous as the second two are. Yet sayeth *Rasis* in his book of the pestilence, to *Mansor* the king, that the carbuncle is deadly and most perilous.[64] And *Avicenna* affirmeth the black to be incurable, specially when a Fever Pestilence do reign. Sometime it is drawn back again into the body, then no remedy. Sometime it happeneth in the most noble places, as near the heart, the throat, most perilous, with sudden stopping the spirits of life. Some pestilent sores do come in the cleansing places, as arm holes, flanks, etc. And when nature is so strong to cast it forth with a red color, palish, or yellowish, the cure is not then very hard.

ANTONIUS:

It should seem to be most hard. You have showed more perils than helps hitherunto. But if there be any remedies, what are they? I pray you tell them, for in that point you may do much good.

MEDICUS:

Even as I have rehearsed before, so will I again begin in the cure of the carbuncle of the opening of a vein, and if none other thing do let, as extreme weakness, etc., then let the patient bleed until the defection of the spirits or nearhand swooning. Let it be done on that side grieved or afflicted, as I have said before in the fever Pestilence of the *Mediana*, etc. Also forget not eight special things. First the substance, as compass, length, depth, hardness, etc. Second, the matter whereof it is bred, as blood, etc. The third as accident, through the dolor, as a fever, redness, etc. Fourth to know it from a cause, whereof a doubt might arise thereof. And this is the difference between them.[65] A carbuncle in the beginning is very hard, flaming red, extreme pain, etc., as I have said before, and will come quickly to his head. But *Cancer* is not so red, neither so painful, yet much harder and longer time or it cometh to the head. But when it beginneth to wax soft, then it ripeth faster than the carbuncle. The fifth, of the causes efficient, whether it be ripe through concoction or no, or the qualities of the corrupted humors, or hardness, etc. The sixth, in what place it is, in place of peril or no. The seventh is to work by incision, plaster, etc. The eighth is good diet, as air, meat, drinks, sleep, etc. These are very good observations, worthy of memory in this case.

And now followeth a peril to the *Surgeon*, which must be richly rewarded, for he putteth his life in danger in that he helpeth the sore body infected. He ought to be provident that doth take this matter in hand, and before he cometh to the pinch to eat his *antidotari* of *Methridatum*, or to have a Sponge with strong vinegar applied to his nostrils to arm himself against the poisoned air, and to take his lance in his hand, according to the art, taking heed that in lancing he cut no vein or Sinew, which have society with each other; therefore, lance not very deep. This is no strange thing after bloodletting, to lance the sore, to let forth the matter. In some it will come forth abundantly, when it is ripe or rotten. In other some not, because the humors are gross and baken together, or the running matter far in, or scant ripe, and nothing will come forth but salt, sharp, filthy, stinking water. Then beware of any thing that might drive it back again into the body, as cold, bole armeniac, etc. Then the incision must be made in the lowest place, so that thereby the matter may the sooner avoid, and must be made in the form crooked if it be not in a place full of sinews. If it be, then make the incision long, after the matter is run forth. Then cover it with lint dipped in this following, which is excellent good, yea, if the matter be stubborn in the sore: take Quince seed, Galls, of each three drams; Myrrh, *Olibanum* and Aloes, of each two drams and a half; Alum two drams; *Aristolochia* the round roots, *Calamint*, as much; *Calamint*, one dram and a half; *Chalcanthum*, a scruple, all beaten finely. Then temper it together in a little Red Wine, made in small rolls. You may keep them dry, and then in this case dissolve it or part of it in the water of stilled milk. Apply this with lint into the sore. Also in this case to wash the sore with a sponge dipped in the warm waters of Dragons, Scabious, sweet wine, *Aristolochia* and *Comfrey*, or their decoction. And to have the roots of *Comfrey*, of Lilies, of Mallows, sodden in white wine until they be soft, then stamped and drawn through a strainer. Put thereunto barley meal and honey of roses. This is a very good thing to apply to the sore after the washing for twelve hours and will digest it. Another good medicine, both to ripe and assuage the pain: mallows, violets, camomile, of each half an handful; dill, half as much. Seethe them and bray them; then add to them barley meal, and oil of roses, flax seed, bean meal, of each three ounces. Seethe them in sweet wine, until they wax thick, and make plaster. And to the places about the roots of the carbuncle, round about it, this is good both to eradicate and defend the same. Seethe four oranges in vinegar or sorrel, and put a little bole armeniac to it. Dip a cloth or flax in it, and apply it round about the sore: many times renew it. In this cure, read Master *Thomas Gale*'s worthy book.

And to take away the hard crust of the carbuncle, do thus: take ceruse, vermilion, sublimated, of each three drams, beaten finely in powder, and part of this may be cast upon the same. And to this may follow mallows, violets, lettuce, of each one handful; sodden in mutton broth the yolks of three eggs, barley meal, oil of roses, and fresh butter, of each three ounces. This plaster applied on will take away the Pestilent crust. Also the *emplastrum* of *Diachylon parvum,* two ounces; with *Ammoniac* and *Galbanun,* of each one ounce; made in a plaster, applied to the place; or a plaster of figs, Dove's dung, and Valerian roots, and the roots of mallows made and applied upon the sore are very good ripers and do much prevail in this cure and further to bring the cicatrix if need require. Take oil of Myrrh; of roses, of violets, of each two ounces; sheep's Tallow three ounces; goat's tallow one ounce and a half; juice of Coleworts three ounces. Seethe them together softly, until the juice be consumed. Then put thereunto half an ounce of Vermilion, ceruse as much, and two drams of litharge of gold, and seethe them unto a blackness. Stir them with a stick. Then put to them six ounces turpentine, and as much Wax as shall suffice to make it in the form of a cerate. And this will make a strong cicatrix. And when the matter hath run much and is past venom, then this is a powder most precious to cast in, and dry it by little and little: take Ashes of Dill, of burnt lead, of *Terra lemnia,* of each one dram; litharge of silver, flowers of pomegranates, and galls without holes, of each two drams; Ceruse, Crevishels,[66] Snails' horns, rock Alum burnt, of each two scruples beaten in powder. This is the powder, and hereafter followeth a good ointment to heal the sore: oil of Roses, two ounces; Ceruse, burnt lead, Litharge, of each one a scruple; red Roses, two scruples in powder; the roots of the great *Comfrey*, and the flowers of Pomegranates, bole Armeniac, of each one scruple; the seed of Purslane two grains; white wax as much as shall suffice, and make this ointment in a Leaden mortar if it may be. Among all simples, *Simphatum* called *Comfrey* is greatly lauded for the healing or helping of the carbuncle, being ground or beaten between two stones and warm applied to the place. So is the herb called *Scabious* in the same manner. So is the Lily roots roasted and bruised and warm laid on. Let not the great white onion roasted and the pith in the middest being taken forth, stopped with good Treacle or *Mithridatum* warm and applied to the place, be forgotten, for some use none other things for the carbuncle, to cure it.

Also consider this to keep the body temperate in eating: beware of repletion; light Fish with tart sauces, Limondes, Sorrel, Oranges, thin wine with water, but no Sugar or sweet things. Forget not sweet perfumes of Rose water, cloves, Maces, Vinegar in a perfuming pan, and have the stomach anointed with oil of Maces, and the complete ointment of roses, of each two scruples, and *Gallia muschata*, ten grains, and dip in a linen cloth in white wax, oil of Roses, white and red Saunders, and the powder of oriental Pearls, fine bole Armeniac, and the sweet wood of Aloes with Rose water, made warm in a little vessel upon charcoal. And be not without a good Pomander made of Storax Calamint, three drams; *Ladanum*, half an ounce; flowers of water Lilies, Violets, the wood of Aloes, Spikenard, of each a dram and a half; the three Saunders, of each half a dram; Cinnamon, two scruples; Mastic, twenty grains; white Poppy seed, Camphor, of each a scruple; Amber and Musk, of each three grains; with rose water in a warm Mortar, make Pomander. Make a hole in it, and put a silk lace through it, and wear this against corrupted air.

The body must have benefit by purgation with clyster or suppository or some potion, as the syrup of roses solutive, three ounces;

confection of Hamech, five drams; and water of Endive, four ounces; mingled together, and drink at once in the morning. Or *Benedicta laxativa,* with water of Bugloss. Be not without *Manus Christi,* to eat oftentimes, and the conserve of Roses, to eat before meat daily. Beware of much sleep, which will make the heat double about and within the heart, for sleep draweth in heat, and in time of waking, it is spread abroad, and the heat draweth to the extremes, as hands, head, and feet. Sir, forget not this, I pray you.

ANTONIUS:

No master Doctor, I warrant you, I have noted it well, and though it help not me, yet I trust it shall do good to others when I am gone.

MEDICUS:

Now sir, I will take my leave for a time. My calling is such that I must depart, and diverse of my patients diligently do look for me as the birds do for the day after a cold Winter's night. And as time and occasion shall serve, I will return. I have hidden nothing from you that may be a means to your health, for when life is gone, farewell altogether, wife, children, gold, lands, treasures, and all the golden glory of this world, and friends also. Therefore, seeing life is the best jewel which brings delights to the heart, pleasures to the eye and ear, sweet savors to sense of smelling, and many hidden treasures, knowledge to the virtue of understanding, what is he that would make such an exchange if it were possible to the contrary?[67] To forsake his golden bedecked bed with sweet sleeps, to lie utterly lost, rotten, forgotten, and stinking in a filthy pit of darkness, enclosed and wrapped with Worms. As by example, we may see the multitude of graves in every church yard, and great heaps of rotten bones, whom we know not of what degree they were, rich or poor in their lives. Therefore sir, to conclude, pluck up that weak heart, rejoice, be glad, and cast away all care, I warrant you.

Antonius:

Gramercies, master doctor, I have put you to pain with much talk and questions. I will keep them in memory. They shall not be forgotten of my part. Even so, forget not your promise in coming to me again. My trust is in you. We shall make daily exchange: cunning for gold, and love for labor. Yours I am. Have, take you that to buy you a new Mule, a footcloth, and a gown.

Medicus:

What mean your mastership? Well, give me your hand, and here is mine with my heart also, ever yours at commandment as your own.[68] Thus fare you well until my return. In the meanwhile, pass the time with some pleasant company. Eat good broth made of Chickens, lean Mutton, roast a little Partridge. Eat light leavened bread. Beware of gross meats, Beef, Pork, etc., and Sallettes, strong wine, Spice, sweet meats, and raw fruits. I pray you remember this, and drink your *Diacodium* at night, to reconcile sleep again, and be somewhat laxative.

Antonius:

I thank you most heartily. Fare you well.

Medicus:

Crispine where are you? Is it not time to depart? We have tarried here very long, but not without gain.

Crispine:

Sir, I have thought it a month since our coming hither. You have been sent for eight times this afternoon, and two of your patients are dead this day.

Medicus:

That is no marvel, for who can hold that will away? I shall have more work than I can put my hand unto. It is now a golden world with me, and with you also.

CRISPINE:

God continue the same. I would thousands were sick, but I would have none dead but the beggars that do trouble the world and have no money to pay.[69] I pray you, what think you of master *Antonius?* Shall he escape it or no?

MEDICUS:

I have his plentiful reward, and money for you also. I have had long talk with him. But to be plain with you, I think never to see him again alive. He was past cure or I came to him, and he could not scape; therefore I kept him with long talk, but I spake but softly.

CRISPINE:

Then I perceive your talk was unprofitable to him, yet I wrote it in a little paper book in my hand.

MEDICUS:

Not unprofitable, if the Physician come in the beginning or augmenting of the sickness. But in the full state of this sickness, it is most dangerous, because death will prevent it, or it cometh to the declination. Oh, it is a strong poison if the Pestilence creep to his heart.

CRISPINE:

This man loved you well in his life. Will you not be at his burial Master Doctor?

MEDICUS:

He loved me as I loved him: he me for health, and I him for money. And they which are preservers of the life of man ought not to be present at the death or burial of the same man; therefore, I have taken my leave; I warrant you *Crispine.* I will return to him no more. Thus, fare you well till the morrow in the morning.

CRISPINE:

I must also depart to my shop. I have much business to do. I will come to you at your commandment, master Doctor. Thus fare you well.

[Scene change to the home of *Civis* and *Uxor*]

CIVIS:

Good wife, the daily jangling and ringing of the bells, the coming in of the minister to every house in ministering the communion, in reading the Homily of death, the digging up of graves, the sparring in of windows, and the blazing forth of the blue cross[70] do make my heart tremble and quake. Alas what shall I do to save my life?

UXOR:

Sir, we are but young and have but a time in this world. What doeth it profit us to gather riches together and can not enjoy them? Why tarry we here so long? I do think every hour a year until we be gone. My heart is as cold as a stone and as heavy as lead, God help me. Seeing that we have sent our children forth three weeks past into a good air and a sweet country, let us follow them. We shall be welcome to your brother's house. I dare say my sister will rejoice in our coming and so will all our friends there. Let us take leave of our neighbors and return merrily home again when the plague is past and the dog days ended, and there you may occupy your stock and have gain thereof.

CIVIS:

Oh wife, we know not our return, for the Apostle sayeth to you that will say, "today or tomorrow, we will go to such a city and buy and sell and have gain and know not what shall happen tomorrow. What is our life? It is as a vapor that appeareth for a little time and afterward vanish away; for that, ye ought to say, if the Lord will and if we live, we will to this or that place,"[71] and if it please God, we will both depart and return again at his good will and pleasure, for we are in his hands whether soever we do go. And I trust it is not against God's commandment or pleasure that we depart from this infected air.

Uxor:

I know not what God will in our departing, but my flesh trembles when I do hear the death bell ring.

Civis:

Yes surely, we have the Apostle saying (for our defense in flying), "no man ever yet hath hated his own flesh but nourished and cherished it,"[72] therefore, who can nourish his flesh in a corrupted air, but rather do kill it? Further, I heard a doctor of Physic say that one called *Galen* in a book of Treacle to one *Pison* his friend that the Pestilence was like a monstrous hungry beast, devouring and eating not a few but sometimes whole cities that by respiration or drawing in their breath do take the poisoned air. He lauded *Hippocrates*, which sayeth that to remove from the infected air into a cleaner, thereby sayeth he, they did not draw in more foul air, and this was his only remedy for the plague, to them that did remain. He commanded not only simple wood to be burned within the city of *Athens* but also most sweet flowers and spices, perfumes, as gums and ointments to purge the air. And wife, fear of death enforced many holy men to fly, as Jacob from his cruel brother Esau, David from Saul, Elias from Jezebel.[73] The Christian men for fear of death did fly the tyranny of the Papists, and although these men did not fly the Pestilence, yet they fled all for fear of death, and so will we by God's grace observe such wholesome means and obey his divine providence. Also, I will leave my house with my faithful friends, and take the keys of the chests with me. Where are ourzhorses?

Uxor:

Our things are ready. Have you taken your leave of your neighbors, man?

Civis:

I have done, so now let us depart, a God's blessing good wife.

Uxor:

Give me my horse, *Roger.*

Roger:

Mistress, he is here ready at your hand, a good gelding. God bless him and sweet Saint Loye.

Civis:

Bring forth mine also, and let the servants forget nothing behind them, specially the steel casket. Let us ride fair and softly until we be out of the town.

Uxor:

How pleasant are these wheat fields garnished with fair plants and flowers. The birds do sing sweetly and pitifully in the bushes. Here are pleasant woods. Jesus, man, who would be in the City again? Not I, for an hundred pound. Oh, help me! My horse starteth and had like to have been unsaddled. Let me sit faster, for falling.

Civis:

He is a bird-eyed jade, I warrant you, and you are no good horsewoman, for I did never see you ride before in all my life, but exercise will make you perfect. Your mother was a good horsewomen and loved riding well as any gentlewoman that ever I knew in my life. Well, she is gone and we must follow; this is the world.

Uxor:

I never was so far from London in all my life. How far have we ridden already, I pray you?

Civis:

Wife, we have ridden ten miles this morning.

Uxor:

What town is this, I pray you sir?

Civis:

This is Barnet, where Samuel your son was nursed,[74] and yonder is Richard Higmer's house. We will see him as we do return home again. We will not tarry now because every Inn is pestered with Londoners and carriers, and it is early days. How like you this town, Dame?

Uxor:

A pretty street, but me think the people go very plain. It is no city, as I do suppose by their manners. What house is this at the town's end, compassed with a Moat?

Civis:

Here dwelleth a friend of ours. This is called the fold.

Uxor:

What great smoke is in yonder wood? God grant it be well.

Civis:

It is nothing but making of Charcoal in that place.

Uxor:

Why, is Charcoal made? I had thought all things had be made at London, yet I did never see no Charcoals made there.[75] By my truth I had thought that they had growen upon trees and had not been made.

CIVIS:

You are a wise woman. They are made of wood. But how like you this Heath? Here was foughten a fearful field called Palm Sunday battle in King Edward the fourth's time. Many thousands were slain on this ground. Here was slain the noble Earl of Warwick.[76]

ROGER:

If it please your mastership, my grandfather was also here, with twenty tall men of the Parish whereas I was born, and none of them escaped but my grandfather only. I had his bow in my hand many a time. No man could stir the string when it was bent. Also his harness was worn upon our Saint George's,[77] back in our church many a cold Winter after, and I heard my grandame tell how he escaped.

CIVIS:

Tell, *Roger,* I pray thee, how he did escape the danger?

ROGER:

Sir, when the battle was pitched and appointed to be foughten, near unto this Windmill, and the Summons given by the Harottes of arms that spear, pole-ax, blackbill, bow and arrows should be set a work the day following, and that it should be tried by bloody weapon, a sudden fear fell on my grandfather, and the same night when it was dark, he stole out of the earl's camp, for fear of the king's displeasure, and hid him in the Wood. And at length he espied a great hollow Oak tree with arms somewhat green, and climbed up, partly through cunning, for he was a thatcher. But fear was worth a ladder to him, and then by the help of a writhen arm of the tree he went down, and there remained a good while and was fed there by the space of a month with old Acorns and Nuts which squirrels had brought in, and also did in his Sallet keep the rain water for his drink, and at length escaped the danger.

Civis:

So he might, for any stripes that he had there. He was well harnessed with a Tree. But I never read this in the Chronicle.

Roger:

There be many things (and it shall please your Mastership) which are not written in the Chronicles I do think are as true, as John your man do read unto me when we do go to bed almost every night. I shall never forget them. Farewell, good John.

Civis:

What are they, *Roger?*

Roger:

Marie, sir, he told me in the old time how Horses, Sheep, Hogs, Dogs, Cats, Rats, and Mice did speak, and I do partly believe that, for as much as our Parrot will say, "Parrot is a minion," and "Beware the Cat," and she will call me "*Roger*" as plain as your Mastership, and although Dogs have lost their speech, yet they do understand. When I do whistle, Truly will come. He will fetch my glove, my bolt in the water, or stoop or lie down when I bid him, and surely he which do understand and hear what I do say, may speak also, but that there are so many languages now adays, he can not tell which to speak and to leave all alone and turneth all to plain barking, as women do, when as they do fall from reasoning into scolding.

Civis:

Thou foolish knave, what meanest thou to speak thus? Dogs did never speak. They do want reason, for there are three things to be considered in each living creature. The first is vegetable, wherein man, Dog, and tree, are all one. The second is sensible. In this, man and dog are all one. The third is where man excelleth all other creatures, where he have reason and judgment, having act to do well, and power to do evil. Through this reason, man do speak. The beast wanteth reason; therefore he speaketh not, etc. But Dogs are taught by custom and not moved by reason.

ROGER:

Well sir, our John's book shall confound your talk, for I did see it in writing, and that which is written I will believe and follow by God's grace, and no more.

CIVIS:

Why, will you do no more for me than I have commanded you by writing? You are an honest fellow?

ROGER:

When I came to you first, you gave me a scroll of parchment, wherein said you, "do no more but as this commandeth, and I will ask no more of thee but allow thy service." Now in case your Mastership with your horse fell both into the mire over the ears, if it were not in my writing to help you both forth, I have done you no evil service. Ha, ha, ha. How crack you this nut?

UXOR:

It were a good deed to crack your pate, you saucy varlet. God's dainty Jack-sauce, whence came you?

ROGER:

Forsooth out of the country, Mistress *nisibecetur* as fine as five pence. How prettily you can call "varlet," and swear by "God's dainty." God bless you. I did never see you stumble before.

UXOR:

Out rogue and slave! Avante villain! Out of my sight, knave!

ROGER:

I think you learned your Rhetoric in the university of Bridewell. You were never well wormed when you were young.

UXOR:

Sir, you do ride too fast. Have you not heard what this honest man have said to me?

CIVIS:

Dame, all things must be taken in good part. I heard nothing. If any thing be amiss, at our return it shall be amended. We must have one riding fool by the way so that it be done merrily and exceed not. Well, fellow, you do believe that beasts will speak because it is written so of them?

ROGER:

That I will. If that my Mistress will hold her peace, I will prove it.

UXOR:

I pray you, give ear to no such trifles and lies, good husband.

CIVIS:

I pray you be content. It is as good to hear a lie which hurteth not as sometime a true tale that profiteth not. Tell on gentle *Roger,* a God's name. Ride near, and let us be merry.

ROGER:

It so chanced in the pleasant time of May, a lusty young Lion after his prey or new eaten spoil did lie him down to sleep, and yet being asleep, the beasts that were nearhand did quake and tremble in beholding of his most fearful countenance and fled away. The poor silly Mouse crept out of her small cave and came softly, thinking no harm, and played about the Lyon, and piped merrily, wherewith the Lion awaked suddenly and was angry, caught the Mouse forthwith, thinking to have devoured it. But this poor Mouse kneeled down upon her knees, and held up her hands, saying, "I have offended your lordship. I pray you therefore forgive me, and let me have my life, and once I shall requite it you," whereat the Lion smiled and let her pass away in peace. Within few days, the same Lion was taken in a strong Net, thinking never to have been delivered, and cried most fearfully with desperation. But gentle, Margery Mouse with all speed came running, and with sharp filed teeth did gnaw and shred the strong cords which entrapped the Lion, wherewith he stood at liberty and went his way. This is true, when Mice and Lions did speak. I will abide by the same, sir, if it shall please your Mastership.

Civis:

No surely, Lions nor Mice did never speak, *Roger.* But some wise man have written this to this end, that like as cruelty is to be utterly avoided, even so ingratitude is to be abhorred. We may hereby consider that very poor men in the time of trouble may help the mighty and strong, and oftentimes do indeed. Why should then the great lord forget the benefit of a poor groom which many ways may pleasure him (if the simple Mouse were from the Lion)? Then the gentleman were most wretched, in occupation and drudgery most vile. If poor and simple men in the time of extreme persecution by God's providence have delivered the oppressed (which persecuted or oppressed) since are come to great promotion, both spiritual and temporal, do forget the same benefits again, it were not only the parts of infidels but also more ungrateful than beasts, as horses which have rescued their masters in battle, and dogs which would never eat after their master's death but die upon their graves. Another kind of ingratitude is with Judas: when one bestow a benefit upon a man, the same man to invent to murder his friend. As if a man in the time of cold should find a snake and, for foolish pity, put him into his bosom to warm him. I think his nature is to sting the man. Or if a Shepherd should bring a young Wolf up among his Lambs and give him Milk, surely he would fall to blood at length and kill the Shepherd himself.

ROGER:

Sir, you have well expounded my tale. Now I know your meaning. I perceive it is not good, keeping of such unkind beasts. They are very costly and perilous and would have Jack Drake's medicine. Sir, upon a time when quackling Ducks did speak and Hens cackling could talk, which indeed are continual companions because they are Fowls (Marie, of sundry kinds, and names), for Ducks and all waterfowls do not only take the benefit of goodly ponds, rivers, and pleasant waters in the time of hot Summer with many dainty meats, and at their pleasures, they do take the commodity of the land also. The land birds do but only live upon the land as footmen. (As for Hawks and flying birds of the wood, which daily persecuteth each other, as murderers do innocents or cruel rich men the poor that would live in rest, I meddle not withal.) Upon a time the Drake with his Duck and his neighbors the Geese, being pleasantly disposed (as Judas was in playing the traitor) only to destroy the landfowls to the end that they might enjoy both land and water together at their pleasure, after the example of covetous men that would have all things in their hands, and when one man have any good profitable trade to live upon, they will covet or use the same although their poor neighbors do perish, and that is the cause of much trouble good master, nowadays, that every calling do pinch and pull each other, and where the hedge is lowest, that commonly is soonest cast to ground, but the strong stakes will stand in the storm. (I speak not of the lusty Lawyers, nor the mighty merchants, no, no. I will observe nothing in them. Let every Fat stand upon his own bottom.) Now, said the Drake to the land fowls, "Good cousins, we are much bound unto you for your daily entertainment in good cheer, and daily company. We with our wives and children are much bound unto you. You are most natural unto us. We daily feed and take of your commodity, and come at our pleasures. Now therefore, take part with us, and use your pleasure upon the Water. There is plenty of young fry and fish, great store, salad herbs of sundry kinds, good against every wound or grief, both meat and medicine, etc. Oh Lord, what pleasure is there to be had. Come sweethearts, and let us take our progress to the pleasant river of Tagus, where as the sands of that flood are precious gold. There is both pleasure and riches. Go and gather wealth and treasure. Here is poverty; there is sweetness. And here but stinking dunghills; there is liberty. And here in bondage, there is joy of the mind, and here daily fear of the Fox that false traitor." This sweet tale pleased well the landfowls (as it is oftentimes seen that fair words make fools fain);[78] notwithstanding, the Cock said unto the Drake, Gossip, "Our bringing up have been by land, and our fathers also. We can not swim; we have no webs in our feet to row withal as you have. We fear drowning."

"What?" said the Drake? "What needeth these words among friends? Use maketh perfectness; we will teach you to swim by art, as well as we do by nature (nothing is too hard to willing minds). Well, let us go together." "Have with you," said the Cock. Then, very womanly, the Duck did take the Hen by the hand following their husbands, which were arm and arm, walking before the Chickens, and the Ducklings followed in a goodly train, as it had been to a sumptuous Marriage between the Cock's eldest son with the pale face and the Drake's daughter with the pretty foot.[79] At the waterside, the Drake with all the water fowls did stoop low and receive their carriage, and when they were all a cock-horse together, they went into the water. And eftsoons, when the Drake gave his watchword, the water fowls did all sink at once, and all the land fowls were suddenly in a wreck, and many of them perished, and some with much ado came to land, as the Cock and the Hen, which returned home with care and shame, and lived long in lamentation, and remained solitary, without company of water fowls.

The Fox, which had games a both sides, made the league with a learned oration painted full of Rhetoric between them, declaring what unity was between brethren, and the fruits and peace, and so reconciled the waterfowls to land, where was a feigned truce, taken with much dissembling, yet very good cheer, shaking of hands, kissing, etc. Great was the feast at the Cock's place. The Nightingale was there to pleasure them with Music, much dancing, and after the same a costly banquet. As you know the manner of the waterfowls to commonly sit near the ground, but landfowls do mount up to perch, and so they did, and when all were at rest, secretly the Cock sent by the Cat a token to come and do execution among the grateful traitors. The Cat was glad, and ran to the Fox, finding him in sacrifice and prayer, and shortly declared the ambassage. The Fox at the first refused so heinous and bloody a deed, declaring his indifference and righteousness like a father, and also what evil opinion many creatures, causeless, had in him. "Marie," said he, "I love the Cock and his wife very well. I also know how the Waterfowls have done. I have made the unity between them. I will therefore not be seen in this matter myself, but two of my sons shall do the feat, go before, and climb in at the window, and open the door." So *in fine* it was done. Suddenly the waterfowls paid for the Malt grinding and were slain like flattering, ungrateful villains. And this is John Drake's medicine.

Civis:

This tale is well told *Roger.* I thank thee. Ungrateful people and flatterers be most wicked, and the children of Judas. If any man be prepared by another man and made rich, if this rich man should forget that benefit to his friend if he fell into poverty, whether would the poor man's lack more vex him or the ingratitude of him that he hath pleasure? (Which perhaps hath sayed, if ever I have such a Marriage, yea or such a ferme, and in case if he be of the clergy, such a bishopric, prebendary, etc., thou shalt not want as long as I can help. I will never forget your courtesy showed to me in these my days of trouble.) How sayest thou to this question, *Roger?*

Roger:

Sir, saving your reverence, you may call it ingratitude, but, slandering no man in my judgment, it is plain knavery. Therefore, it is good trying of friends before need do require, as the man which taught his son to kill a swine and put him in a sack all bloody, and secretly to prove his friends which of them would help not only to hide the slain man but also help to convey him in safety; and to conclude, in the time of trouble, among many he found but one.

Civis:

Marie, God defend that murder should be cloaked by friendship, which although it be, yet God often himself will take vengeance, be it never so close, as example in Cain. I like not this example of thine.

Roger:

I have better in store, if you will here it.

Civis:

Say on a God's name. It is good passing the time. But me think we ride too fast. We have day enough. How do you wife? What cheer with you?

Uxor:

Well sir, I thank you. I hear your talk well. God be with our friends at home, and forgive our foes, and end these plagues at London, and amend all people that through sin have moved God to plague us.

Civis:

It is well said good wife. Amen. Amen. Remember your talk goodman *Roger*.

ROGER:

Sir, in our country there was a man which by occupation was a Friar (or, Religion, whether you will). I did know him well. He wore a grey coat, well tucked under his corded girdle, with a pair of trim white hose. The knave had a good leg (for his brother was a Yeoman of the Guard, which was a great wrestler). Marie, this Friar, although he did rise to the Choir by dark night, he needed no candle, his nose was so red and bright, and although he had but little money in store in his purse, yet his nose and cheeks were well set with coral and rubies, and I do remember the gentleman had one great orient pearl in his right eye. He never travelled without *Aqua vitae* and spectacles and fine Needles, with a quarterstaff in his neck, which he called a bless-beggar.[80] He had many proper collations and pardons in store. He sung his pricksong very trim; he would have been loath that any should have sung one note above him in the Choir. He was well beloved in the country, specially among women. A close man, he was never without a bale of dice. Marie, he used no foisting nor cogging. He played well at tables, and of all meats he most loved a fat Pig and a pudding, but he might not away to eat Communions nor read the scripture; it ever went against his stomach, but he was cockhope for Portas matters and cakes. I dare say he could raise beelzebub and bring devils to creep and crouch in a circle. Also he had the Foolosophers' stone,[81] and taught many his secrets therein.

Upon a time this holy Friar in the month of June traveled in his pleasant progress, with his boy following him, which was indeed his sister's son, one young Renob by name, a pretty young stripling, and as they had walked from the morning until ten of the clock, after the Friar had said our lady Matins, with a Collect of Saint Francis his patron, he sat down under a hawthorn tree to rest with his boy also and gave ear to the pleasant charm of sweet birds, much commending the Cuckoo because she kept so constant her plainsong, when the Nightingale did sing the descant.

"Oh," said the boy, "this were Paradise. If here were meat and drink for our relief, I would desire no better dwelling."

"Yes," said the Friar. "It were better to be a Pope—which is above all men, Angels and devils—which have the Keys of heaven gates under his girdle, to whom the kings of the world do service."

"That is past my reach," said the boy. "I lack friends, age, and learning to take that dignity."

"Who will find fault and if thou wert the Pope, my poor boy?" said the Friar. "By my preferment, what kindness wouldest thou show to me, being so much thy friend?"

"Sir," said the boy, "you should be a Latro[82] Cardinal on my right hand and be half with me in my kingdom."

"Remember," said the Friar, "your promise. Give me thy hand my lad. I promise thee I will make thee Pope."

Then he raised Sir Sathanas, the patron of Popes, transformed the tree where the boy was into kingly palace, with Saint Peter's throne, with infinite of the clergy, among whom sat this young Pope. Forthwith came the Friar in this golden dream. Very lowly he kneeled and put the Pope in remembrance who he was and what he had done, hoping to be gratified, to whom sir Pope said, "I know thee not thou lousy beggar and false Friar. I am descended of kingly parentage, advanced by God and learning. Away with thy black curse, away." Forthwith the Friar by subtle calculation withdrew this delusion of his master the devil, and the late pope with his pomp became again the Friar's boy, sitting in a Birch tree, to whom the Friar said, "Now you false vile boy, I know what you would have done if you had been Pope. Come down, in the devil's name, and carry my wallet. And first for your knavery, I will make you a banquet of birch." And thus my young master was served in this sort.

Civis:

Honors do change manners, yet pride will have a fall. I do remember a poor young man by fortune was advanced into promotion, to whom one of his old fellows came and spake homely unto him, after the old fashion, as when they dwelt together. In scorn the rich man answered disdainfully, after this manner, "Take me as I am, and not as I was. We are now no fellows. It is come to pass." To whom the other made answer thus again: "Sometime thou wart, yet now thou art not. And now thou art that then thou werst not, and what thou shalt be, tell thou canst not; although a churl's heart, live you mayst not."

Well, well, God send every ship to a good Haven and send us peace and cease this plague, that we may return home again to our old acquaintance. For this week I do remember twenty good fellows met together at one banquet, my very friends, Merchants and others. You know them well, *Roger:* towards young men and honest, great doers, close and just, witty, I warrant you, to prevent any proviso in the loan of money by month or year. No state or time will nip them. They can wisely color the matter, for, *Roger,* that is an art among merchants not to be revealed. God send me into their company again. Notwithstanding, I have been no great doer in lending forth money.

ROGER:

Master, it giveth me in mine heart that you shall never meet altogether again.

CIVIS:

Wherefore?

ROGER:

Sir, upon a time a number of Foxes assembled together at a great banquet, where as was great plenty of lamb's flesh, hens, etc. In the end of the feast, this blessed company, loath to depart, inquired of old Reinold the day wherein they should meet again to be merry. "I will tell you," said Reinold, "when we shall meet again," and so trained them up to an high mountain, where as there were many highways derived into sundry countries. "Farewell," said he, "my children, and follow your father's steps. Go every one a sundry way, for we shall never meet again at a banquet until we do meet together in the Skinner's shop." Sir, I have weighed the matter. I warrant you it will prove so. One of late departed, I will not name unto you, which is dead and buried, my fellow John did read his Epitaph to me.

CIVIS:

What was it I pray thee?

ROGER:

No sir, you will be angry then.

CIVIS:

Surely, I will give no place to anger to chafe my blood; it is perilous in the Pestilent time. For next to the serving of almighty God, and my Christian duty to my neighbor, I will give myself only to mirth, which is the greatest jewel of this world.[83]

ROGER:

Sir, thus it was, an Epitaph of one that was a great usurer, covetous, merciless, and churlish, but passing rich. He knew no end of his goods. It made him look aloft, and many louted full low at his presence. And thus it was written of him:

> Here lieth Gathrall that never did good.
> A gentleman degenerate, yet sprung of good blood.
> Merciless, an usurer all the days of his life
> An oppressor of poor men, a mover of strife,
> A Papist of religion, a soldier of Rome,
> Here dwelleth his carcass til the day of doom.
> Deprived of riches, spoiled of fame,
> Nothing left in memory, but an evil name,

His judgment we commend to the seat divine,
Yet he lived like a wolf, and died like a swine.

CIVIS:

Who was this made upon, *Roger?* I pray thee tell me.

ROGER:

No, so God help me, I will not name him, inquire it out. But I heard a friend of mine say that he had written a book against Extortioners and Usurers, which if they amend not, he will name them and paint them forth, not only them, but their parents, which are dead, which used that vile trade of usury, procuring God's vengeance, in casting the Pestilence upon cities, towns, and countries, causing poverty, breaking up houses most ancient, selling to lend upon gain, destroying hospitality, with infinite encumbrances by forfeitures, statutes, etc. Oh that the usurers' goods were confiscated after their deaths to the common poor, as in case they had slain themselves, and that they had no power in law to be will unto their children that which was gotten in serving the devil, which would not prosper to the third heir, for "evil gotten goods are evil spent," said our curate upon Sunday. "Oh, that the burying were turned into open casting forth among dead cattle and not numbered in the Christian fellowship after death, which in life have been so wicked." So said our Curate. Sir, you heard not how a man of late did let forth his Cow by the quarter and by the year?

CIVIS:

No, I pray thee tell me.

ROGER:

There was a man of late which had one hundred pound which he called his Cow, and secretly did lend her forth, sometime by the week, and his price was ten shillings the week, and when her milk became dearer and many fasting days at hand, he called for his Cow and said that she gave indifferent milk. But said he, "I must put her into a better pasture, and she shall give more Milk by five shilling in the week, etc." And at length white meat became a little better cheap, because of the great plenty of such kine in the town, that his Cow was brought home again, because that she was letten so dear. Now, because she had done him good service, and he had no more but her at home, and calf he had none by her to keep up the stock. His servant loved milk well, and could get none of that Cow. When his master was from home, stole the Cow and ran his way, and hitherto hath not been found, neither Cow nor man, and all the milk is gone.

Civis:

A marvelous thing, good lord. What would such grafters do if they had many cattle or kine in store?

Roger:

They would destroy all a commonwealth, but we see what mischief they have done.

Civis:

It is time to bait our Horses in this town. If there be any good meat, we will dine. Prepare *Roger*, for we have far to ride this night. Know what company is in the Inn and whether the house be infected or no?

Roger:

Sir, I was in the hall, and there sitteth our host, a pleasant merry man and a good companion, I warrant him. I see by his nose that of all pottage he loveth good ale. He is Monsieur Grandpaunch. He hath chafed the Parson wondrously, which with a pair of spectacles playth at tables with him. He stealeth fast the table men from him. Our hostess hath a sharp nose, thin lipped, a proper young woman, with a shrill voice like a Cat, but when she is pleased I warrant her to be a pleasant woman, and full of meritrix. The good man of this house bringeth up youth very well and is very loving to his son, and I perceive he will bear much with him.

Civis:

Wherein?

Roger:[84]

When I came into the hall, my young master leaned upon his father's shoulder, with his cap upon his head, sitting and coughing like a lout.

Civis:

Call the chamberlain, and let us have a chamber severally.

Roger:

With all speed, a God's name. Chamberlain, prepare your chamber with all things accordingly in the same for my master and mistress. Whip master Hosteler with a cast of legerdemain.[85] Bestir you, sirrah, and make twelve pence of three bottles[86] of stinking Hay and a peck of Oats. You can make a stoned horse a gelding, and a longtail a curtal. You know my meaning well enough. Hem sirrah, I say nothing but mum. I have seen you often in Smithfield.

Uxor:

What, sir sauce? You take upon you to play the Controller? Go quietly about your own business, and let the Hosteler alone.

Roger:

Mistress, it is merry when knaves are met. I did see him once ask blessing to twelve Godfathers at once.

Civis:

This is a comely parlor, very neatly and trimly appareled, London-like. The windows are well glassed, and fair clothes with pleasant borders about the same, with many wise sayings painted upon them.

Uxor:

I pray you husband, what is that writing in those golden letters?

Civis:

Melius est claudus in via quam cursor praeter viam. That is, "better is an halting man which keepeth the right way than the swift runner besides that wandereth astray."

Uxor:

What is that man, I pray you?

Civis:

Non hominis consuetudinem sed dei veritatem sequi oportet, which is, "It behoveth us not to follow the constitutions or customs of men but to follow the truth of God's word." And also there is a good saying following the same: *Doctrinis variis and peregrinius ne circumferamini.* That is, "Be not led or carried about with diverse or strange doctrine." Here is more following, written upon the chimney good wife, which I will keep in store. Oh God what serpents they are, lord defend me from them. I will read it to myself: *O mulier omne facinus ausa est plus quam omne, verum nihil est peius, nec erit unqan mulierae inter hominum calamitatis.*[87]

Uxor:

Well man, well. Truth seeketh no corners. I perceive there is some naughty matter; that I know not but by one thing that I do hear you read make me think all the rest is not well, because the first word is stark naught, and that is "*O mulier,*" which I am sure is nor ever was good. I pray you husband, what picture is that following?

Civis:

Oh wife, it was the picture or *Effigium* of a noble man,[88] which in his days served a most noble king and was like the cutter down of trees by the ground. But if God had not upon some secret purpose prevented his labor in the wood of Antichrist, he would have utterly eradicated the roots with all Papistry, which daily springeth out in every corner to the hurt of better fruits, but by God's grace they shall be confounded, as God will.

Uxor:

What picture is that, which have a gray hoar head, a long gown, and a lock of gold linking his lips together, with many goodly books before him, and a pair of blind spectacles upon his nose, with a golden pen fallen from his hands?

Civis:

Oh wife, wife, it is a Candle covered with a Bushel, and the noble Talent of wisdom hidden, which must make great accompts for keeping silence.

Uxor:

Sir, in that table environed round with antiques of sundry portraitures, the ground thereof is hooping Russet, are three pictures, black, scholar-like, or in mourning clothing. The first of them with a Rake in his hand with teeth of gold do stoop very low, groping belike in the lake after something that he would find, and out of this deep water above the Rake, a little steeple. The second gapeth up towards the heaven, holding the lap of his gown abroad, as though he would catch something, and towards the same lap or spread gown doth fall, as it were, a church with a steeple and choir, etc. The third man standeth in poor apparel, with a book in his right hand and his left hand upon his breast with a lamentable countenance in simple apparel. What meaneth this husband?

Civis:

Dame, I dare say but little to this matter to others, but to you, I will speak a little, and not so much as I do think. The first man is one that hath but a very small learning, lesser wit, and less honesty. He hath no virtue to prefer him to living, but only the name and title of a priest or minister. He would fain have a benefice or personage of some pretty donative. He cannot get it at the Bishop's hands. He lacketh God's plough. This fellow raketh with the Devil's golden rake even in the conscience of the covetous patron's or confounder's heart, which giveth the benefice. He playeth *Simon Magus*. He will buy it and with *Judas* the other will sell it, and at length it is gotten for gold and spent with wickedness to the slander of the church. God defend us from such rakers and Simoniacs.

The second is sick of the mother, and, like unto heirs when as the fathers have left them fair lands, they mourn of the chine[89] and are never contented but wimper and whine until the mothers are dead, and when it so cometh to pass, their wicked covetousness by one means or other cometh to shame and poverty.[90] This honest man gapeth for a vowson of a benefice before it is fallen and doeth catch it or it cometh to the ground, before the death of the discumbent. He will not suffer it to fall into relapse.

This man is a steward to a great man, or keepeth his hall, garden or barns, or is a wiseman and a good husband. Look where his master is patron; there he hopeth to be person.[91] He gathereth for his young masters, his patron's sons. His patron must be his executor or some of his master's kinsmen. This fellow walloweth in benefices, as the Hedgehog doeth with apples upon his pricks, and hath the benefit but of the apple in his mouth. He getteth nothing of his promotions, but only one little benefice. Yet his master will snatch at that, either to save the wool or lamb. And so he hath only the shells or glorious titles of promotion, but the giver hath the sweet kernels. God amend this, good wife.

The third is one which showeth the state of learned men, laboring long time in study and divine virtue, which are wrapped in poverty, wanting the golden Rake or gaping mouth. This man hath very few to prefer him to that promotion. He smiteth himself upon the breast. He weepeth and lamenteth that vice should thus be exalted, ignorance rewarded with glory, covetous men spoiling the Church by the names of Patrons and givers, which are extortioners and sellers, they care not to whom, so that it be raked. Well, well, God of his mercy, amend this evil Market.

Uxor:

Upon that wall is painted a man's skin, and tanned, colored like unto Leather, with the skin of the hands and feet, nails and hair remaining, and the skin is spread abroad, in the which is written certain words, which I do not understand.

Civis:

Wife, I wish more such leather, or else fewer such carcasses as such leather hath contained in it. It is the Skin of a wicked Judge, a Lawyer, which played on both hands. This gentleman loved gold above God and cruelty above Justice. Both his ears were stopped, his eyes open. He had respect of persons, specially who brought in lucre and made him humble courtesies. Them he would defend, although their causes in righteousness deserved it not. The innocent he oppressed that wanted, and undid many a man. His master being a great prince (in the whole multitude of the people, and specially of the Lawyers to certify them. And to decline from evil and do good, to have the ears open, to hear both rich and poor alike in the seat of judgment, to have lame hands in taking of money, which is the root of all evil among them) commanded his Skin to be flain from his flesh, he being yet living, roaring with blood running from his body, and died in a case most miserable—upon whose Skin is this writing, hanging in the Judgment hall, before the place of Justice: *Iudex qui non queret veritatem, debet excoriari.* A Judge which will (for lucre) not seek out the truth (in the law) ought to have his Skin flain from his body.

Uxor:

Here standeth a woman of most excellent form in shape and fairness in beauty, with a crown of rich gold, with seven precious stones fixed in the border of her crown, covered with a costly mantle from her paps downward. Her breasts naked, the right breast giveth milk unto the mouth of the young child on the right side, and from the left breast floweth blood, into the mouth of an other child. What meaneth this?

CIVIS:

It is a goodly picture and signifyeth the estate of an university or multitude of scholars, which cometh to be nourished in learning.[92] Which mother, the university, being crowned with the seven liberal arts fixed in her crown, and as many as taste of her doctrine, in the better part in virtue to this end to do well be blessed, they do taste upon the right breast, but the left breast yieldeth forth doctrine of Errors, Magics, Papistry, etc., to this end to persecute, rob and spoil Christ's Church. God grant that both these breasts may give good milk to nourish the people of God, in one holy doctrine to each vocation, to agree in unity like brethren, and that the universities may teach the learned acts and one true religion in this Christ our lord.

UXOR:

What is that picture, which grafteth a golden Imp upon a Leaden stock with a bag of money of great bigness hanging about his neck?

CIVIS:

It should seem to be a pitiful case. It is a noble covetous Senior, which for gold's sake do make disparagement of his blood, marrying and selling his son and heir unto some Extortioner or shameless usurer's daughter, whose fruits are so infected on the mother's side that they will become as counterfeit, crafty, compounded metal and never come to the true touchstone again.[93] The fine metal is so corrupted through covetousness and natural conjunction, as we do see grafts of trees fix young Imps, although the Imp be of a fine Pippin and grafted into an evil stock. You shall know that fruit by the tree, a plague prepared for gentlemen for their abuse.

Uxor:

Upon that Table before you is painted a naked man, lying down wounded, upon whom feedeth many Flies with full bellies, and there commeth another man, which with a green branch of Rosemary beat them away.

Civis:

It should appear by the circumstance that it is not hurtful to keep officers still in place, for when they have filled their purses and have all things accordingly, they are well, and if they be removed eftsoons, the new hungry Flies will vex the body of the commonwealth and never cease until they be also satisfied, etc.

Uxor:

Yet what is that man I pray you, that sitteth in a rich throne asleep, and one do blow in his ear with a pair of golden bellows, and another do pick his purse?

Civis:

That same is a mighty person overcome with adulation or flattery, careless, swimming in pleasure and vainglory, whom his men do use like an honeycomb, and daily spoil him of his riches by sundry frauds, which he perceiveth not.

Uxor:

And what meaneth yonder Mule, holding his head so low, with a plain black footcloth, shod with golden shoes?

Civis:

Wife, silence now is best. I will say nothing to the matter. The Mule carrieth a Master that will do nothing but for gold, and the fools of the world that love debate and strife must shoe this Mule.

Uxor:

Here is a row of pictures like Prelates painted one by another in the border, in three parts. The first are barefooted men bareheaded, long garments, and books in their hands, Some of them are bloody. The second company are mitered, and shod with Shepherd's hooks in one hand and books in the other hand. The third sort have Swords in their hands, crowned with triple crowns, clothed in kingly robes, with frowning faces, and books under their feet. And next after them sitteth an old mangy slave, naked, with a triple crown, making or patching of a Net, from whom goeth as it were men laden with towns, woods, and treasure.

Civis:

Wife, this is the true Church of God and the malignant Synagogue of Antichrist figured. First the true Preachers and martyrs of God's church, simple men, which followed most nearest the testament of Christ. After this persecution, then entered Confessors, good men, which lived well, and, according to the Apostle's doctrine, were good Shepherds, withstood the Wolves of heresies, etc., kept hospitality, and live accordingly, and were as Lambs and good Wheat. Then for the sins of Princes and wickedness of men came in Wolves among Lambs. Darnel choked the Lord's field: oppressors of Princes, emptiers of Purgatory, and Pillars of hell, raisers of debate, shedders of blood, makers of Martyrs, men of war, destroyers of the true church, erectors of Idols, usurpers of kingdoms, and treaders of God's truth under their vile sect, which sect kings have kissed—such is the pride of the Pope.

Then the Pope sitteth all naked, working. Now through God's word, Antichrist is revealed, and seen what he is: foul, loathly, clothed in shameful decrees, wicked laws, and filthy life, and is despised of many nations, save of his own children. Now patcheth his old Bottles, which will keep no new wine. Neither can he well piece Christ's pure cloth and his ragged traditions together. Neither will his Net pleasure the Church, in which Net he have taken the servants of Christ, shed their blood. He may be rather called a murderer than a fisher. He never had Saint Peter's Net, since the Pope came to the church of Rome. Now clouteth he a net, with his rotten Decrees, Councils, glossing it with God's word, like the Angel of darkness transformed into the similitude of an angel of light. But his nakedness is seen, for all his title of his holiness and rich Crown. Now as many as will not obey his mastership, he giveth away their kingdoms, dukedoms, provinces, and goods, after the example of his patron, not Peter, which forsook worldly things, but rather Satan, which would have given Christ much riches to have honored him. But the lands of Princes are too heavy to be carried with his Porters and also too hot to be trodden upon of any of his messengers. His Net is very good to catch the great Uncle[94] withal and some of his lawless countrymen, to store[95] the Pope's holy ponds at Rome.

Uxor:

I will ask but one or two questions, and now our dinner is ready, I pray you. What meaneth yonder Shepherd to clip the Sheep so near that he bleedeth? It is well painted.

Civis:

It seemeth a covetous landlord that do so oppress the tenant with fine, rent, bribe, etc., whereby he and his family do live in great misery like slaves with continual penury and affliction of mind, and he will never suffer the wool to grow to the full staple, at length to his own decay.

Uxor:

What meaneth yonder fool that stand upon the tree and cutteth the arm asunder whereupon he standeth, with a sharp ax, and is falling down?

Civis:

Under that predicament is comprehended all traitors against Princes: children against parents, servants against Masters, poor against rich, tenants against lords, etc., whereupon they do live, and have their stay in this world, and will seek their hurts, which indeed is their own decay, loss, and destruction in the end.

Uxor:

Good God, what meaneth that bloody naked picture, with a sharp rod in each hand, wounding his body, and spoiled of all his apparel?

Civis:

God send peace in the Christian realms, good dame. That do signify by the circumstance of some old wise painter that when the body or state of any Realm or Realms of vicinity or nearness together, being as hands to one body or helpers to each other, if they be at strife, the whole body whereupon they are derived shall eftsoons through the same be ruinated and brought into peril. In this matter I will talk no further as now. Let us go to dinner, a God's name. *Roger*, what good fellow is here to keep me and your mistress company?

Uxor:

Husband, in this fine border is curiously painted a house builded of stone and with many strong doors and windows, barred and railed with strong iron bars,[96] and before one of the doors standing a man, with a yellow cap, in a plain poor coat with white sleeves, and a little boy standeth behind him with a fair gown in his arms, merchant like, in a fine black cap, and over the door is written, *Veritas non querir angulos*. I know not the meaning.

Civis:

Indeed "truth seeketh no corners," as these evil disposed vile thieves do, although it was meant to help some honest decayed citizens, that they should not be utterly destroyed of pitiless creditors, but after they might rise up again. Now the bankrupt is in durance, hath lost his credence. He is in prison, whereas his credence is spoiled and gone. No man will trust him. But that inn hath a privilege to increase many guests by this means, that they may have liberty with a little Applesquire to be his keeper, which changeth his apparel and countenance, creeping into corners, making bargains in every place, taking up every commodity, refusing nothing. All is fish that cometh to the net. He setteth hand and Seal to everything. He sweareth he would not lose his credence for thousands. He giveth sweet words. He knavishly robbeth, undoeth, spoileth the widow and the honest, pitiful merchant or true citizen, and when he hath undone them, he runneth to his place again, as the Fox doeth to his hole, and liveth by the spoil.

UXOR:

What meaneth this strange picture? Here standeth a man double, or in two twins, back to back. The one side is lusty, fair, rich and young, and beautiful. The other side seemeth sick, foul, poor and old. In the young man's hand was a grasshopper, and in the old man's, an Ant without feet.

CIVIS:

In that table is lively declared mankind, both the time of his youth in felicity, with the careless grasshopper, gathereth nothing but spoileth: house, land, etc., in banquets, dice, apparel and harlots, etc. And when age commeth, he would be thrifty, and then can get no more; then, the lame, footless ant. Then maketh he exclamation, saying "Oh what goods did my father leave me? What good counsel my friend gave me, but I esteemed none of them both, but *in fine* lost both riches and friends, and now I am in great poverty, sickness, and age. Let other men take example by me, and remem ber the wisdom of Solomon, saying *Vade ad formicun ô pigar and considera vias eius et disce sapientiam, etc.* Go thou, idle body, to the Ant. Consider and mark well her ways, and learn wisdom. She hath no guide, prince, nor law giver, but gathereth in summer to keep her in winter, etc.[97]

UXOR:

There is also painted a lusty young man, stooping down to a vessel, in which swimmeth both Eels and Snakes. He seemeth to catch one of them. What meaneth that?

Civis:

Ha, ha, ha, it is merrily handled, forsooth. It is one that is overcome either with love or covetousness. He goeth awooing, my ding ding, and if he speedeth my darling, what getteth he, my sweeting? Forsooth, either a serpent that will sting him all his life with cruel words or else sweetheart with pleasant speech, that when he thinketh her most sure, he hath but a quick Eel, you know where. Ha, ha, ha.[98]

Roger:

Sir, there is one lately come into this Inn in a green Kendal coat, with yellow hose, a beard of the same color (only upon the upper lip), a bald chin, a russet hat, with a great plume of strange Feathers, and a brave scarf about his neck, in cut buskins. He is playing at the treetrip with our host's son. He playeth trick upon the Gittern, and dance Trenchmore and Hey de Gie,[99] and telleth news from Terra Florida. He looketh asquint. I did see him give the good man a piece of Unicorn's horn, good against poison. He seemeth a pretty Scholar. But I heard him pray the chamberlain in his ear to lend him six pence upon a pressing iron, which chamberlain refused the gage.

Civis:

Roger, call him to dinner. It is some pleasant fellow and lacketh money belike through travail. The poor man is driven to his shifts and would make other men merry when he weepeth in his heart.[100]

Uxor:

Good husband, call in some grave company. What should such Jacks and tosspots do here? He seemeth to be some thief or ruffian. Fie on him, varlet, fie, fie.[101]

ROGER:

By our Lady, I will fetch him into dinner. He is a good companion for me. We shall hear news.

CIVIS:

Go thy ways, quickly.

ROGER:

Sir, my master and my mistress pray your mastership to take the pains to come to their chamber whereas you shall be heartily welcome to their dinner.

MENDAX:

Sir, I will wait upon them, but first I will upon this Whetstone, sharp my knife.

ROGER:

Sir, here is this gentleman come to keep you company.

CIVIS:

He is most heartily welcome. Set him a chair. Give him a trencher and a napkin. I pray you take part of such as God have sent. If it were at London, I might make you better cheer, but here I can not.

MENDAX:

Here is good cheer. I was there within these ten weeks that I would have given twenty shillings for such a loaf as this, whereas no such cheer was to be had.

CIVIS:

Where was that, I pray you gentle Master? I can not tell what to call you, nor of what country you are.

Mendax:

Sir, I was born near unto Tunbridge, where fine knives are made. My name is *Mendax*, a younger brother lineally descended of an ancient house before the Conquest. We give three Whetstones in Gules, with no difference, and upon our crest a left hand, with a horn upon the thumb and a knife in the hand. The supporters are a Fox on the one side and a Friar on the other side.[102] And of late I travelled into Terra Florida, whereas I felt both wealth and woe. The black Ox never trod upon my foot before a Dog have but a day.[103] We are born all to travail, and as for me I have but little to lose, yet I am a gentleman and can not find in my heart to play the slave or go to Cart. I never could abide it, by the Mass.

Civis:

You speak like a wise man. I perceive by your behavior, you have been well brought up.[104] I pray you where is that land?

Mendax:

Many hundred miles beyond *Torrida Zona*, or the *Equinoctial* line, in the *longitude* near unto the Pole *Antarctic*. It is seventeen thousand miles long and is in the part named *America*, and by the way are the Islands called *Fortunata*, or *Canaria*, whose West parts be situated in the third climate.

Civis:

It was a dangerous travel into that country. Where landed you, at what place?

Mendax:

We sailed to the Islands of *Porto Santo*, and then to *Medeira*, in which were sundry countries and Islands, as *Eractelenty*, *Magnefortis*, *Grancanary*, *Tenerife*, *Palma*, *Ferro*, *etc.*[105] And our Captain went with his soldiers to land, and at our first coming near unto a river, in one of these Islands, as we refreshed ourselves among the Date trees, in the land of *Palms*, by the sweet Wells, we did to the great fear of us all see a great battle between the Dragon and the Unicorn, and as God would, the Unicorn thrust the Dragon to the heart, and again the Dragon with his tail stung the Unicorn to death. Here is a piece of his horn. The blood of dragons is rich. That battle was worth two hundred marks to our captain.

Then we traveled further into *Tenerife*, into an exceeding high mountain, above the middle region, whereas we had great plenty of Alum, and might well hear an heavenly Harmony among the stars. The Moon was near hand us with marvelous heat. And when we came down at the hill foot, grow many gross herbs, as Lovage, *Laserpitium*, *Acanthus*, and *Solanum*, and, whether it was by the eating of *Solanum* berries or no, there was a very mighty man, naked and hairy, in a great sleep, whom we gently suffered to lie still. He had a great beard, in which a bird did breed and brought her young ones meat. Our captain declared unto us that the spials had viewed the land, and how that our enemies were at hand.[106] The next day, most fearful people, painted with sundry colors, approached in strange beasts' skins, with Flint, so were their shafts and Darts, with whom we fought and slew, and took some. And yet the people so assaulted us that with much difficulty we recovered our barks.

And then we sailed forth, and chance to let fall our sounding lead, new tallowed, whereupon did stick gold. With all speed we sent down our Divers, and so within three days we gathered thirty hogsheads of fine gold, besides two butts of orient Pearls. All the shore was full of Coral. From thence we sailed to the great Isle, called *Madagascar* in *Scorea*,[107] where were kings, Muhamitans by religion, black as Devils. Some had no heads but eyes in their breasts. Some when it rained, covered all the whole body with one foot. The land did abound in Elephants' teeth. The men did eat Camels' and lions' flesh. Musk and Civet in every place did abound, and the mother of pearl the people made their platters to put in their meat. They dwell among spice. The ground is moist with oil of precious trees. Plenty of wine out of grapes as big as this loaf; much Pepper; they can not tell what to do with sugar, but that their merchants of *Maabar,*[108] twenty days journey off, do come and take of their goods, frankly for nothing, but some of them do bring iron to make edge tools, for which they have for one pound, twelve pound of fine gold. Their pots, pans, and all vessel is clean gold, garnished with Diamonds. I did see swine feed in them.

CIVIS:

Did you see no strange Fowls there, and Fishes?

MENDAX:

In the Isle called *Ruc,* in the great *Canes* land,[109] I did see Mermaids and Satyrs, with other fishes by night come four miles from the sea and climbed into trees and did eat Dates and Nutmegs, with whom the Apes and the Baboons had much fighting, yelling, and crying. The people of that land do live by eating the flesh of women.[110] In this land I did see an Ape play at tick-tack and after, at Irish on the tables[111] with one of that land, and also a Parrot give one of their gentlewomen a checkmate at Chess.

CIVIS:

God keep me from those cruel people.

MENDAX:

But sir, as for birds, they are not only infinite in numbers but also in kinds. Some voices most sweet and some most fearful, Nightingales as big as Geese, owls greater than some horse, and there are birds that do lie in a rock, where Dragons are, whose Feathers in their wings are thirty foot long, the quill as big as a Cannon royal. Also I heard Parrots dispute in Philosophy, fresh in Greek.

CIVIS:

I pray you, is there any plenty of precious stones?

Mendax:

Very many, but hard to come by, but in the Island *Zanzibar* is much plenty of Ambergris that they make clay for their houses withal. There if we had holden together like friends, we might have gotten a great kingdom. Oh my heart, it maketh it bleed when I do remember it. Every man is but for himself. You may consider what division is. Emeralds, Rubies, Turquoise, Diamonds and Sapphires were sold when we came thither first for the weight of iron. A thousand rich Turquoise were sold for four pence: to be short, one with another after three shillings and four pence a peck. Our men gathered up carbuncles and Diamonds with rakes, under the spice trees.

Civis:

How chance you brought none home into this realm?

Mendax:

Oh sir, we filled two ships with fine gold, three ships with Ambergris, Musk and Unicorns horns, and two tall barks with precious stones, and sailed by the Adamant stones, which will draw iron unto them and so cast away the greatest riches in Heathenness or Christendom.[112] After that evil chance, we came upon the mainland of *Cuba*, in the great and mighty land of *America*, where as the people called the *Cannibals* do dwell in caves, rocks, and woods there, as women will eat their own children, and one man another, and they are Giants most high and fearful. All go naked. They neither know good humanity, humane policy, religion, law, nor chastity. One is equal with another. The strongest of body are chief, for there all is ruled by force and not through reason, after the manner of swine. Children love their fathers no more than pigs do the boars, for they say lust causeth generation. And when their parents are very old, they bring them to an exceeding high mountain, whereas is a great tower builded upon a rock, under which tower is the golden mine, in which mine there be two great monstrous dragons keeping the same, which will never suffer the children to come to receive the benefits of that place until such time as they have slain their parents, and cast their flesh into the cave, and wash the Dragons' Images (which are within that tower made of precious wood) with the blood of their said parents.

From thence we traveled into an Island, where as it never raineth but once a year, and that is in the month of July, where as *Nilus* runneth, by giving benefit unto the plain country, where as spice of all kinds doeth grow. In that Island doeth grow Hops most plentifully, which they do call *Lupulum.* A little before our coming was a great wind which had shaken down much fruit and precious spice and many hundred cart loads of good Hops, after which fell down plenty of rain, raising a mighty flood, incontinent succeeded a burning heat, for it is under the *Equinoctial* line, or *Torrida Zona. In fine,* through this concoction of the sun moving this boiling of the water, through the help of much Spice, I never drank such Hippocras, Wine, nor Beer. The Flemmings have found out the commodity and care to transport no more Hops hither unto us. And if good luck had been our good lord, we had made ourselves and all the Christian kingdoms forever.

Civis:

Alas, alas, what was that? I pray you, tell me. I am sorry that you and your friends have traveled thus long and have been in danger for nothing. But I perceive you have been a great traveler and have seen many Countries, Woods, and Rivers.

Mendax:

Non finis erit si prosequar omnia verbis,
Flumina et specos, campos, silvasque lacusque,
Colles, apricosque siunosque undeque portus.
Omnia sunt vidi.[113] Now let them go.

I have seen those things and many more. Sir, in the lands beyond *Cuba,* or as the Cosmographers call *Lamiam* or *Janican,* where as the people do curse the Sun at noon because it burneth them, there are many Islands among them. There is a fleeting Island, swimming above the sea, by what means I know not; whether occasioned by cork, wool, etc., it would by the wind shift from place to place. Some said it was a shred off the banks of Paradise, broken through the force of Ganges and so in continuance brought down. It was not broad. In that Isle were but few people, and the men of that place do by proper art with a sharp Flint stone worm the women and prettily cut their tongues, and take forth a small Serpent alive, and heal their tongues again with herb of grace. This Island hath many rich stones, gold and spice in it, with precious trees, as *Agallicum* and *Guaiacum*. In that Isle, there had been some French men, whose skins were clean cast off, in the manner of Snakes. Marie, they were full of holes. This *Guaiacum* did much pleasure to them belike. But as we were devising how to steal this land away and bring it forth to the main Sea with our Pilots, two things letted our purpose: the one was, the haven mouth was too straight; the second, the people were too vigilant, and letted our purpose. But I trust I and my companions will make one lusty voyage and give an onset for all: we will either win the saddle or lose the horse.

We are none but good fellows. Of my part I will do what lieth in me to make many prentices free and cause other good young gentlemen in selling their land to get thousands. If men knew as much as I do in this matter, they had rather venture the best joint[114] than be from thence. It is almost heaven. And if we do want by the way, let every man keep close, and there we may chance to find some little fleeting Islands by the way, wherein good Sugar, spice, Silk, Linen, etc., do grow, ready made, and that will make ready money, and money maketh a man.[115] Oh, that young men would believe me and follow me, I would make them Lords.

Uxor:

Good husband hearken in your ear. I would speak with you, sweetheart.

CIVIS:

Speak on your mind, good Susan. What is the matter, woman?

UXOR:

Sir, this is a blind-eyed, shameless ruffian—a rogue, I warrant him, and a thief. This knave is able to make children run from their parents, servants rob their masters, young heirs to sell their lands, men to run from their wives, and women also. You may know by his Arms of what stock he cometh. I warrant him from drowning and dying of the Pestilence. Oh villain, he will be hanged. I dare say he knoweth all kinds of thieves, vagabonds, rovers, and hazarders. I like not his words, nor his bragging countenance. Let us hence.

CIVIS:

Well, much good do you. You have taken much pain, but small profit. You have traveled far, and may speak by authority. Come, take away. Pay the reckoning. *Roger,* horse, horse, and away.

ROGER:

All things are ready sir.

CIVIS:

Fare ye well gentle friend.[116]

MENDAX:

I thank you of your gentle company, good gentleman.

UXOR:

Whose fair field is yonder? I would fain know it. And let trifles pass. I will not believe them. Let foolish things go, and talk of matters profitable.

ROGER:

Mistress, do you not know it? It is my master's. I am his baily there. He had a good bargain, I assure you. It was in mortgage to him these two years. I would he might find the like purchase. All yonder town is his. He hath raised the rent one hundred marks a year more than it was. There were good living in the plague time. For there are large pastures, and the houses are down, saving the manner place, for the careless have forfeited their leases and are gone a begging like villains, and many of them are dead for hunger.

UXOR:

Whose Oxen are these, *Roger*?

ROGER:

My master's also, for he that hath money shall have land and worship. My master is a close wiseman and lieth in the wind of them that will buy money for land. He can handle a young gentleman trimly and ride him with a golden snaffle. He knoweth upon which side his bread is buttered well enough, I warrant you. My master rised so early this morning that he noddeth as he rideth.

UXOR:

Sir, me thinks you totter as you ride. What, are you asleep? Do you not hear your man's prating? He is pleasantly disposed. He would make me believe that you were a great landed man and had much cattle in store. Why sir, how do you that you speak not to me?

CIVIS:

Wife, wife, God send us good luck. Do you not see yonder cloud in the West towards the North, coming hither?

Uxor:

Most fearful God, send us good luck. Sir, it is a sudden change. I will hide my face. It feareth me so much.

Roger:

I am forty years old, but I did never see the like but once, and that was between Godmanchester and Godmanshill, a little from Cambridge, as I traveled to Wolpit fair to buy Colts, and there appeared a strange form, as me thought, a great number of steeples were broken, and many naked Friars, Bishops, and the Pope himself did wring their hands. In ragged clothes, they looked all very lean, and then it thundred and lightened, in which storm many Geese were killed and also sheep and Lambs. The year after was the tumbling down of Abbeys and the reformation for the Church matters; but this passeth. For the precious passion of Christ, let us run away with speed. I do see a fearful thing in the cloud appearing, a black lean naked body, very long, riding upon a pale, miserable, foul jade. He hath also three darts in his left hand. The one is coal black, the other blood red, and the third is a dark pale. He hath no flesh upon him. Me thinketh that I do see a great fire and many fearful monsters in the same follow him, with a fearful voice, saying "all the wicked shall come to us. We are swallowed in the second death."

Civis:

Let us take this house. Ride apace. The storm doeth begin most fearful. God help us. What shall we do or whether shall we fly? Jesus, Jesus, what a thunder is this, as heaven and earth should go together. Lord how the lightning falleth from heaven. All this region is upon a flaming fire. The birds fall from the trees. Look how the cattle tremble, and trees are pulled up by the roots, and the houses are burnt with celestial fire.

UXOR:

Let us depart from these trees, for I have heard say, to sit under a white thorn is most safe and surest in a tempest. I have many goodly jewels against lightning, as the carbuncle, Emerald, Hyacinth, with Amber and gold. God and Saint Barbara defend us. I have a Saint John's Gospel about my neck, and a pair of bracelets of Coral about mine arms.[117] Oh God defend us. I am sorry that we came forth.

ROGER:

Master and Mistress, come into this valley, and let us sit in that same deep close pit under the hillside until this storm be past. Saint George to borrow.[118] Merciful God, who did ever see the like?

CIVIS:

I think it be the day of judgment. The earth doeth quake, the heaven doeth burn, and me think I do see the fearful horseman lighted in the valley, with a marvelous fearful saying, *"En adsum vobis, mors ultima linea rearum, etc."*[119] Oh where shall we hide us from him? He casteth forth his three darts and taketh them up again. He is in a great rage. Behold how he destroyeth man and beast in this valley. This is come in a moment. Who would have thought it in the morning? None of us. He draweth near. I know him well. It is merciless Death, most fearful. I am afraid of his presence. He bendeth his black dart against me. I have no target to bear it off.

UXOR:

Good husband, remember that I am young, and with child, also you are well stricken in years; therefore, play the man, and take *Roger* with you, and entreat him, and if he will needs have you, yet for God's sake be not acknowen that I am here for fear that he kill me and your child also.

Civis:

Keep you close under that Cloak, and stir not, I pray you.

Roger:

I cannot abide him. I will run away, for poverty and death will part good fellowship. Sir, shift for yourself, and draw your sword against him.

Civis:

Alas, my wife in my trouble is too faint-hearted and will not keep me company.[120] My servant is run away from me. Whither may I fly from death? If I do run, he is too swift for me. If I turn my back, he will cowardly kill me. If I do submit myself to him, he is merciless. I perhaps shall persuade him with my gold. I have an hundred pounds in Angels. I will give it him to save my life. Oh, he is here. Sir, most humbly here upon my knees, I desire your lordship to pardon me and suffer me to live still in this world, and here I offer unto you this purse of gold. I shall always do you service and love you with all my heart and be at your Lordship's commandment and to my power seek to please you as my good lord and Master.

Mors:

You are well overtaken. I am glad that we are met together. I have seen you since that you were born. I have threatened you in all your sicknesses, but you did never see me nor remembred me before this day. Neither had I power to have taken you with me until now, for I have commission to strike you with this black dart, called the pestilence. My master hath so commanded me, and as for gold, I take no thought for it. I love it not. No treasure can keep me back the twinkling of an eye from you. You are my subject, and I am your lord. I will cut off your journey and separate your marriage, but not cut off your years, for they are determined when I should come. This is your appointed time, and when the time shall be appointed me, I will smite your wife, children, and servants. They shall not be hidden from me. I will find them forth, be they hidden never so secret, or flee never so swift or far off, for I am so swift that in the moment of an eye I can compass the whole world, and am of so wonderful a nature that I can be in sundry places at once and in sundry shapes. In flames of fire, I oftentimes do consume mankind. In the water I do kill them. I am marvelous in work. I spare nothing that hath life but I bring to an end and to mine own nature, which is death.

Civis:

Sir, I most humbly desire you to suffer me to return home again into the city, and let my goods in order to the use of my wife and children to pay my debts and then godly to depart this world. I desire no more.

Mors:

I must dispatch and strike you with this black dart. I have much business to do with the other two darts.

Civis:

Oh fearful Death. What is these two other darts in thine hand?

Mors:

I will smite thee with this pestilent dart, as I have done to many kingdoms, cities, and people, both man and beast, young and old. With this pale dart, I will destroy infinite numbers with hunger. They shall perish for lack of food, in destruction of corn, cattle, wine, oil, fruit, herb, grass, fowl, and fish. I will make them eat their own flesh and make their own children to be sodden and roasted for them. With this third dart, I will in battle slay in number more than the Stars of heaven and bathe myself in blood. I spare not one, neither Prince nor Peasant, against whom I do cast this dart. I have no respect of any person; be they never so noble, rich, strong wise, learned, or cunning in Physic, they shall never prevail against me, but I will overcome them. I come into the King's chamber at the time appointed in force of Physic and cast my dart that none shall see but feel. I often come into the counting house and suddenly kill the money teller. I overthrow the Dancer and stop the breath of the singer and trip the runner in his race. I break wedlocks and make many widows. I do sit in judgment with the Judge and undo the life of the prisoner and at length kill the Judge also himself. I do summon the great Bishops and cut them through their rochets. I utterly blemish the beauty of all Courtiers and end the misery of the poor. I will never leave until all flesh be utterly destroyed. I am the greatest cross and scourge of God.

Civis:

What is the cause, O fearful Death, that thou doest scourge the face of the earth with thy Darts, and who hath sent thee for that purpose?

Mors:

Neither is the saying of the Philosophers or Poets true, which compt that I come by chance to mortal things, or inquiring the cause of the matter, or *Deprivation in materia,*[121] or of generation and corruption. And some other do affirm that I do come through the concourse of the stars, infecting the air and poisoning living things, and therefore the Heathen in fearful Tragedies and stories have admonished the vain world to repent by setting forth of me, Death.[122] Some of them daily had the dead heads of their parents brought to their tables to mortify their vanities withal. And all these men whom I have slain were Heathen men.

But I am the messenger of God, his scourge and cross to all flesh good and bad, and am the end of life, which do separate the body from the soul. I am no feigned thing by the wise brains of the Philosophers but only through the disobedience of your first parents Adam and Eve through whose fault all flesh is corrupted and subject to me, Death: for through sin came death. Truly my master's anger was so great in your parents that he suffered me to plague with my hand the best in his church, as Abel, Isaac, Jeremy, Zechariah, John the Baptist, and Jesus Christ, his only son, which suffered me. And seeing that my master hath commanded me not to spare his only child, with his Apostles and holy Martyrs, dost thou think that I should bear with thee or suffer any in this wicked world? He sent me to Sodom with his Angels to burn them, to drown bloody Pharaoh, and to slay the kings of the Heathen. Also I was at their ends, although all flesh doth abhor me. Yet Judas and all desperate men did call upon me. Thus do I end both good and bad, but precious in the sight of the lord is the death of his saints, and many be the scourges of wicked men. I am in God's hands, as the sword is in the man of war's, as it is written, "the lord doeth kill and quicken again." And it is he that did create evil, that is, pain or death, light and darkness. And whereas he hath not set his strong angel to bridle me, I am merciless and will kill all whereas the token is not set up or his mark upon them whom he doeth forbid me to touch, and that is not upon thee nor upon many thousands that live most wretchedly.

Thy days are but a span long. Thou art like a flower in the field. Thy days are passed like a shadow. Thou hast run thy race, and thy days are consumed like smoke, and thou shalt scant live to draw thy breath.[123] I must destroy this, thy earthy mansion. I am so commanded. Have, here is thy reward. Suffer it patiently. I must go presently to visit a great number suddenly that do not remember me. I will cut them down with my scythe like grass and kill them with my three fearful darts. The pains of hell do follow me, to swallow up all flesh that doeth not repent them of their wickedness.

CIVIS:

Oh wretched man that I am, whither shall I fly for succor?[124] Now my body is past cure. No Physic can prevail. The sorrows of death doeth compass me round about. The policy of the world with fear bade me fly and use God's means, as Lot did when Sodom was afire. But now do I see, who so escapeth hunger and the sword shall be overtaken with the pestilence. I am at the pit's brink. Now begin I to wax weak in body. I am very dry. My pain doeth increase. He is gone that did strike me, but I do feel his wound that he gave me. Alas, woe is my vile stinking carcass and filthy flesh, conceived and born in sin, deprived of original justice, compared to a beast in Adam, fallen as a rotten Apple from a living tree.

What have I gotten, my Lord God, by my fall? Nothing else but only darkness, care, misery, affliction, sickness, pain, agues, and now in mine heart, Death most painful itself. Now for all my pomp, health, wealth, riches, and vain pleasures of this world: this my body, which I have both costly clothed, well fed, and garnished with all delights, for whose sake I have been covetous and sinned against Jesus Christ to maintain the same body. From henceforth, therefore, now shall I be turned into a stinking carrion for worm's delight, dust, clay, rotten, most vile, forsaken of all men, poor without substance, naked without clothing, sown in dishonor, forgotten of my posterity, not known from henceforth, vanish like a shadow, whither like a leaf, and fade as a flower. Oh uncertain life, but most assured death. Fie on this filthy shadow of this world and flattering of the same with all the instruments of the flesh.[125] Oh Lord, although I be in this extreme trouble, yet have mercy upon me, according to thy great mercy and loving kindness. For I do make my prayer in the time of trouble, trusting that thou wilt hear me.

ROGER:

Mistress, the fearful thing that talked with my Master is gone. Let us go hear what news with him.

UXOR:

I am glad it is past. Thanks be to God. I will go with speed to see my husband, for he hath been in great danger.

Roger:

Sir, I am glad that he is gone, the devil go with him. Hath he taken all your gold?

Civis:

No, I have my gold in store, for in the world I found it, and in the world I must leave it. It is but vain and can not help in the time of this my trouble. God hath prevented me and summoned me to appear before his seat. This death hath smitten me. I must die.

Uxor:

Alas my good sweet husband, what aileth you? Or what would you have me do for you to help you in this case?

Civis:

Help me into some house whereas I might send for some man of God to be my heavenly Physician, teaching me the way to the kingdom of Christ.[126]

Roger:

Here is a house at hand, and here is your horse also. We will help you up and carry you to this place.

Uxor:

Now sir, you be come here into this place. For God's sake, discomfort not yourself. I trust you shall do well. You shall want nothing that may be had for money, gold and silver. I will send for your own brethren and sisters. You shall have with all speed the best learned Physicians in this Realm. In the meantime, drink Dragonwater and Mithridatum mingled together to put this passion from your heart. Ride, *Roger,* and seek a Physician with all speed.[127] Spare not the horse.

CIVIS:

Soft sirrah, and speak with me, and do what that I do command you, in the name of Jesus Christ.

ROGER:

Sir, look what your mastership shall command me to do; that will I do with all speed and tarry not.

CIVIS:

Go thy ways, and pray master *Theologus* to come to me that I may have his counsel. Pray him to come with speed. Deliver him this token.

ROGER:

I shall. In the meantime, good master, be of good cheer, for God's sake.

UXOR:

Alas what shall I do, and my poor children?

CIVIS:

I have set my worldly things in order, for so hath God's word taught me to do.[128] I thank God, and my debts shall be truly payed, and whatsoever any poor man doeth owe me, I do forgive them, and restitution shall I make with all speed to as many as I have wronged. And I shall leave plenty to you and my children, requiring you to live according to God's commandment, obeying him all the days of your lives, and remember death, and to do to all men as you would be done unto:[129] to live chaste, either in Marriage or a life sole; use prayer; and chaste your bodies with abstinence. Be pitifully minded, and hate vice. Beware of wicked company. Love well the temple of God. Visit the prisoners and helpless. This is good Religion in the eyes of God. As near as you can, keep the commandments of the almighty God, and beware of idleness and pride of heart. Lament no more good wife. For who can keep that must needs away? Methink I hear *Theologus* come.

THEOLOGUS:

Sir, God the heavenly Physician bless you and give you the perfect consolation of conscience in Christ his son and give you grace meekly to bear this his cross.

CIVIS:

You are heartily welcome, dear *Theologus*. I have thought it long since I did send for you.

THEOLOGUS:

Your man declared to me by the way a pitiful story which happened to you this day. Further, I had sooner been with you, but one master *Antonius* sent for me, but or I came, he was dead, and *Avarus* and *Ambodexter* is in his house, preparing a solemn funeral for him.

CIVIS:

Oh sir, then I have no cause to rehearse the matter new again, but seeing my flesh is near the pit, and in a manner my breath faileth me, being wounded with death, and that I am of two parts, body and soul, the one past all cure, the other in hope of salvation, I desire, if it please God, that I may live to the end of your orations. Declare unto me, what is the cause of sin?

THEOLOGUS:

The Devil was the first cause of sin, as it is written in Genesis how with a lie he deceived the woman, and they that commit sin are of the Devil, for he hath sinned from the beginning of the world and is the first author of sin. The second cause was man, declining from

God and crediting the Devil, by which man, sin entered into the world and all the calamities and crosses therein, as sorrow, dread, fear, poverty, sickness, and death itself, all to punish sin.

Civis:

Oh lord, how I have erred. I had thought God had been the cause, as when I read these words, "*Indurabo cor Pharaonis*" (I will indurate the heart of Pharaoh) with such like places[130] and his induration was the cause of his sin, and who did indurate him but God? And when it is said, "*ne nos inducas im tentationem*" (neither lead us into temptation, etc.); here I gathered it was God that led us into temptation, for which cause, we desire him not to lead us into temptation, etc.

Theologus:

You have mistaken those places, for God is not the author or cause of sin, for he did so much abhor the same that nothing could pacify his wrath under heaven, no merit or work, but only the blood of Jesus Christ his son. And for this word "I will indurate," the very word in Hebrew is "I will suffer Pharaoh's heart to be hardened." And so it was in the Lord's prayer, it is "*Ne sinas nos induci*" (neither suffer us to be led or fall into temptation, etc.). Therefore my brother, it was the will of Satan and man that caused sin.

Civis:

Why, hath not man will to do good again, if he lust?

Theologus:

No, if he had the election to will, as first he had, he would do the like; therefore, it is in a sure hand, even in God's, and not in ours.[131] As when men do speak the truth, it is not of their own will or power but the heavenly spirit in them, and by almighty God are all the steps of men directed. Though man fall into sundry temptations, he shall not be cast off, for the Lord putteth under his hand, which is a great comfort to us in trouble when we are underneath the cross. Without him we can do nothing that is good. No man can take any good thing upon him, except it be given to him from heaven, and no man, dear brother, can come to the son of God, unless the father hath drawen him, and not his will, which is most wicked from his youth upward, as appeareth in our vile nature, thought, word, and deed. And whosoever hath not the spirit of Christ is not of Christ, but those which are led of the spirit of God are the sons of God, and this commeth not by man's will and power.[132]

For the worldly minded man doeth not understand or perceive those things that are of God's spirit, without which he can not be saved, be he never so learned, and can dispute of the soul, making distinctions of knowledge and judgment, calling it the mind, or intellection, or reason, or desire, which is the will, under whom the affection is governed, whose spring is the heart. All these make not to the heavenly purpose but rather standing upon such trifles doth hinder the way to salvation in Christ and rob him of his passion, when we do attribute freedom or freewill to come of ourselves, but that we are in God's hands as his instruments, through him to work such things as best may please him. And he withdraw his holy hands, we can do no good. Therefore, submit yourself to Christ and his will, for our wills are malignant and damnable in his eyes. Forsake your prave will, and humbly submit yourself to Jesus Christ, saying now before our death, "Our Father which art in heaven, hallowed be thy name. Thy kingdom come. Thy will be done, in earth as it is in heaven, etc." And thus I do conclude of free will in us and faithfully look for the reward, not of works but of mercy only, only purchased by the Sacrifice of Christ, thanking him that he hath made you merciful to your brethren in this world, which was the fruits of faith, by which faith in his blood we are saved and shall receive our alms or reward, and not our duty, for we are unprofitable when we have done our best.

Civis:

What reward is that, I pray you? Or what promises are granted by Christ?

Theologus:

The reward is the remission of sins and life everlasting, granted by the father for Jesus Christ's sake, freely without our works, for there is none other salvation under heaven given to men but only Christ. In him we do merit, as when we are merciful, we have a promise of this present life and the life to come. And in this world also an hundredfold, and in the world to come everlasting life. And who that giveth one of these little ones a cup of water for my name's sake shall not lose his reward. And he commanded to give, promising it shall be given to them again. And further he sayeth, break the bread to the poor, and it shall be to thee like a garden. He sayeth not, let thine executors or assigns give the poor when thou art dead, but thou must do it thyself in this world, now while it is light, for the night is at hand. I mean death, when thou canst not work.[133] Remember Dives lost the time and could not call it back again, which waileth in hell, hath no reward, for he trusted not God, nor rewarded any man. Further, reconcile thyself to thy brother, for else thou canst not please God, though thou wroughtest all good works and gave thy body to be burned, for charity is so precious in God's eyes that who so want it can not reign with Christ. Therefore, forgive from thy heart, and thou shall be forgiven. Make not thy will upon goods gotten by usury, nor by anything that falsely in bargaining thou hast taken from thy brother, for then thou shalt not dwell in God's tabernacle. Neither shall thy children prosper upon the earth, but God will hate them to the third and fourth generation for thy sin.[134]

Examine well thy conscience. Death hath wounded thee, which is common to all flesh. In thus doing, thou shalt pass from death to everlasting life by Christ and never taste upon the second death among the impious or castaways. Confess thy sins from thy heart—ask mercy—be they never so red, and many in number. Jesus hath washed them in his blood, and sprinkled them with Hyssop, and made them as white as snow.[135] Now, play the man in Christ. Fear not to depart this world. Christ is gone before with his holy Apostles, Prophets, Martyrs, Confessors and Virgins, penitent thieves, and harlots also. There is the army of angels before his throne, with Joy incessantly honoring him. Hell gates are sparred, Satan beaten down, thy sins razed, the good Angel at hand to conduct thee to that blessed land of rest. Here is nothing but labor, days of care, sin, wretchedness, a thousand crosses, the snares of the devil, and many vanities, the flesh most inconstant, the world a place of misery and sin. Bid it farewell, taking thy leave with the badge of a Christian man, of Christ crucified. Remember that promise made in thy Baptism. Arm thyself with the breastplate of faith, continue to the end, and thou shalt receive a crown of life, thy cross taken away. Cast thy whole care upon Christ and he shall deliver thee at hand and give thee the holy resurrection of body and soul to dwell in one forever with him.[136]

CIVIS:

Oh what comfort in conscience I have received. First, I render thanks to God the father, the son, and the holy ghost. Secondly, blessed be the hour of your coming hither in this time of my trouble with this holy consolation in Christ, in whom I do believe, renouncing the world, the flesh and the devil, believing all the articles of my Christian faith, acknowledging the blessed Sacraments to be the instruments to everlasting life and salvation in Christ, by the which God doeth work in his Church to the world's end, to them that shall be saved. One Trinity and three distinct persons coequal in unity; in one essence and being is my God. The father created me, the son redeemed me, and the holy ghost sanctified me and inspired me, whereby I know that I am his elected. And one undefiled mother the Church hath thus taught me, in that blessed book of Patriarchs, Prophets, Martyrs, and Jesus with his Apostles, which is God's work. Now master *Theologus*, my time is at hand. I pray you, say something of the resurrection, and then let us pray in the name of God together, that it may please him to forgive me my sins, which I have committed against heaven and earth, and to receive my soul into his blessed hands.

THEOLOGUS:

Good brother, not only the doctrine of Prophets and the Evangelists do promise the Resurrection to come, of some to salvation and some to damnation, but the same resurrection is most manifest.[137] As for example, Christ himself and other, did rise, and were seen to many in Jerusalem. And by the space of forty days, he taught the Apostles and was conversant with them, and then ascended into glory, until the time appointed to judge the quick and the dead, when he shall send his angels to gather all flesh under heaven from the four winds and sit down in judgment, saying, "Come to me you blessed of the father, and receive the kingdom prepared for you from the beginning." Further he sayeth, "This is the will of my father, which hath sent me, that all that do see the son and believeth in him shall have everlasting life, and I will raise him in the last day." And the holy Apostle Saint Paul most heavenly doeth preach the resurrection to the Corinthians. "Thy dead shall live," sayeth Isaiah, "and thy slain shall rise again, and those which sleep in the dust shall rise, the earth shall cast forth their dead bodies." "I will create both heaven and earth new," sayeth the Lord, "and put the old out of my remembrance." "Many," sayeth Daniel, "that lie asleep in the dust shall be wakened again, some to life everlasting and other to reprobation." God sayeth, "I will open their tombs and bring them forth." And the holy man Job sayeth, "I know that my redeemer liveth, and that in the last day, he shall raise me again out of the earth and I shall be clothed again with my Skin, and in my flesh I shall see God, whom I shall see with these same eyes and with none other."[138] These are comfortable and most true places of holy scripture for the resurrection of the dead. You are assured in conscience of this blessed resurrection, and life everlasting in Christ Jesus our lord.

CIVIS:

Yea forsooth, dear *Theologus*, but my speech is almost past. Yet I thank God I know you all, and I beseech him to bless you, and when my spirit is gone, I pray you bury my body with comeliness, not with pomp, and use it as an instrument wherein the soul hath dwelled and which the soul shall possess again in honor, in that blessed resurrection.

THEOLOGUS:

Let us most humbly here upon our knees with our hands lifted up towards the heaven desire God the father for Christ's sake to receive your soul into his glorious kingdom.[139] O dear citizen rejoice and be glad that thy labor is almost past. Rest is at hand. Fear not the pain of death, for it is impossible to escape that which cannot be fled or avoided. For it is written, "Who is that man that liveth and shall not see death?"[140] None, no not one; therefore, suffer it my sweet heart patiently, and that is an argument of good conscience and of an heavenly mind.

Your wife mourneth immoderately, oh God. All flesh was born to die. This happened to our parents, as father, mother, etc., and shall not fail to all that shall follow, unto the end of the world or coming of Christ. For surely, sweet life was never without the exception of bitter death. It is no novelty, therefore, when we do hear tell of the departure of any of our friends. Let us not fall into a sudden passion, as onely the high priest did, which hearing of the death of his children, fell down and brake his neck, but rather constantly with wise *Anaxagoras*, which hearing of the death of his beloved son, said to the messenger, "This is no new tidings, nor strange to me. As soon as he was born, I knew that he should die, for of nature's law is learned, life to be taken and resigned, and no man die but he which have lived."[141]

Oh leave your lamenting, good mistress. Why rage you like one which have no hope? Be absent, or use moderation. Remember holy Job: the same days when the Lord permitted Satan not only to destroy his servants and cattle but also, before age in the lusty time of youth in the feast day at one table, his dear children of his body were all broken in pieces and slain with the violent fall of the house. What did he, rend his hair or flesh? No, no. He considered who sent them, and who did take them—even the Lord, whom he most obediently suffered and reverently thanked. Further, good sister, remember Saint Jeremiah, taking God to witness of an holy woman, whose husband was dead, whom he most tenderly loved, by whom she had but two sons of singular beauty wanting no gift of grace or of nature, which both died the same day wherein their father departed. "When this Cross was," sayeth Saint Jeremiah, "who would not have thought that she would have fallen mad, in rending her hair, breasts, clothes and skin, running up and down, wailing and crying, with pitiful wringing of hands. What did she? First, she weeped not one tear, but most soberly, with a womanly countenance, she humbly kneeled upon her knees, holding up her hands, rendering thanks, and making prayers to almighty God, saying, 'most humbly I thank thee good lord, for that that it have pleased thee to take me into thy service. I am sped, oh Lord, for thou hast discharged me,'" etc. Take also for an example, the most worthy constancy of that patient woman, which without much lamentation did with her own eyes behold her dear children slain, their members cut in pieces, and boiled in cauldrons.[142] Mark how constantly of late years, children did see the flesh of their fathers, mothers, etc., burn in the fire, most patiently suffering. And again, fathers beholding their children do the like. What, did they roar like Lions, etc? No, no, but rejoiced, that God had of their blood and stock erected a people to reign with him in life, which witnessd him in death. The examples should move all Christians. Perfect mortification is not much to lament for, our friends dying, but rather by the example of their deaths, to remember our end, and then we shall not sin. Therefore, better it is to go to the house of mourning than to the house of banqueting.

And when it shall please God to call your husband away, and the days of forgetfulness shall approach, as everything under heaven have the time, both of mourning and rejoicing, when you do behold yourself in a glass, remember your face shall be lean and pale, your nose rotten, your teeth stinking and black, your eyes dim and blind, your ears deaf and running, your hairs fallen away, your veins broken, your sinews relaxed and wasted, bones corrupted, bowels full of rheums, and all your flesh consumed. Behold, behold, you damosels of vanities and lusty youth, the pleasure of this world, how it endeth with stink, filth, etc., not reserved after death to any good purpose, as timber when it is cut down, but because it is so vile and will infect the air, the corpse is enclosed in a pit, as we daily see, where as it consumeth, as I have said.

Remember this: be not proud of noble parentage, of riches, beauty, or cunning, but rather consider where are the old lusty kings, queens, lords, knights, ladies. Where are the old courtiers and valiant men of war? Where are the Mayors of cities, lawyers, bishops, Physicians? Where are all the pleasant Musicians? Where are become the old commons in every kingdom? Where is become the Pope's rotten holiness, with all the infernal malignant synagogue of antichrist, etc.? All are gone and passed like shadows, wasted and come to nothing, as Saint Augustine affirmeth. "Oh man," sayeth he, "go to the charnel-house or graves. Take up the bones. Mark well if thou canst know the master from the servant, the fair from the foul, the rich from the poor, the wise from the fool, etc. Thou canst not do it; it is impossible to know them."[143]

Well, world. Well. What doest thou promise unto all them which do love thee? Perhaps much riches or dignity? How noisome to the soul is riches, the very minister of, or to, all civil rule and mischief, as damnable usury, adultery, treason, murder. It maketh one proud, high minded, and forgetful of himself. It deludeth him with flatterers and curtsies of Hypocrisy. It is the mother of vainglory and nourisher of pride and idle life and loathly gluttony. It is remembered by our master Jesus Christ, which calleth it thorns, and by his Apostles, which nameth it the root of all ill. It is the master of some rich men and women, which keepeth it to their great hurt.[144] And the foolish prodigal waster, which commonly succeedeth the gatherer, spendeth it soon away in wickedness, as it is said, "Easy gotten goods are soon spent"; therefore sufficient, or a mean, is well to a Christian man (for sundry causes), for they that will be rich fall into sundry temptations, cares, broken sleeps.

He gapeth and looketh for much and spendeth little. He cannot be merry (for fear of loss). The more he getteth, he is never satisfied that is a covetous man but still desireth and never pacified, like unto the dry man in a hot burning fever.

Riches hath poisoned the church and transformed the clergy, specially in Rome among the Popes and many great men, whose ancestors did keep plentiful houses of the one half, which now is come to pass that nowadays in keeping hospitality or ministering of charity but break up houses and hurt many poor even for the love of one glutton, himself which will not well spend it, nor for his children which can not well use riches. For we do see how God doeth plague the seed of extortioners, vile usurers, etc. What if they had mountains of gold? So, increased dolor of mind and death stealeth on all flesh like a thief and smiteth the money-lover, the usurer, the oppressor, the golden watchman, the great officer, merchant, the wise gentleman, that hath purchased so much. What is the end of this gear? A dead carcass and scant a good winding sheet. Out of the door he must to grave. He shall fare well, *Gloria mundi,* and welcome silly worms. I pray God that this turneth not to damnation.

Oh, what is become of rich *Senior Antonius'* Treasures, *Capax, Rapax, Tenax, Ambodexter?* (Ill gotten goods are worse spent.) Sour sweetness and slipping Ice, the golden entangled hook, and the drink of *Midas* hath utterly destroyed him, and before ever he was aware, death hath slain him. He loved so well this world and life in the same that if his Physician might have saved his life, he would have lost one of his hands and suffered his flesh to have been cut with some broken bones, with the continuance of pain, ache and grief, with dreadful sleeps. And when he did see no remedy, the terror of conscience tormented him, vexed him, and overcame him, made him rage, and curse the time of his birth. His life was so horrible in the eyes of God and man, whose judgment I do commend to God, but surely great plagues do remain for the ungodly. Therefore let us be converted and turn clean from our sins and wickedness, and so there shall no sin do us harm. Let us fast and pray, hate evil, and cleave to good, make restitution, forgive our enemies, abhor vice, and be sorry that we can not be sorrier. Remember our accompts, and come betimes unto the Lord. Make no tarrying to turn unto the Lord. Put not off from day to day. For suddenly shall his wrath come and in time of vengeance shall he destroy us and "except we do all repent, we shall perish," sayeth Christ. Let us repent therefore, and turn unto God that he may forgive us that our sins may be done away, that we may say, "From plague, pestilence, and famine, from battle and murder, and from sudden death, oh Lord deliver us. From hardness of heart and contempt of thy word and commandment, which is the greatest cause of the wrath and indignation, oh good Lord deliver thy people, for thy holy name's sake. Amen. Amen."

Almighty and most dear father of heaven, we most humbly beseech thee for Jesus' sake, have mercy upon this thy servant, which now is nailed to the painful cross of death, for Adam's offence.[145] Impute no sin unto this penitent, which most willingly hath submitted himself to thy fatherly correction, but behold thy son on the right hand, the only Mediator for all the elected, whose names are written in the book of life. Let this thy servant, we beseech thee most mighty God, have clean remission and forgiveness of all his sin, by thought, word, and deed, committed against thy divine Majesty.[146] Now in this peril of death, assist him with thy holy angel, command Satan to depart, make clean his conscience with a glad mind to rejoice only in thy mercy, for vain is the help of man, but thy mercy doeth endure for ever. We are thy people and the Sheep of thy pasture. To thee we shall give praise for ever and ever. Amen.

Civis:

Amen, Amen. Lord receive my soul into thy hands, thou God of truth.[147]

THEOLOGUS:

The mighty God of Angels[148] and the former of all things visible and invisible, in whose hands is only life and death, light and darkness, and all the motions of the soul and body, without thee most mighty God, all things had been nothing, and of nothing all things are made by thee. Without thy Christ and thy blessed spirit, which is one coeternal trinity, all flesh were accursed, all consciences molested, and all souls utterly damned.[149] From light into darkness, from freedom into everlasting reprobation, but by Jesus Christ thine only son, we thank thee dear father of all mercy, that now it hath pleased thee to take to thy mercy at this present time our brother, whom thou hast elected, consecrated, and now he shall by thy mercy and pity be sanctified unto thee to be a citizen of eternal glory. Now do flesh and blood forsake him and all his worldly strength faileth him.[150] Now is the Organs yielding up the heavenly sound. His soul cometh now unto thee. Good Lord, receive it to thy mercy, into thine everlasting glory whereas Abraham, Isaac, and Jacob are continually. To thee, oh heavenly father, be incessant honor and glory. Amen.

The end of the Dialogue.

A Copie of a letter, to Frances Barlow, by W. B.

When the time of trouble draweth nere, good *Frances Barlow*, as death, which shall separate the soul from the body, if we be not ware and wisely provident, we shall stand in great danger of losses: first we shall lose our health, strength and beauty, wherein we have delighted, and all our senses, as pleasure of speech, joy of heart, and the comfortable sight of the eyes, wherewith we do daily behold all the pleasures of this world, etc.[151] We shall lose all our further treasures, lauds and substance, and also our lives, and as dung be cast into the earth, and finally our souls banished from God's blessed presence or resting place. Therefore let us call, my Frances, to our remembrance, the fearful curses of almighty God against our sins, and the cause of our plagues, which is our abominable living, in sinning against God in thought, word, and deed, against heaven and earth, in pride, wrath, idolatry, fornication, swearing, lust, gluttony, and stopping of our ears against grace, and the word of truth.

Let us call to remembrance how that we have done wrong to each other, in word and deed, in slandering or in hindering by bargaining, etc., our brethren, for whom Christ hath died, whom we have hated and not pitied in their extreme sorrows and adversities, and have not payed their labours and travels. Let us repent and call for grace, and restore now, while we are in the way of grace, and in that, that we can not make satisfaction for our sins by no merits of alms, prayers, oblations, etc., which are unclean in God's eyes. As concerning the remission of our sins, as Job sayeth, "How can he be clean that is born of a woman? Behold, he will give no light unto the Moon, and the stars are unclean in his sight. How much more, man a worm; even the son of a man, which is but a worm,"[152] which in beholding of his sin hath no cause, but to dispair, and to be damned. What remedy in this case? None, but with all speed by faith, lift up your head, and behold even Jesus Christ on God's right hand, pleading our case, excusing us to his father, which prayeth to him for us, and is heard, and Satan beaten down, and God's Angels set at our bedside with spiritual armor for us in this battle of death against Satan, to conduct us to that happy land.

Let us kneel down and first say whatsoever God doth send to us, life or death, his name be praised. His will be done in earth as it is with his Angels in heaven, desiring him to be fed with his lively word, and blessed sacrament, the immortal food for the soul, passing all worldly treasures or physic for the body, and that it would please him to pardon our trespasses and offences in thought, word, and deed, against his divine majesty, even as we do forgive our enemies such faults as they do here in earth against us, and that in the time of agony or pains of death, he suffer us not to fall into temptation, or be overladen under our cross but that his hand may help us and deliver us from this vile life full of miseries and bring us into the land of the living. In doing this, you shall be most happy and blessed. Let us submit ourselves to him that hath made us. We have not made ourselves. We are his vessels and are in his sight and cannot flee from his presence nor run beyond that race, which he hath appointed us.[153] He bringeth death, and restoreth again to life in the resurrection. Oh, be content to render the same talent, which was but lent unto you, even your body, the gifts of nature and grace: commit wife, children, and all to him.[154] He doeth no wrong; he taketh but his own. Remember, he brought you in hither naked, and how you do live but a small time, and are full of misery, like a flower for the time and shall pass away like a shadow.[155] Alas, we do deserve great punishment, but he plagueth us not according to the gravity of our sins, for then were we damned, or like unto Sodom that perished without hands in the day of God's wrath and vengeance.

Consider, Frances, that this is no news or marvelous chance that you should change your life. Well it happened to all your forefathers, from Adam to kings and all the nobles of the earth, and to the poor also. All flesh is grass, and worms are the companions to the corpse in dark grave or house of clay.[156] Yet there is a day which God hath appointed which none can tell but himself, in which he will judge both the quick and dead, and call all flesh before him: both his very elect and the merriless reprobates, and then body and soul shall remain immortal together and have life everlasting. This hold fast, dear Frances, as an anchor in this storm, from death to life everlasting. Hold fast the twelve articles of the Christian faith. Pray to the end only to God the father by Christ. Remember his promises, that at what time soever a sinner doth repent, he will forgive. Call; he will answer unto thy soul. Knock and he will open.

This time of your adversity and plague of the pestilence doth make you forget all pleasures and delights past. Even so, remember this world is the more slippery, and the pleasures do compass all understanding to God's elected.[157] Because I will conclude, the time draweth at hand of our deliverance. Cast your care onely upon God almighty. Look not back again. Beware of by-paths either upon the right or left hand, but tread in the true path or very way of Jesus Christ himself. I pray you, let Ambrose Barnes read the 11 Chapter of Saint John's Gospel, and the first Epistle to the Corinthians, Chapter 15. If the time had not been so much spent, and the venom so dangerous, and the parties so weak and feeble, I would have caused you to have been letten blood and given you pills *contra pestem,* with cordials accordingly by God's grace, if that would have done you any good. But take this cordial in good part. Thus, God give you the crown of life, which Jesus Christ without our deservings, hath purchased for us in his precious blood. His name be praised. Amen.

Your W. B.

Fare ye well. We must follow when it pleaseth God.

To his loving friend and brother, Master William Conscience, Minister, W. B. sendeth Salutation.

If the almighty God do take care for the fowls of the air and flowers of the field, and provideth nourishment for them, how much more for his beloved men, that do faithfully serve him in the holy ministry of his word and sacraments, visiting the sick and burying the dead?[158] The Captain that doeth but serve a mortal Prince—howsoever he speedeth, life or death, behaving himself wisely and valiantly against the enemy—is worthy of worldly fame and honor; much more the Lord's armored knight, being his Angel and mouth between him and his people that stand in danger, is worthy in Christ to be numbered, crowned, and placed among his Angels immortal. By this, I know that you are no hireling, but (under Christ) the true Shepherd in that, that you fly not from your fold when that Wolf Satan with his companion Death, do work their violence against the flesh & soul.[159] In this case, remember these words: *Nolite eos timere qui occidunt corpus,* etc: fear not them which do kill the body. They cannot kill the soul. In this, we do see what the power of death is, not only to kill in us the four

Elements (whereof the body is framed) by sword, fire, water, sickness, etc., but the soul is not made of any of them, but the Creator of all things hath made it most pure of nothing, upon which soul, death hath no power, because it is of nature immortal. But so long as body and soul are together, and not divided, that is called man. And whatsoever things are seen with bodily eyes are ordained for the same body, and the body for the soul, and the soul for God[160] The life of the body is the soul, and the life of the soul is God, so, for sin the body is ruinated, and shall be in dust until the resurrection. But in the fall or death of the body, the soul dieth not but is delivered, when the snare of this flesh is broked.[161] The flesh with the senses are dead, but *Anima cum ratione sua,*[162] do still live; therefore, I trust and know that you do consider wisely three things. The first is, the world, with the wretchedness therein, worthy to be despised. The second, our own knowledge of ourselves, our sin, our sickness, and whereof we are made, even of repugnant elements. Thirdly is, to lay hand of eternal blessedness, remembering the merciful promises of God, as, "Come to me all you that are heavy-laden either with affliction of mind, poverty in Christ, sickness or death, and I shall refresh you."[163] This is the very Physician of the soul, even Christ, and the perfect quietness of conscience. God hath given you a talent full godly. You do lucrify the same and hide it not. Therefore, it shall be said most joyfully, "It is well done, good servant and faithful. Thou hast been faithful; in little; I will make thee ruler ouer much. Enter into thy master's joy." And again, "He which doth continue to the end shall have the crown of life."[164] Be patient, my brother (Conscience), and settle your heart, for the coming of the Lord draweth near, and blessed are the dead, which die in the Lord, for they shall reign with Christ in glory, his name be ever praised, and his will be fulfilled. Amen. Be of good comfort, and cast away fear. Be merry. Let not the Pestilent corpses nor the noise of bells terrify you.

Inter mortales te non mihi charior ullus:
Te plus, quam verum diligo amoque fratrem.[165]
Finis.

Colendissimo fratri suo in Christo, Magisto Richardo Turnero Theologo, Guilhelmus Bullenus. S. P. D.[166]

Reverendissime, et observandissime frater, puto te literas meas recepisse, in quibus tibi scribebam, regimen contra pestem, ac idcirco modo non ero prolixiorim febre pestilenti. Nam omnis febris quam pestilentem vocamus provenit e putredine quae fit ab excessum humidi. Hac vero (ut inquit Galenus) febrem ex plurima humiditate putrefacta, prouenire prutrefacta sine dubio potius quam a calore aucto fatendum est humiditas.[167] Ideo materia est putrescens in venis unde calor naturalis valde afficitur & uno die omnes virtutes decidunt urinae sunt foetentes, etc. Galenus, Avicenna, Rasis, Trallianus, etc. affirmant: in febre pestilenti est multitudo obstructionum et praecipuè ubi materia urgit ad cutim et caput. Multitudo materiae et cruditatum in causa est.

Cura est, prohibere putredinem.[168] Obstructiones igitur sunt aperiendae, cum humorum evacatione. Sed si natura movit, tunc nihil movendum est. Hoc est autem remedium ut inquit. Johannes Baptist. Monta. Vironensis. Rx:[169] Syrup de Cichorio cum Rhabarbaro, ℥ 1 ß;[170] aqua Boraginis, acetosae, ℥ 3; in quibus citrum sit impositum et decoctum deinde unguentum pectorale contra pestem. Rx: unguenti Rosacei confortativi mesues, ℥ 1;[171] specierum-cordialium, ℥ 1; Sandalorum alborum, ℈ 1;[172] Rosarum siccarum ℥ ß; misce simul artificiose et fiat linimentum pro corde, et pro toto regione ventris. Mirum est hoc remedin contra venenum pestis.[173]

Quod ad rationem victus attinet, ubi est maxima putredo (ut inquit Hippocrates, 17 Aphorisms) ubi coruptihumores et putridi nihil, perniciosius quam instituere tenuem victum, quia inter, exhibeas ius pulli, et ponas semper in tuo cibo praeter acetosam succum citri. De reliquo velim tibi persuadeas quemadmodum legisti im Galeno, etc.

Vale et vale iterum (eruditis vir) sisque; bono animo. Nunc literas concludo. Nam plura non opus habeo scribere, ne tuis optimis occupationibus (in ui nea domini) importune nunc obstrepere vi dear. Martij. Incarnati. 1564.

Tuus ad omnia Guilihelmus Bullenus.

Amantissimo ac probissimo viro magistro T. Gaylo Chyrurgo. Guilihelmus Bullenus. *Salutem Plurimam Dicit.*[174]

Bonam valetudinem, cum corporis tum animi a deo opt. max. tibi precor (optime vir). Nihil est hoc tempore quod tibi scribam, quàm quòd libellum quem mihi donasti, legi, et iterum legipro quo tibi ago gratias et habem ut pro sumno munere. Nam ex eo et intellexi amorem et animu~ quem erga me geris, et operam tuam perspexi non solum mihi sed omnibus qui ubique sunt Anglis futuram utilitati. Nostrum enim omnium haberi possunt amatores et cultores, libri tui insignissimi. Quamobrem quid magis mihi gratu esse potuit hoc munere, praesertim cum a tali Chirurgo mihi datum sit? cujus rei nunquam me capiet oblivio, sed quantum potero gratias referri libenti animo faciam. Opto te bene valere, ac interim me tibi comendo doctissimo viro magistro Bactero[175] humillime meis verbis gratias agi meque plu rimum comendare desidero.

Martii *28*. Anno incarnate, *1564*.
Tibi deditissimus Guilihelmus Bullenus.

The Table of this present book.[176]

4

Plague Orders

Queen Elizabeth I: Orders thought meet (1578)

In 1563, Queen Elizabeth I not only contracted and nearly died from smallpox but she also experienced the first visitation of plague during her reign. It was the worst in memory, and the new queen saw her nation suffer. In that year, Elizabeth I adjourned parliament (STC 7962.5); her Privy Councilors William Cecil and Ambrose Cave drafted a short set of regulatory orders for the cities of London and Westminster and the duchy of Lancaster (STC 16704.9); and the Church of England issued a national form of prayer and fasting, *A Form to be used in Common prayer* (in this volume). But these measures were immediately deemed lacking, and between 1563 and 1578, cities and towns across the country worked to solidify their local plague policies. A large-scale change came in 1578, with the second major visitation in Elizabeth I's reign and with the first ever nationwide plague orders, *Orders thought meet*. Modeled on Continental regulations, the English orders are seventeen in number, addressed to the justices of the peace in all counties in the nation. These orders support a human to human contagion theory over both the competing "miasma" theory that air tainted by putrefaction was the primary cause of plague and over those theories that focus on the role of the astrological influences prominent in Moulton's plague remedy in this collection. Utilizing the practices of quarantining homes, collecting taxes to assist the poor, recording and reassessing local and national strategies, and making the positions of plague Watcher, Searcher, and Examiner nationally recognized, these orders were a break with the past in many ways.

Not only interdisciplinary and comprehensive, the orders were also flexible. Built within them was a provision for change, empowering local officials to add to them as they saw fit. In addition, appended to them was a set of medical prescriptions for the plague, *an advice set down upon her Majesty's express commandment,* to be posted with the orders in markets and churches, and therefore free of charge. The orders endured. Elizabeth I reissued the 1578 orders and the plague remedies that accompanied them (STC 9187.9) in each of the major outbreaks in her realm, and the kings that followed her did the same well beyond England's last battle with plague. See, for example, the 1592 (STC 9199); 1603 (STC 9209); 1625 (STC 9244); 1641 (Wing [2nd ed.], E2791C); and 1666 (Wing [CD-ROM, 1996], E819) versions. Compare these orders with the 1563 schedule of plague prayers (chapter 2) and with the plague remedies supplied by Thomas Moulton (chapter 1) and William Bullein (chapter 3).

Orders thought meet by her Majesty and her privy Council to be executed throughout the Counties of this Realm, in such Towns, Villages, and other places, as are or may be hereafter infected with the plague, for the stay of further increase of the same.

Imprimis, all the Justices in every County as well within the liberties as without, immediately upon knowledge to them given, shall assemble themselves together at some one general place accustomed, being clear from infection of the plague, to consult how these orders following may be duly put in execution, not meaning that any Justices dwelling in or near places infected shall come thither while their coming may be doubtful. And after their

ORDERS,

thought meete by her

Maieſtie, and her priuie Councell, to be

executed throughout the Counties of this Realme,

in ſuch Townes, Villages, and other places, as are, or
may be hereafter infected with the plague, for
the ſtay of further increaſe of the ſame.

Alſo, an aduiſe ſet downe vpon her
Maieſties expreſſe commaundement, by the beſt learned in Phyſicke within this Realme, contayning ſundry good
rules and eaſie medicines, without charge to the meaner
ſort of people, aſwell for the preſeruation of her good
Subiects from the plague before infection,
as for the curing and ordring of them
after they ſhalbe infected.

Imprinted at London by Chriſtopher Barker, *Printer to the Queenes
moſt excellent Maieſtie.*

Fig. 6. *Orders thought meet,* title page, STC 9187.9. Reproduced by permission of the Huntington Library, San Marino, California.

first general assembly, they shall make a distribution of themselves to sundry limits and divisions, as in other common services for the County they are accustomed to do for the prosecution thereof.

2. First, they shall inquire and presently inform themselves by all good means what Towns and Villages are at the time of such assembly infected within every their Counties and in what Hundred or other division the said Towns and Villages are and how many of the same places so infected are corporate Towns, market Towns, and Villages, and shall consider of what wealth the inhabitants of the same Towns and Parishes are to be able to relieve the poor that are or shall be infected and to be restrained in their houses.

3. Item, thereupon after conference used according to the necessity of the cause, they shall devise and make a general taxation either by charging the Town infected with one sum in gross or by charging the special persons of wealth within the same, to be forthwith collected for the rate of one month at the first, and so if the sickness shall continue, the collection of the like sum or of more or less, as time and cause shall require, and the same to be every first, second, third, or fourth week implored to and for the execution of the said orders. And in case some of the said Towns infected shall manifestly appear not to be of sufficient ability to contribute sufficient for the charges requisite, then the taxation or collection shall be made or further extended to other parts or in any other further limits as by them shall be thought requisite where there shall be any such Towns or Villages so infected and unable to relieve themselves. And if the said Towns be situated in the borders and confines of any other shire, then as the Justices shall see cause and need for the greatness of the charge requisite that the parts of the Shire joining to the Town infected be not able, they shall write their letters to the next Justices of the other Shire so confining to procure by collection some relief, as in like cases they are to relieve them in respect of near neighborhood of the place and for that the same infection may be the better stayed from the said adjoining places, though they be separated by the name of the County.

4. Item, they shall cause to be appointed in every Parish as well infected as not infected certain persons to view the bodies of all such as shall die before they be suffered to be buried and to certify the Minister of the Church and Churchwarden or other principal officers or their substitutes of what probable disease the said persons died, and the said viewers to have weekly some allowance and the more large allowance where the Towns or Parishes be infected during the infection towards their maintenance, to the end they which shall be in places infect may forbear to resort into the company of others that are sound, and those persons to be sworn to make true report according to their knowledge, and the choice of them to be made by direction of the Curate of the Church with three or four substantial men of the Parish. And in case the said viewers either through favor or corruption shall give wrong certificate or shall refuse to serve being thereto appointed, then to cause them to be punished by imprisonment in such sort as may serve for a terror to others.

5. Item, the houses of such persons out of the which there shall die any of the plague, being so certified by the viewers or otherwise known, or where it shall be understood that any person remaineth sick of the plague, to be closed up on all parts during the time of restraint: viz. six weeks after the sickness be ceased in the same house, in case the said houses so infected shall be within any Town having houses near adjoining to the same. And if the infection happen in houses dispersed in Villages and separated from other houses, and that of necessity for the serving of their cattle and manuring of their ground, the said persons cannot continue in their houses, then they to be nevertheless restrained from resorting into company of others either publicly or privately during the said time of restraint and to wear some mark in their uppermost garments or bear white rods in their hands at such time as they shall go abroad, and if there be any doubt that the masters and owners of the houses infected will not duly observe the directions of shutting up their doors, specially in the night, then shall there be appointed two

or three watchmen by turns, which shall be sworn to attend and watch the house and to apprehend any person that shall come out of the house contrary to order, and the same persons by order of the Justices shall be a competent time imprisoned in the stocks in the highway next to the house infected, and furthermore, some special mark shall be made and fixed to the doors of every of the infected houses, and where any such houses shall be Inns or Alehouses, the signs shall be taken down for the time of the restraint and some cross or other mark set up in the place thereof to be a token of the sickness.

6. Item, they shall have good regard to choose honest persons that either shall collect the sums affected or shall have the custody thereof, and out of the said collection to allot a weekly proportion for the finding of victual or fire or medicines for the poorer sort during the time of their restraint. And whereas some persons being well disposed to yield alms and relief will be more willing to give some portions of victual as corn, bread, or other meat, the same shall be committed to the charge of some special persons that will honestly and truly preserve the same to be distributed as they shall be appointed for the poor that are infected.

7. Item, to appoint certain persons dwelling within the towns infected to provide and deliver all necessaries of victuals or any matter of watching or other attendance to keep such as are of good wealth being restrained at their own proper charges and the poor at the common charges, and the said persons so appointed to be ordered not to resort to any public assembly during the time of such their attendance, as also to wear some mark on their upper garment or to bear a white rod in their hand to the end others may avoid their company.

8. Item, that in the shire Town in every County, and in other great towns meet for that purpose, there may be provision bespoken and made of such preservatives and other remedies, which otherwise in meaner towns can not be readily had, as by the Physicians shall be prescribed and is at this present reduced into an Advice made by the Physicians and now printed and sent with the said

orders, which may be fixed in market places, upon places usual for such public matters, and in other towns in the bodies of the parish churches and chapels, in which advice only such things are prescribed as usually are to be had and found in all counties without great charge or cost.

9. Item, the Ministers and Curates and the Churchwardens in every Parish shall in writing certify weekly to some of the Justices residing within the Hundred or other limit where they serve, the number of such persons as are infected and do not die and also of all such as shall die within their Parishes and their diseases probable whereof they died, and the same to be certified to the rest of the Justices at their assemblies, which during some convenient time would be every twenty-one days, and thereof a particular book kept by the Clerk of the peace, or some such like.

10. Item, to appoint some place apart in each parish for the burial of such persons as shall die of the plague, as also to give order that they be buried after sun setting and yet nevertheless by daylight so as the Curate be present for the observation of the rites and ceremonies prescribed by the law foreseeing as much as conveniently he may, to be distant from the danger of infection of the person dead or of the company that shall bring the corpse to the grave.

11. Item, the Justices of the whole County to assemble once in twenty-one days to examine whether those orders be duly executed and to certify to the lords of the privy Council their proceedings in that behalf, what towns and villages be infected, as also the numbers of the dead, and the diseases whereof they died, and what sums of money are taxed and collected to this purpose, and how the same are distributed.

12. Item, the Justices in the Hundred where any such infection is, or the Justices next adjoining thereunto, to assemble once a week to take accompt of the execution of the said orders and as they find any lack or disorder, either to reform it themselves or to report it at the general assembly, there to be by a more common consent reformed.

13. Item, for that the contagion of the plague groweth and increaseth no way more than by the use and handling of such clothes, bedding, and other stuff as hath been worn and occupied by the infected of this disease during the time of their disease, the said Justices shall in the places infected take such order that all the said clothes and other stuff so occupied by the diseased, so soon as the parties diseased of the plague are all of them either well recovered or dead, be either burnt and clean consumed with fire or else aired in such sort as is prescribed in an especial article contained in the Advice set down by the Physicians. And for that peradventure the loss of such apparel, bedding, and other stuff to be burned may be greater than the poor estate of the owners of the same may well bear, it is thought very good and expedient if it be thought meet it should be burnt, that then the said Justices, out of such collections as are to be made within their Counties for the relief of the poorer sort that be infected, allow also to them such sum or sums as to them shall be thought reasonable in the recompense of the loss of their said stuff.

14. Item, the said Justices may put in execution on any other orders that by them at their general assembly shall be devised and thought meet, tending to the preservation of her Majesty's subjects from the infection, and to the end their care and diligence may the better appear, they shall certify in writing the said orders newly devised, and if any shall willfully break and contemn the same or any the orders herein specified, they shall either presently punish them by imprisonment, or if persons so contemning them shall be of such countenance as the Justices shall think meet to have their faults known to her Majesty or to the Council, they shall charge and bind them to appear before us and the contempt duly certified, that there may be a more notorious sharp example made by punishment of the same by order of her Majesty.

15. Item, if there be lack of Justices in some parts of the shire or if they which are Justices there shall be for the time absent, in that case the more number of the Justices at their assembly shall make choice of some convenient persons to supply those places for the better execution hereof.

16. Item, if there be any person Ecclesiastical or lay that shall hold and publish any opinions (as in some places report is made) that it is a vain thing to forbear to resort to the infected or that it is not charitable to forbid the same, pretending that no person shall die but at their time prefixed, such persons shall be not only reprehended but by order of the Bishop, if they be ecclesiastical, shall be forbidden to preach, and being lay, shall be also enjoined to forbear to utter such dangerous opinions upon pain of imprisonment, which shall be executed if they shall persevere in that error. And yet it shall appear manifestly by these orders that according to Christian charity, no person of the meanest degree shall be left without succor and relief.

17. And of these things above mentioned, the Justices shall take great care as of a matter specially directed and commanded by her Majesty upon the princely and natural care she hath conceived towards the preservation of her subjects, who by very disorder and for lack of direction do in many parts willfully procure the increase of this general contagion.

An advice set down upon her Majesty's express commandment by the best learned in Physic within this Realm, containing sundry good rules and easy medicines without charge to the meaner sort of people, as well for the preservation of her good Subjects from the plague before infection, as for the curing and ordering of them after they shall be infected.

Preservative by correcting the air in Houses.[1]

Take *Rosemary* dried, or *Juniper, Bay leaves,* or *Frankincense;* cast the same on a Chafin dish, and receive the fume or smoke thereof. Some advise to be added *Lavender* or *Sage.*

Also make fires rather in Pans to remove about the chamber, than in Chimneys, shall better correct the air of the Houses.

Take a quantity of *Vinegar,* very strong, and put to it some small quantity of *Rosewater;* ten branches of *Rosemary.* Put them all into a basin. Then take five or six *Flint stones,* heated in the fire until they be burning hot. Cast them into the same *Vinegar,* and so let the fumes be received from place to place of your house.

Perfuming of apparel.

Such apparel as you shall commonly wear, let it be very clean, and perfume it often either with some red *Sanders,* burned, or with *Juniper.* And if any shall happen to be with them that are visited, let such persons as soon as they shall come home shift themselves and air their other clothes in open air for a time.

Preservation by way of defense in open air and common assemblies to be used outwardly.

It is good in going abroad into the open air in the streets to hold some things of sweet savor in their hands or in the corner of a handkerchief, as a sponge dipped in *Vinegar* and *Rosewater* mixed, or in *Vinegar,* wherein *Wormwood* or *Rue,* called also *herb of grace,* hath been boiled.

Preservative by way of inward medicine.

Take a quantity of *Rue* or *Wormwood* or of both and put it into a pot of usual drink, close stopped. Let it lie so in steep a whole night, and drink thereof in the morning fasting.

In all Summer plagues, it shall be good to use *Sorrel sauce* to be eaten in the morning with bread, and in the fall of the leaf to use the juice of *Barberries* with bread also.

Men's bodies are apt to take
infection either
By the constitution of the heart, the vital spirits being weak, and the natural heat feeble, in which case things Cordial are to be used.
By Repletion, the body being filled with humors, either
Good, and then is the party to be let blood.
Evil, and then is he to be cured with medicine purgative.

Preservatives Cordials.

Mithridates Medicine.

Take of good *Figs,* not worm-eaten, clean washed; of *Walnuts,* the kernels clean picked; of either of them an hundred; of the leaves of green *Rue,* otherwise called *herb of grace,* the weight of two scruples; of common Salt, the weight of four drams. Cut the *Figs* in pieces and stamp them and the *Walnut* kernels together in a mortar of Marble or wood a good space until they be very small, and then put your *Rue* leaves unto them. Stamp and stir them well together with the rest. Last, put in the Salt and stamp and stir these things together until they be incorporated and made of one substance. Of the which, take the quantity of two or three *Figs* every morning fasting. To children, the half will serve, and he that listeth to increase or diminish the substance of this Medicine shall easily do it by taking of a greater or less quantity of the simples according to a due proportion.

A well appointed Medicine to preserve.

Take the finest clear *Aloes* you can buy, in color like to a Liver and therefore called *Hepatica;* of *Cinnamon,* of *Myrrh,* of each of these, the weight of three French crowns or of the twelve pence of our money; of *Cloves, Maces, Lignum Aloes,* of *Mastic,* of *Bole Oriental,* of each of these half an ounce. Mingle them together and beat them into a very fine powder. Of the which, take every morning fasting the weight of a groat of this in white wine delayed with water, and by the grace of God you shall be safe from the plague. No man which is learned, if he examine the simples of this medicine, whereof it consists, and the nature and power of them, can deny but that it is a medicine of great efficacy against the plague, and the simples whereof it is made are easily to be had in any good Apothecary's shop, except *Bole Oriental,* which is used in the stead of true *Bolus Armeniac,* whereof we have seen great store in the shops of master *Rich,* the Queen's Majesty's Apothecary and master *Morgan's* in *Cheapside.*

Take a dry *Fig* and open it and put the kernel of a *Walnut* into the same being cut very small; three or four leaves of *Rue* commonly called *herb of grace;* a corn of Salt. Then roast the *Fig,* and eat it warm. Fast three or four hours after it, and use this twice in the week.

Take the powder of *Tormentil,* the weight of six drams with *Sorrel* or *Scabious* water in Summer and in Winter with the water of *Valerian* or common drink.

Or else in one day they may take a little *Wormwood* and *Valerian* with a grain of Salt. In another day they may take seven or eight berries of *Juniper,* dried and put in powder and taking the same with common drink or with drink in which *Wormwood* and *Rue* hath been steeped all the night.

Also the treacle called *Diatessaron,* which is made but of four things of light price, easy to be had.

Also the root of *Enula Campana,* either taken in powder with drink or hanged about the breast.

Likewise, a piece of *Arras* root[2] kept in the mouth as men pass in the streets is very good *Cordial.*

Take six leaves of *Sorrel.* Wash them with water and *Vinegar.* Let them lie to steep in the said water and vinegar a while. Then eat them fasting, and keep in your mouth and chew now or then either *Setwall* or the root of *Angelica* or a little *Cinnamon.*

Take the root of *Enula Campana* being laid and steeped in vinegar and gross beaten. Put a little of it in a handkerchief, and smell to it if you resort to any that is infected.

For women with child, or such as be delicate and tender and cannot away with taking of medicines.

Make a toast of white or of the second bread, as you think good, and sprinkle on it, being hot, a little good wine *Vinegar* made with Rose leaves, and for want of it, any good common or used *Vinegar,* and spread on the toast a little Butter, and cast thereon a little powder of *Cinnamon,* and eat in the morning fasting. The poor, which can not get *Vinegar* nor buy *Cinnamon,* may eat bread and Butter alone, for Butter is not only a preservative against the plague but against all manner of poisons.

When one must come into the place where infectious persons are, it is good to smell to the root of *Angelica, Gentian,* or *Valerian,* and to chew any of these in his mouth.

An other preservative for the poor.

It shall be good to take a handful of *Rue* and as much common *Wormwood* and bruise them a little and put them into a pot of Earth or Tin, with so much *Vinegar* as shall cover the herbs. Keep this pot close covered or stopt, and when you fear any infection, dip into this *Vinegar* a piece of a sponge and carry it in your hand and smell to it, or else put it into a round ball of *Ivory* or *Juniper* made full of holes of the one side; carrying it in your hand, use to smell thereunto, renewing it once in a day.

To be used after infection taken.

For as much as the cause of the plague standeth rather in poison than in any putrefaction of humors as other agues do, the chiefest way is to move sweating and to defend the heart by some cordial thing.[3]

Suppository.

If the Patient be costive and bound in his body, let him take a *Suppository* made with a little boiled *Honey* and a little fine powder of *Salt* and so taken in at the fundament and kept till it move a stool.

An excellent Medicine made without charges.

Take of the powder of good *Bayberries,* the husk taken away from them before they be dried, a spoonful. Let the Patient drink this, well mingled in a draught of good stale Ale or Beer, which is neither sour nor dead, with a draught of white Wine and go to bed and cast himself into a sweat and forbear sleep, as is aforesaid.

Another sovereign remedy that is a stilled water.

Take the inward bark of the Ash tree, a pound of Walnuts with the green outward shell to the number of fifty. Cut these small. Of *Scabious,* of *Vervain,* of *Petimorel,* of *Houseleek,* of every one of a handful; of *Saffron,* half an ounce. Pour upon these the strongest *Vinegar* you can get; four pints. Let them a little boil together upon a very soft fire and then stand in a very close pot, well stopped, all night upon the embers. Afterward, distill them with a soft fire and receive the water close kept. Give unto the Patient, laid in bed and well covered with clothes, two ounces of this water to drink and let him be provoked to sweat, and every six hours during the space of twenty-four hours give him the same quantity to drink. This Medicine, for the worthiness thereof and because it will stand the maker thereof in little charge, it shall be very well done to distill it in the Summer when the *Walnuts* hang green on the tree, that it may be ready against the time that occasion serveth to use it.

1. Bloodletting.

If the Patient be full of humors which be good, let him immediately be let blood upon the Liver vein in the right arm or in the Median vein of the same arm (if no sore appear) in the first day.

2. Medicine Purgative.

For the poor, take *Aloes* the weight of six drams. Put in the pulp of an Apple. And for the richer, *Pills* of *Rufus* to be had in every good Apothecary's shop.

After letting of blood and purging (as shall be needful) some of the forenamed Cordials are to be used.

These preparations thus used the first day that the Patient shall fall sick, as cause shall be to use the one or the other (no sore appearing), in which case if the sore shall appear, they are both to be forborn. The next is to use all means to expel the poison and to defend the heart by Cordials.

3. Medicament Expulsive.

The poison is expelled best by sweatings provoked by posset Ale made with *Fennel* and *Marigolds* in Winter and with *Sorrel, Bugloss,* and *Borage* in Summer, with which in both times they must mix the treacle of *Diatessaron,* with weight of nine drams, and so to lay themselves with all quietness to sweat one-half hour, or an hour, if they be strong. For they that be neither full of humors nor corrupt in humors need neither purging nor letting of blood, but at the first plunge may move themselves to sweat with Cordial things mixed with such things as move sweat and are before declared.

What is to be done when there is any rising or swelling in any part.

Then if by these three means the poison be expelled outward by Botches, carbuncles, or marks called God's marks, according as nature doth expel, so must the further proceedings be, providing still that they continue still in the use of the cordial and moderate sweating now and then all the time that the sores be in healing, which must by the Surgeon be handled with great discretion.

Medicine to be used in ordinary diet.

It is thought that the power of hart's horn hath a special prerogative to be used all the time of their sickness in their broths and supping, which in Summer must ever have *Sorrel, Borage, Bugloss,* and in winter, *Betony* and *Scabious* or *Morsus Diaboli.* And if their abilities do not serve, let them use it with *Aleberries* made with a little *Nutmeg* or one *Clove* or with *Caudles* in like manner made with *Cloves, Maces, Nutmegs, Sanders* or such like.

Both to preserve and cure the sickness.

Take an egg and make a hole in the top of it. Take out the white and yolk. Fill the shell with the weight of two French crowns of *Saffron*. Roast the said egg thus filled with *Saffron* under the embers until the shell begin to wax yellow. Then take it from the fire, and beat the shell and *Saffron* in a mortar together with a half a spoonful of *Mustard* seed. Take of this powder a French crown weight, and as soon as you suspect yourself infected, dissolve it into ten spoonfuls of posset Ale and drink it lukewarm. Then go to bed and provoke yourself to sweating.

To be used in the first time of the Sickness.

Another is to take five or six handfuls of *Sorrel* that grows in the field, or a greater quantity according as you will. Distill more or less of the water thereof, and let it lie infused or steeped in good *Vinegar* the space of twenty-four hours. Then take it off and dry it with a linen cloth. Put into an alembic and distill the water thereof. And as soon as you find yourself touched with the sickness, drink four spoonfuls of the said water with a little sugar, and if you be able, walk upon it until you do sweat. If not, keep your bed and, being well covered, provoke yourself to sweating, and the next day to take as much again of it a little before supper.

Item, to provoke vomit with two ounces of rank oil or walnut oil, a spoonful of the juice of *Celandine,* a half a spoonful of the juice of radish root, so that the party infected do walk and not sleep, is better than any letting of blood or any purging, for the disease neither can suffer agitation of humors, nor when one is infected, hath no time to bleed or to purge.

Outward medicines for to be applied to the sore.

The first.

Take of *Scabious* two handfuls. Stamp it in a stone mortar with a pestle of stone if you can get any such, then put unto it of old swine's grease salted, two ounces, and the yolk of an egg. Stamp them well together and lay part of this warm to the sore.

The second.

Take of the leaves of *Mallows,* of *Camomile* flowers, of either of them an handful; of *Linseed* beaten into powder, two ounces. Boil the *Mallow* leaves first cut and the flowers of the *Camomile* in fair water standing above a finger's breadth. Boil all them together until all the water almost be spent. Then put thereunto the *Linseed.* Of *Wheat* flour, half an handful; of swine's grease, the skins taken away, three ounces; of oil of *Roses,* two ounces. Stir them still with a stick and let them all boil together on a soft fire without smoke, until the water be utterly spent. Beat them all together in a mortar until they be well incorporated together and in feeling smooth and not rough. Then make part thereof hot in a dish set upon a Chafin dish of coals, and lay it thick upon a linen cloth, applying it to the sore.

Another excellent medicine to ripen and bring out the Sore.

Take a white *Onion* cut in pieces; of fresh butter three ounces; of *Leaven* the weight of twelve pence; of *Mallows,* one handful; of *Scabious,* if it may be had, one handful; of *Cloves* of garlic the weight of twenty drams. Boil them on the fire in sufficient water and make a poultice of it, and lay it warm to the sore.

Another.

To the sore itself, do thus: take two handful of *Valerian,* three roots of *Danewort,* a handful of *Smallage* or *Lovage,* if you can get it. Seethe them all in butter and water and a few crumbs of bread and make a poultice thereof and lay it warm to the sore until it break.

Another for the same.

If you can not have these herbs, it is good to lay a loaf of bread to it, hot as it cometh out of the oven (which afterward shall be burnt or buried in the earth), or the leaves of *Scabious* or *Sorrel* roasted, or two or three *Lily* roots roasted under embers, beaten and applied.

A general medicine for all sorts of people taken with the plague, to be had without cost.

Take of the root of butterbur, otherwise called pestilent wort, one ounce; of the root of great *Valerian*, a quarter of an ounce; of *Sorrel* an handful. Boil all these in a quart of water to a pint. Then strain it and put thereto two spoonfuls of *Vinegar*, two ounces of good *Sugar*. Boil all these together until they be well mingled. Let the infected drink of this, so hot as he may suffer it a good draught, and if he chance to cast it by again, let him take the same quantity straight way upon it, and provoke himself to sweat, and he shall find great help.

Time of continuance apart from common assemblies.

Such as have been infected should keep their house without being conversant with the whole until the sores shall have left running and be perfectly whole and sound, which in sanguine and choleric persons will be healed sooner than in melancholic and phlegmatic complexions.

Such persons may not well be conversant with them which are not infected, for the space of one month.

Infected clothes.

The contagion, suspected to remain in clothes either woolen or linen, cannot well be avoided by better means than by fire and water, by often washing and airing, the same in frosts and sunshine, with good discretion, and burning the clothes of small value.

Imprinted at London by Christo-
pher Barker, Printer to the Queen's
most excellent Majesty.

5

Plague Bills

Worshipful Company of Parish Clerks: The Number of all those that hath died (c. 1583)

The bills of mortality in England took form as local governments sought methods for alerting citizens to plague-time dangers and as Privy Council members looked to protect the monarch, the court, and the nation. Under King Henry VIII, for example, Thomas Cromwell required this form of record-keeping for London, but it was not until Elizabeth I's reign that local officials across the nation were uniformly required to give written account of plague deaths. Soon after the issue of Elizabeth I's 1578 *Orders thought meet*, bills were regularly printed for wider distribution. *The Number of all those that hath died* (STC 16738.5) is both representative and unusual. It is an annual bill for multiple parishes, and such bills would become increasingly popular by the end of the century, but the bill is rare for its time, when it was routinely the case that bills recorded deaths for single parishes and existed in manuscript form. This bill is of special value because within it the author explains the need for just such record keeping, and by way of comparing plague years, cites the number of plague dead in 1562–63, from the first Elizabethan visitation.

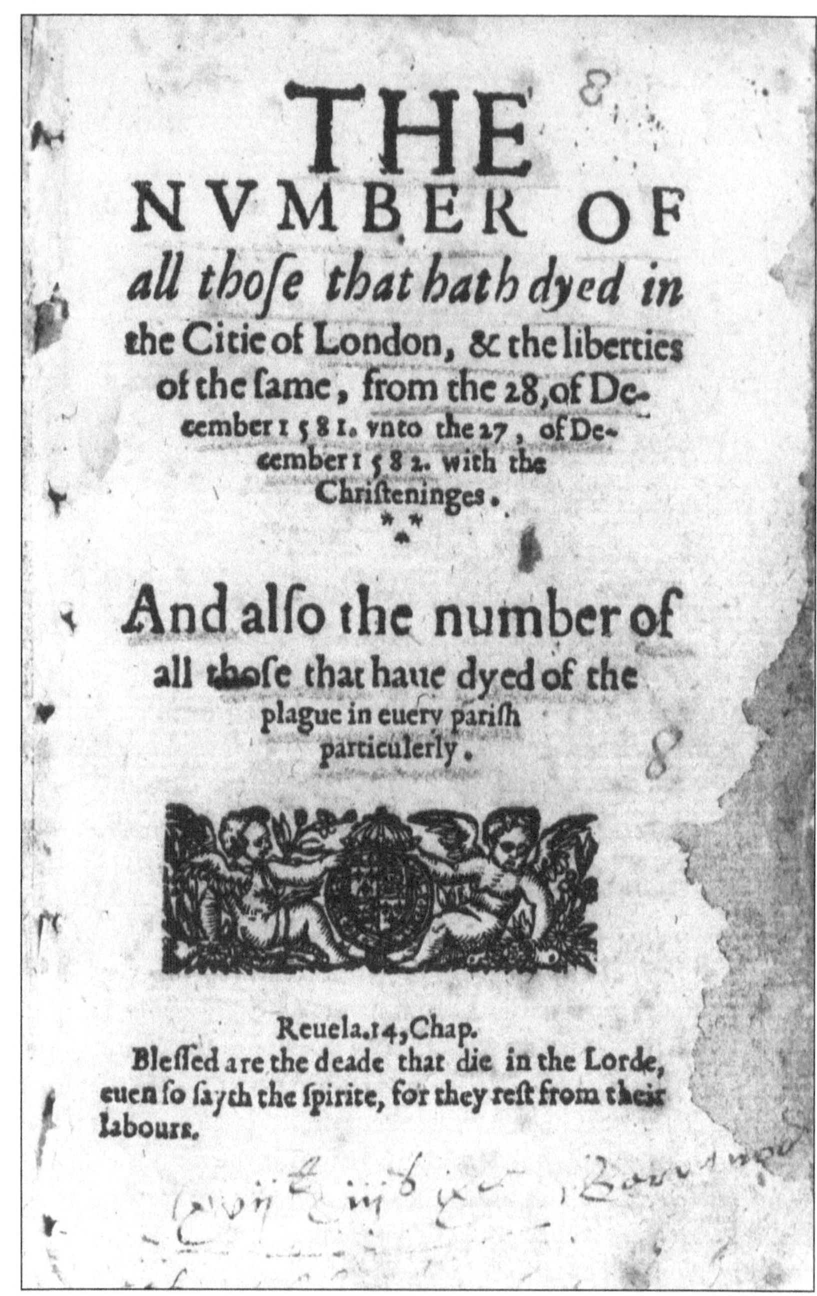

THE
NVMBER OF
all thoſe that hath dyed in
the Citie of London, & the liberties
of the ſame, from the 28, of De-
cember 1581. vnto the 27, of De-
cember 1582. with the
Chriſteninges.

And alſo the number of
all thoſe that haue dyed of the
plague in euery pariſh
particulerly.

Reuela.14, Chap.
Bleſſed are the deade that die in the Lorde,
euen ſo ſayth the ſpirite, for they reſt from their
labours.

Fig. 7. *The Number of all those that hath died,* title page, STC 16738.5 (2nd ed.). Reproduced by permission of the Guildhall Library, City of London.

It is useful to compare this early bill with previous manuscript bills and with the numerous annual bills from the seventeenth century. See for example, Herbert Barry, "A London Plague Bill for 1592, Crich, and Goodwyffe Hurde," *English Literary Renaissance* 25.1 (1995): 3–25; Worshipful Company of Parish Clerks, *A generall bill for eight weeks shewing all the burials and christninges within the city of London and the liberties thereof* (1603; STC 16743.1); Henry Chettle, *A True bill of the whole number that hath died* (1603; STC 16743.2); H.C., *London's Lord have mercy upon us* (1637; STC 4273); and *The mourning-cross: or, England's Lord have mercy upon us* ([1665] Wing M2991B). Due to the range of spellings used for early parish names, those listed here were cross-referenced with STC 16743.1, noted above, and with parish names supplied by John Stow in *A Survey of London* (1603).

There is dead this year, that is to say, from the 28 of December 1581 unto the 27 of December 1582 within the City and the liberties of the same: 6930.

Of the Plague	3075
Christened	3503
Parishes clear of the plague	5
Out-Parishes	430
Of the Plague	239

Here followeth the Parishes with their numbers that hath buried of the Plague.

A.

Allhallows Barking	60
Allhallows in Bread Street	3
Allhallows the More	30
Allhallows the Less	7
Allhallows Honey Lane	1
Allhallows Lombard Street	7
Allhallows Staining	67

Allhallows in the Wall	13
Albons in Wood Street	16
Andrew Eastcheap[1]	29
Andrew Holborn	89
Andrew Wardrobe	97
Andrew Undershaft	24
Alphege at Cripplegate	7
Anne at Aldersgate[2]	35
Anne at Blackfriars	21
Augustine at Paul's Gate	clear
Antholin at Budge Row[3]	clear
B.	
Bartholomew Hospital	14
Bartholomew at the Exchange	10
Benet Finck	11
Benet Grace Church	11
Benet Paul's Wharf[4]	20
Benet Sherehog	4
Bride Parish	124
Botolph Aldgate	158
Botolph Aldersgate	72
Botolph Bishopsgate	60
Botolph Billingsgate	7
C.	
Christ's Church	50
Christopher at the Stocks	1
Clement by Eastcheap	3
D.	
Dennis Backchurch	25
Dunstan in the East	35
Dunstan in the West	47
E.	
Edmund in Lombard Street	6
Ethelborow in Bishopsgate Street	15
F.	
Faith under Paul's	21
Foster in Foster Lane	4
G.	
Gabriel Fenchurch	5

George by Pudding Lane[5]	2
George in Southwark	74
Giles at Cripplegate	186
Gregory by Paul's	22
H.	
Helen in Bishopsgate Street	7
J.	
James Garlickhithe	11
John Evangelist	2
John in Walbrook	9
John Zachary	25
K.	
Katherine Coleman	33
Katherine Cree Church	57
L.	
Lawrence in the Jury	15
Lawrence Pountney	13
Leonard in Eastcheap	2
Leonard Foster Lane	54
M.	
Mary Aldermary	6
Mary Aldermanbury	26
Mary Abchurch	40
Mary Bow	clear
Mary Botolphe[6]	2
Mary Colechurch	1
Mary Hill	27
Mary Mounthaw	1
Mary Staining	4
Mary Somerset	26
Mary Woolchurch	2
Mary Woolnoth	4
Magnus	15
Magdalen in Milk Street	2
Magdalen in Old Fish Street	27
Martin Ludgate	50
Martin Orgar	6
Martin Outwich	17
Martine Vintry	13

Martin in Ironmonger Lane	2
Margaret in Lothbury	3
Margaret New Fish Street	12
Margaret Pattens	12
Margaret Moses in Friday Street	clear
Matthew in Friday Street	clear
Michael in Basinghall	17
Michael in Cornhill	15
Michael in Crooked Lane	3
Michael in the Querne	7
Michael Queenhithe	25
Michael in the Royal[7]	12
Michael in Wood Street	6
Mildred in Bread Street	6
Mildred in the Poultry	6
N.	
Nicholas Acon	12
Nicholas Golden Abby[8]	14
Nicholas Willows[9]	3
O.	
Olave in Hart Street	23
Olave in the Jewry	8
Olave in Silver Street	16
Olave in Southwark	383
P.	
Pancras	6
Peter in Cheap[10]	4
Peter in Cornhill	20
Peter Paul's Wharf	3
Peter the Poor	3
S.	
Saviours	72
Sepulchres	362
Stephen in Coleman Street	33
Stephen in Walbrook	5
Swithin at London Stone	2
T.	
Trinity	4
Thomas Apostle	5
Thomas Hospital	19

I have here set forth the Parishes and the numbers, according as the same came unto me in the weekly reports. And thereof have drawn the total sum that every Parish hath buried of the Plague.

The causes why I have at this present set forth the Parishes particularly where they have died of the Plague.

The first cause is for that it is reported in the Country that there hath died such an infinite number here in London as thousands in a week, and therefore I have set down the Parishes for the sure justifying of the number and true certificate of them that have died of the Plague, that those that see and read the same may not only be reasonably certified but also may rebuke those persons that have given forth such reports.

Secondly, for that it is said of some that it was but in a few Parishes.

Thirdly, for that it was amongst the poor and simplest and most basest people as beggars and suchlike.

Fourthly, that they were children and servants, and none of any countenance and calling.

Fifthly, for that it is also said that every Parish hath not given a just certificate of those that died of the plague, that here in viewing of the Parishes and the number thereunto annexed, they may see the truth, and if there by any fault committed, it may be reformed.

The number that died of in the time of the great Plague.

There died in London and the liberties thereof in the year of our Lord 1562, from the first of January unto the last of December 1563, of all diseases, twenty thousand three hundred, three score and twelve.

And of the Plague, being part of the number aforesaid, seventeen thousand four hundred and four.

Christ in the Revelation 22 Chapter sayeth, "Behold, I come shortly, and my reward is with me, to give every man according as his work shall be."

6

Plague Literature

Thomas Dekker: The Wonderful Year (1603)

By the late sixteenth and early seventeenth centuries, the depiction of plague in literature had undergone serious revision. In these works of prose and poetry, plague visits London as a tyrant, usurping the position of the queen or king. He comes dressed in battle gear. He comes to rape and pillage. He comes hungry, ready to gobble up all bodies until his gorging leaves graves spilling forth, overstuffed. And he comes with his own legions, not clearly to do God's bidding and with no explanation for his actions. He reigns, reminding Elizabethans of Christopher Marlowe's Tamburlaine and reminding us of Shakespeare's *Richard III.* The tyrant plague is a gobbler of good rules, an abuser of custom, and a consumer of civilization, and it is dramatist Thomas Dekker who gives us the most complete picture of this literary version of the bubonic plague in his prose pamphlet, *The Wonderful Year* (1603). This is the first of Dekker's many plague pamphlets, pieces intended as short entertainments during plague visitations.

These facts are enough to secure a place in this collection for *The Wonderful Year,* but the content alone does so, capturing the final Elizabethan plague visitation and pointing to a grim future of plague outbreaks under the Stuarts. This was a future that saw the increasing specialization of efforts to deal with the plague as well as corporal punishment for those who refused to obey quarantine laws. *The Wonderful Year* is anything but "wonderful" by our sense of the term, offering none of the pleasant dialogue or consolation that is the primary purpose of Bullein's earlier writing. Dekker does offer humor, but it is rooted in pain and never offers the reader a break from the grim realities of plague-time. It is a seventeenth century critique of earlier efforts, literary and civic, to offer healing in plague-time. If the reader has an uncomfortable moment of jaw-dropping amusement at the expense of sufferers acting out antic displays of plague-time desperation, then Dekker has achieved his purpose, which is never as clear as those works that precede his in this collection. For all of these reasons, *The Wonderful Year* is one of the most difficult of readings presented here in spite of its being the latest, written by a dramatist who knew how to compose a clear sentence. It is also one of the most rewarding of reading experiences. Although it does not offer the hope of Moulton's plague remedy, of Bullein's morality tale, of the Church of England's service of prayer and fasting, or of Elizabeth I's plague orders, it does provide a more realistic depiction of individual suffering in plague-time when the victim faces the horror of a death delivered by a force that is wholly incomprehensible in its cruelty and unyielding in spite of all remedies, prayers, and orders.

Of the three identical 1603 copies of Dekker's *The Wonderful Year,* the one transcribed here is STC 6536.5.

To His Well Respected Good *friend,* M. *Cuthbert Thuresby, Water Bailiff of London.*

Books are but poor gifts, yet *Kings* receive them: upon which I presume you will not turn *This* out of doors, yet cannot for shame but bid it welcome, because it brings to you a great quantity of my love, which, if it be worth little (and no marvel if *Love* be sold under-foot when the God of *Love* himself goes naked), yet I hope you will not say you have a hard bargain, sithence you may take as

THE

VVonderfull yeare.

1603.

Wherein is ſhewed the picture of *London*, ly-
ing ſicke of the Plague.

*At the ende of all (like a mery Epilogue to a dull Play) cer-
taine Tales are cut out in ſundry faſhions, of purpoſe
to ſhorten the liues of long winters nights,
that lye watching in the darke for vs.*

Et me rigidi legant Catones.

LONDON
Printed by Thomas Creede, and are to be ſolde
in Saint Donſtones Church-yarde
in Fleet-ſtreete.

Fig. 8. *The Wonderful Year,* title page, STC 6536.5. Reproduced by permission of the Folger Shakespeare Library.

much of it as you please for nothing. I have clapt the *Cognizance* of your name on these scribbled papers; it is their livery, so that now they are yours, being free from any vile imputation, save only that they thrust themselves into your acquaintance. But general errors have general pardons, for the title of other men's names is the common *Heraldry* which all those lay claim to, whose crest is a Pen-and-Inkhorn. If you read, you may happily laugh. 'Tis my desire you should, because mirth is both *Physical* and wholesome against the *Plague,* with which sickness (to tell truth) this book is (though not sorely) yet somewhat infected. I pray, drive it not out of your company for all that, for (assure your soul), I am so jealous of your health that if you did but once imagine there were gall in mine Ink, I would cast away the Standish, and forswear meddling with any more *Muses.*

To the Reader.

And why to the *Reader?* Oh good Sir! There's as sound law to make you give good words to the *Reader* as to a *Constable* when he carries his watch about him to tell how the night goes, though (perhaps) the one (oftentimes) may be served in for a *Goose* and the other very fitly furnish the same mess. Yet to maintain the scurvy fashion and to keep *Custom* in reparations, he must be honeyed and come-over with "*Gentle Reader,*" "*Courteous Reader,*" and "*Learned Reader,*" though he have no more *Gentility* in him than *Adam* had (that was but a gardener), no more *Civility* than a *Tartar,* and no more *Learning* than the most errand *Stinkard,* that (except his own name) could never find anything in the Horn-book.

How notoriously therefore do good wits dishonor not only their *Calling* but even their *Creation,* that worship *Glowworms* (instead of the *Sun*) because of a little false glistering? In the name of *Phoebus,* what madness leads them unto it? For he that dares hazard a pressing to death (that's to say, *To be a man in Print*) must make account that he shall stand (like the old Weathercock over Paul's steeple) to be beaten with all storms. Neither the stinking

Tobacco breath of a *Satingull*, the *Aconited* sting of a narrow-eyed *Critic*, the faces of a fantastic Stage-monkey, nor the "*Indeed-la*" of a Puritanical Citizen, must once shake him. No, but desperately resolve (like a French Post)[1] to ride through thick and thin; endure to see his lines torn pitifully on the rack; suffer his Muse to take the *Baston*, yea the very stab; and himself like a new stake to be a mark for every *Haggler*, and therefore (setting up all these rests) why should he regard what fool's bolt is shot at him? Besides, if that which he presents upon the Stage of the world be *Good*, why should he basely cry out (with that old poetical mad-cap in his *Amphitruo*[2]) *Jovis summi causa clarè plaudite:* beg a *Plaudite* for God-sake! If *Bad*, who (but an Ass) would entreat (as Players do in a cogging *Epilogue* at the end of a filthy Comedy) that, be it never such wicked stuff, they would forbear to hiss, or to damn it perpetually to lie on a Stationer's stall. For he that can so cozen himself as to pocket up praise in that silly sort makes his brains fat with his own folly.

But *Hinc Pudor!* or rather *Hinc Dolor*,[3] here's the Devil! It is not the rattling of all this former hail-shot that can terrify our *Band* of *Castalian Pen-men* from entering into the field. No, no, the murdering Artillery indeed lies in the roaring mouths of a company that look big as if they were the sole and singular *Commanders* over the main Army of *Poesy;* yet (if *Hermes'* muster-book were searcht over) they'll be found to be most pitiful, pure, fresh-water soldiers. They give out that they are heirs apparent to *Helicon*, but an easy *Herald* may make them mere younger brothers, or (to say troth) not so much. Bear witness all you whose wits make you able to be witnesses in this cause, that here I meddle not with your good Poets, *Nam tales, nusquàm sunt hîc ampliüs*.[4] If you should rake hell, or (as *Aristophanes* in his *Frogs* says) in any Cellar deeper than hell, it is hard to find Spirits of that *Fashion*. But those Goblins whom I now am conjuring up have bladder-cheeks puft out like a *Swizzers* breeches (yet being prickt, there comes out nothing but wind), thin-headed fellows that live upon the scraps of invention, and travel with such vagrant souls, and so like Ghosts in white sheets of paper, that the Statute of Rogues may worthily be sued upon them, because their wits have no abiding place and yet wander without a passport. Alas, poor wenches (the nine Muses!) how much are you wronged to have such a number of Bastards lying upon your hands? But turn them out a begging, or if you cannot be rid of their Rhyming company (as I think it will be very hard), then lay your heavy and immortal curse upon them, that whatsoever they weave (in the motley-loom of their rusty pates) may like a beggar's cloak be full of stolen patches, and yet never a patch like one another, that it may be such true lamentable stuff that any honest Christian may be sorry to see it. Banish these *Word-pirates* (you sacred mistresses of learning) into the gulf of *Barbarism:* doom them everlastingly to live among dunces. Let them not once lick their lips at the *Thespian* bowl but only be glad (and thank *Apollo* for it too) if hereafter (as hitherto they have always) they may quench their poetical thirst with small beer. Or if they will needs be stealing your *Heliconian Nectar,* let them (like the dogs of *Nilus*) only lap and away.[5] For this *Goatish* swarm are those (that where for these many thousand years you went for pure maids) have taken away your good names. These are they that deflower your beauties. These are those rank-riders of Art that have so spurgalled your lusty winged *Pegasus* that now he begins to be out of flesh, and (even only for provender sake) is glad to show tricks like *Banks* his Curtal.[6] O you Booksellers (that are Factors to the Liberal Sciences), over whose Stalls these Drones do daily fly humming, let *Homer, Hesiod, Euripides,* and some other mad Greeks with a band of the Latins lie like musketshot in their way, when these Goths and Geats[7] set upon you in your paper fortifications. It is the only Canon upon whose mouth they dare not venture. None but the English will take their parts; therefore fear them not, for such a strong breath have these cheese-eaters that if they do but blow upon a book, they imagine straight 'tis blasted. *Quod supra nos, Nihil ad nos* (they say): that which is above our capacity shall not pass under our commendation. Yet would I have these Zoilists (of all other) to read me, if ever I should write anything worthily, for the blame that known-fools heap upon a deserving labor does not discredit the same but makes wise men more perfectly in love with it. Into such a one's hands therefore, if I fortune to fall, I will not shrink an inch but even when his teeth are sharpest and most ready to bite, I will stop his mouth only with this, *Haec mala sunt, sed tu, non meliora facis.*[8]

Reader.

Whereas there stands in the Rear-ward of this Book a certain mingled Troop of strange Discourses fashioned into Tales, Know that the intelligence which first brought them to light was only slying Report, whose tongue (as it often does) if in spreading them it have tript in any material point, and either slipt too far or fallen too short, bear with the error, and the rather because it is not willfully committed. Neither let any one (whom those Reports shall seem to touch) cavil, or complain of injury, sithence nothing is set down by a malicious hand. Farewell.

The Wonderful Year.

Vertumnus, being attired in his accustomed habit of changeable silk, had newly passed through the first and principal Court-gate of heaven, to whom for a farewell and to show how dutiful he was in his office, Janus (that bears two faces under one hood) made a very mannerly low leg and (because he was the only Porter at that gate) presented unto this King of the Months all the New-year's gifts, which were more in number and more worth than those that are given to the great Turk or the Emperor of *Persia*. On went *Vertumnus* in his lusty progress, *Priapus, Flora,* the *Dryads,* and *Hamadryads,* with all the wooden rabble of those that drest Orchards and Gardens, perfuming all the ways that he went with the sweet Odors that breathed from flowers, herbs, and trees, which now began to peep out of prison, by virtue of which excellent airs, the sky got a most clear complexion, lookt smug and smooth, and had not so much as a wart sticking on her face. The Sun likewise was freshly and very richly appareled in cloth of gold like a Bridegroom. And instead of gilded Rosemary, the horns of the Ram (being the sign of that celestial bridehouse where he lay, to be married to the Spring) were not like your common horns, parcel-gilt, but double double-gilt with the liquid gold that melted from his beams,[9] for joy whereof, the Lark sung at his window every morning; the Nightingale every night; the Cuckoo (like a single sole Fiddler that reels from Tavern to Tavern) plied it all the day long. Lambs friskt up and down in the valleys. Kids and Goats leapt to and fro on the Mountains. Shepherds sat piping, country wenches singing. Lovers made Sonnets for their Lasses, whilest they made Garlands for their Lovers. And as the Country was frolic, so was the City merry. Olive Trees (which grow nowhere but in the Garden of peace) stood (as common as Beech does at Midsummer) at every man's door. Branches of Palm were in every man's hand. Streets were full of people, people full of joy. Every house seemd to have a Lord of misrule in it. In every house there was so much jollity. No Screech Owl frighted the silly Countryman at midnight, nor any Drum the Citizen at noon-day, but all was more calm than a still water, all husht, as if the Spheres had been playing in Consert. In conclusion, heaven lookt like a Palace, and the great hall of the earth, like a Paradise.

But O the short liv'd Felicity of man! O world, of what slight and thin stuff is thy happiness! Just in the midst of this jocund Holy-day, a storm rises in the West. Westward (from the top of a *Richmount*) descended a hideous tempest that shook Cedars, terrified the tallest Pines, and cleft in sunder even the hardest hearts of Oak. And if such great trees were shaken, what think you became of the tender Eglantine and humble Hawthorne? They could not (doubtless) but droop. They could not choose but die with the terror. The Element (taking the Destinies' part, who indeed set abroach this mischief) scowled on the earth and, filling her high forehead full of black wrinkles, tumbling long up and down (like a great-bellied wife) her sighs being whirlwinds and her groans thunder, at length she fell in labor and was delivered of a pale, meager, weak child named *Sickness,* whom Death (with a pestilence) would needs take upon him to nurse, and did so. This starveling being come to his full growth had an office given him for nothing (and that's a wonder in this age). Death made him his Herald, attired him like a Courtier, and (in his name) charged him to go into the Privy Chamber of the English Queen, to summon her to appear in the Star-chamber of heaven.

The summons made her start, but (having an invincible spirit) did not amaze her. Yet whom would not the certain news of parting from a Kingdom amaze! But she knew where to find a richer, and therefore lightly regarded the loss of this, and thereupon made ready for that heavenly Coronation, being (which was most strange) most dutiful to obey that had so many years so powerfully commanded. She obeyed Death's messenger and yielded her body to the hands of Death himself. She died, resigning her Scepter to posterity and her Soul to immortality.

To report of her death (like a thunder-clap) was able to kill thousands. It took away hearts from millions, for having brought up (even under her wing) a nation that was almost begotten and born under her, that never shouted any other "*Ave*" than for her name, never saw the face of any Prince but herself, never understood what that strange outlandish word "*Change*" signified. How was it possible but that her sickness should throw abroad an universal fear and her death an astonishment? She was the Courtier's treasure, therefore he had cause to mourn; the Lawyer's sword of justice, he might well faint; the Merchant's patroness, he had reason to look pale; the Citizen's mother, he might best lament; the Shepherd's Goddess, and should not he droop? Only the Soldier who had walkt a long time upon wooden legs and was not able to give Arms, though he were a Gentleman,[10] had bristled up the quills of his stiff Porcupine mustachio and swore by no beggars that now was the hour come for him to bestir his stumps. Usurers and Brokers (that are the Devil's Angels and dwell in the long-lane of hell) quakt like aspen leaves at his oaths. Those that before were the only cut-throats in *London* now stood in fear of no other death. But my *Signior Soldado*[11] was deceived: the Tragedy went not forward.

Never did the English Nation behold so much black worn as there was at her Funeral. It was then but put on to try if it were fit, for the great day of mourning was set down (in the book of heaven) to be held afterwards. That was but the dumb show; the Tragical Act hath been playing ever since. Her hearse (as it was borne) seemed to be an Island swimming in water, for round about it there rained showers of tears, about her death-bed none, for her departure was so sudden and so strange that men knew not how to weep, because they had never been taught to shed tears of that making. They that durst not speak their sorrows, whispered them. They that durst not whisper, sent them forth in sighs. Oh what an Earthquake is the alteration of a State! Look from the Chamber of Presence to the Farmer's cottage, and you shall find nothing but distraction. The whole Kingdom seems a wilderness, and the people in it are transformed to wild men.

The Map of a Country so pitifully distracted by the horror of a change, if you desire perfectly to behold, cast your eyes then on this that follows, which being heretofore in private presented to the King, I think may very worthily show itself before you, and because you shall see them attired in the same fashion that they wore before his Majesty, let these few lines (which stood then as Prologue to the rest) enter first into your ears.

Not for applauses, shallow fool's adventure,[12]
I plunge my verse into a sea of censure,
But with a liver drest in gall, to see
So many Rooks, catch-polls of poesy,
That feed upon the fallings of high wit,
And put on cast inventions, most unfit,
For such am I prest forth in shops and stalls,
Pasted in Paul's, and on the Lawyer's walls,
For every basilisk-eyed Critic's bait,
To kill my verse, or poison my conceit:
Or some smoakt gallant, who at wit repines,

To dry Tobacco with my wholesome lines,
And in one paper sacrifice more brain
Than all his ignorant skull could ere contain.
But merit dreads no martyrdom, nor stroke;
My lines shall live when he shall be all smoke.

Thus far the Prologue, who leaving the Stage clear, the fears that are bred in the womb of this altering kingdom do next step up, acting thus:

The great impostume of the realm was drawn
Even to a head: the multitudinous spawn
Was the corruption, which did make it swell
With hoped sedition (the burnt seed of hell).
Who did expect but ruin, blood, and death,
To share our kingdom, and divide our breath?
Religions without religion,
To let each other blood, confusion
To be next Queen of *England*, and this year
The civil wars of *France* to be played here
By Englishmen, ruffians, and pandering slaves
That fain would dig up gouty usurers' graves.
At such a time, villains their hopes do honey,
And rich men look as pale as their white money.
Now they remove, and make their silver sweat,
Casting themselves into a covetous heat,
And then (unseen) in the confederate dark,
Bury their gold, without or Priest, or Clerk,
And say no prayers over that dead pelf.
True: Gold's no Christian, but an Indian elf.
Did not the very kingdom seem to shake
Her precious massy limbs? Did she not make
All English cities (like her pulses) beat
With people in their veins? The fear so great,
That had it not been physickt with rare peace,
Our populous power had lessened her increase.
The Springtime that was dry, had sprung in blood,
A greater dearth of men, than e're of food.
In such a panting time, and gasping year,
Victuals are cheapest; only men are dear.
Now each wise-acred Landlord did despair,

Fearing some villain should become his heir,
Or that his son and heir before his time,
Should now turn villain, and with violence clime
Up to his life, saying, "Father you have seen
King *Henry, Edward, Mary,* and the Queen:
I wonder you'll live longer!" Then he tells him
He's loath to see him killed; therefore he kills him,
And each vast Landlord dies like a poor slave;
Their thousand acres makes them but a grave.
At such a time great men convey their treasure
Into the trusty City, waits the leisure
Of blood and insurrection, which war clips,
When every gate shuts up her Iron lips.
Imagine now a mighty man of dust
Standeth in doubt what servant he may trust,
With Plate worth thousands, Jewels worth far more;
If he prove false, then his rich Lord proves poor.
He calls forth one by one, to note their graces.
Whilst they make legs,[13] he copies out their faces,
Examines their eye-brow, construes their beard,
Singles their Nose out; still he rests afeard.
The first that comes, by no means he'll allow,
Has spied three Hairs starting between his brow,
Quite turns the word, names it Celerity,
For Hares do run away, and so may he.
A second shown, him he will scarce behold:
His beard's too red, the color of his gold.
A third may please him, but 'tis hard to say,
A rich man's pleased, when his goods part away.
And now do chirrup by fine golden nests
Of well hatcht bowls, such as do breed in feasts,
For war and death, cupboards of plate down pulls.
Then *Bacchus* drinks not in gilt-bowls, but skulls.
Let me descend and stoop my verse a while,
To make the Comic cheek of Poesy smile.
Rank penny-fathers scud (with their half hams,
Shadowing their calves) to save their silver dams,[14]
At every gun they start, tilt from the ground.
One drum can make a thousand Usurers sound.
In unsought Allies and unwholesome places,
Back-ways and by-lanes, where appear few faces,

In shamble-smelling rooms, loathsome prospects,
And penny-lattice-windows, which rejects
All popularity, there the rich Cubs lurk,
When in great houses ruffians are at work,
Not dreaming that such glorious booties lie
Under those nasty roofs. Such they pass by
Without a search, crying, "There's naught for us,"
And wealthy men deceive poor villains thus.
Tongue-traveling Lawyers faint at such a day,
Lie speechless, for they have no words to say.
Physicians turn to patients, their Arts dry,
For then our fat men without Physic die.
And to conclude, against all Art and good,
War taints the Doctor, lets the Surgeon blood.

Such was the fashion of this Land, when the great Land-Lady thereof left it. She came in with the fall of the leaf, and went away in the Spring. Her life (which was dedicated to Virginity) both beginning and closing up a miraculous Maiden circle, for she was born upon a Lady Eve, and died upon a Lady Eve, her Nativity and death being memorable by this wonder: the first and last years of her Reign by this, that a *Lee* was Lord Mayor when she came to the Crown and a *Lee* Lord Mayor when she departed from it.[15] Three places are made famous by her for three things: *Greenwich* for her birth, *Richmount* for her death, *Whitehall* for her Funeral. Upon her removing from whence (to lend our tiring prose a breathing time), stay, and look upon these *Epigrams*, being composed,

1. *Upon the Queen's last Remove being dead.*

The Queen's remov'd in solemn sort,
Yet this was strange, and seldom seen:
The Queen used to remove the Court,
But now the Court remov'd the Queen.

2. *Upon her bringing by water to* White Hall.

The Queen was brought by water to White Hall.
At every stroke, the Oars tears let fall.

More clung about the Barge. Fish under water
Wept out their eyes of pearl, and swom blind after.
I think the Bargemen might with easier thighs
Have rowed her thither in her people's eyes,
For howsoe'r, thus much my thoughts have scanned,
S'had come by water, had she come by land.

3. *Upon her lying dead at* White Hall.

The Queen lies now at White Hall dead,
And now at White Hall living,
To make this rough objection even,
Dead at White Hall at Westminster,
But living at White Hall in Heaven.

Thus you see that both in her life and her death she was appointed to be the mirror of her time. And surely, if since the first stone that was laid for the foundation of this great house of the world, there was ever a year ordained to be wondered at, it is only this: the *Sibil's Octogesimus, Octavus Annus,*[16] that same terrible 88, which came sailing hither in the Spanish Armado[17] and made men's hearts colder than the frozen Zone when they heard but an inkling of it. That 88, by whose horrible predictions, Almanac-makers stood in bodily fear their trade would be utterly overthrown, and poor *Erra Pater* was threatened (because he was a Jew) to be put to baser offices than the stopping of mustard-pots; that same 88, which had more prophecies waiting at his heels than ever *Merlin* the Magician had in his head, was a year of Jubilee to this. Plato's *Mirabilis Annus,* (whether it be past already or to come within these four years) may throw Plato's cap at *Mirabilis,* for that title of wonderful is bestowed upon 1603. If that sacred Aromatically-perfumed fire of wit (out of whose flames *Phoenix* poesy doth arise) were burning in any breast, I would feed it with no other stuff for a twelve-month and a day than with kindling papers full of lines that should tell only of the chances, changes, and strange shapes that this Protean Climacterical year hath metamorphosed himself into. It is able to find ten Chroniclers a competent living and to set twenty Printers at work.

You shall perceive I lie not, if (with *Peter Bales*) you will take the pains to draw the whole volume of it into the compass of a penny. As first, to begin with the Queen's death, then the Kingdom's falling into an Ague upon that. Next follows the curing of that fever by the wholesome receipt of a proclaimed King. That wonder begat more, for in an hour, two mighty Nations were made one. Wild *Ireland* became tame on the sudden, and some English great ones[18] that before seemed tame, on the sudden turned wild — the same Park which great *Julius Caesar* enclosed, to hold in that Deer whom they before hunted, being now circled (by a second *Caesar*) with stronger pales to keep them from leaping over. And last of all (if that wonder be the last and shut up the year), a most dreadful plague. This is the abstract, and yet (like *Stow's* Chronicle of *Decimo sexto* to huge *Holinshed*)[19] these small pricks in this Set-card[20] of ours represent mighty Countries. Whilst I have the quill in my hand, let me blow them bigger.

The Queen being honored with a Diadem of Stars, *France, Spain,* and *Belgium,* lift up their heads, preparing to do as much for *England* by giving aim, whilst she shot arrows at her own breast (as they imagined) as she had done (many a year together) for them, and her own Nation betted on their sides, looking with distracted countenance for no better guests than Civil Sedition, Uproars, Rapes, Murders, and Massacres. But the wheel of Fate turned. A better Lottery was drawn, *Pro Troia stabat Apollo.*[21] God stuck valiantly to us. For behold, up rises a comfortable Sun out of the North, whose glorious beams (like a fan) dispersed all thick and contagious clouds. The loss of a Queen was paid with the double interest of a King and Queen. The Cedar of her government, which stood alone and bare no fruit, is changed now to an Olive, upon whose spreading branches grow both Kings and Queens. Oh, it were able to still a hundred pair of writing tables with notes but to see the parts played in the compass of one hour on the stage of this new-found world! Upon Thursday it was treason to cry "God save King *James,* King of *England,*" and upon Friday high treason not to cry so. In the morning no voice heard but murmurs and lamentation, at noon nothing but shouts of gladness and triumph. *Saint*

George and *Saint Andrew*, that many hundred years had defied one another, were now sworn brothers. *England* and *Scotland* (being parted only with a narrow River, and the people of both Empires speaking a language less differing than *English* within itself, as the providence had enacted that one day those two Nations should marry one another) are now made sure together, and King *James* his Coronation is the solemn wedding day. Happiest of all thy Ancestors (thou mirror of all Princes that ever were or are) that at seven of the clock wert a king but over a piece of a little Island and before eleven the greatest Monarch in Christendom. Now

Silver Crowds
Of blissful Angels and tried Martyrs tread
On the Star-ceiling over *England's* head.
Now heaven broke into a wonder, and brought forth
Our *omne bonum* from the wholesome North
(Our fruitful sovereign) *James*, at whose dread name
Rebellion swooned and (ere since) became
Groveling and nerveless, wanting blood to nourish,
For Ruin gnaws herself when kingdoms flourish.
Nor are our hopes planted in regal springs,
Never to wither, for our air breeds kings,
And in all ages (from this sovereign time)
England shall still be called the royal clime.
Most blissful Monarch of all earthen powers,
Serv'd with a mess of kingdoms, four such bowers
(For prosperous hives, and rare industrious swarms)
The world contains not in her solid arms.
O thou that art the Meter of our days,
Poet's Apollo! deal thy Daphnean bays
To those whose wits are bay-trees, ever green,
Upon whose high tops, Poesy chirps unseen,
Such are most fit t'apparel Kings in rhymes,
Whose silver numbers are the Muses' chimes,
Whose spritely characters (being once wrought on)
Out-live the marble th'are insculpt upon:
Let such men chant thy virtue; then they fly
On Learning's wings up to Eternity.
As for the rest that limp (in cold desert)
Having small wit, less judgment, and least Art,

Their verse! tis almost heresy to hear.
Banish their lines some furlong from thine ear,
For tis held dang'rous (by Apollo's sign)
To be infected with a leprous line.
O make some Adamant Act (n'ere to be worn)
That none may write but those that are true-born,
So when the world's old cheeks shall race and peel,
Thy Acts shall breath in Epitaphs of Steel.

By these Comments it appears that by this time King James is proclaimed. Now does fresh blood leap into the cheeks of the Courtier. The Soldier now hangs up his armor and is glad that he shall feed upon the blessed fruits of peace. The Scholar sings Hymns in honor of the Muses, assuring himself now that *Helicon* will be kept pure, because *Apollo* himself drinks of it. Now the thrifty Citizen casts beyond the Moon, and seeing the golden age returned into the world again, resolves to worship no Saint but money. Trades that lay dead and rotten, and were in all men's opinion utterly damned, started out of their trance, as though they had drunk of *Aqua Caelestis,* or Unicorn's horn, and swore to fall to their old occupations. Tailors meant no more to be called Merchant-tailors but Merchants, for their shops were all led forth in leases to be turned into ships, and with their shears (instead of a Rudder) would they have cut the Seas (like Levant Taffaty) and sailed to the West Indies for no worse stuff to make hose and doublets of than beaten gold. Or if the necessity of the time (which was likely to stand altogether upon bravery) should press them to serve with their iron and Spanish weapons upon their stalls, then was there a sharp law made amongst them that no workman should handle any needle but that which had a pearl in his eye, nor any copper thimble, unless it were lined quite through or bumbasted with silver. What Mechanical, hard-handed Vulcanist (seeing the dice of Fortune run so sweetly, and resolving to strike whilst the iron was hot) but persuaded himself to be Master or head Warden of the company ere half a year went about? The worst player's Boy stood upon his good parts, swearing tragical and buskin oaths that how villainously soever he ranted, or what bad and unlawful action soever he entered into, he would in despite of his honest audience be half a sharer (at least) at home, or else stroll (that's to say travel) with some notorious wicked floundering company abroad. And good reason had these time-catchers to be led into this fool's paradise, for they saw mirth in every man's face. The streets were plumed with gallants. Tobacconists filled up whole Taverns. Vintners hung out spick and span new Jew bushes (because they wanted good wine), and their old rain-beaten lattices marcht under other colors, having lost both company and colors before.[22]

London was never in the highway to preferment till now. Now she resolved to stand upon her pantoffles. Now (and never till now) did she laugh to scorn that worm-eaten proverb of "*Lincoln* was, *London* is, and *York* shall be,"[23] for she saw herself in better state than *Jerusalem*. She went more gallant then ever did *Antwerp*, was more courted by amorous and lusty suitors than *Venice* (the minion of *Italy*). More lofty towers stood (like a Coronet, or a spangled head attire) about her Temples than ever did about the beautiful forehead of *Rome*. *Tyre* and *Sidon* to her were like two thatcht houses to *Theobalds*,[24] the grand Cairo but a hogsty. *Hinc illae lachrimae:* she wept her belly full for all this.[25] Whilst *Troy* was swilling sack and sugar, and mousing fat venison, the mad Greeks made bonfires of their houses. Old *Priam* was drinking a health to the wooden horse, and before it could be pledged had his throat cut. Corn is no sooner ripe, but for all the pricking up of his ears, he is pared off by the shins and made to go upon stumps. Flowers no sooner budded but they are pluckt up and die. Night walks at the heels of the day, and sorrow enters (like a tavern-bill) at the tail of our pleasures, for in the Apennine height of this immoderate joy and security (that like Paul's Steeple overlookt the whole City), behold that miracle-worker, who in one minute turned our general mourning to a general mirth, does now again in a moment alter that gladness to shrieks and lamentation.

Here would I fain make a full point, because posterity should not be frighted with those miserable Tragedies, which now my Muse (as *Chorus*) stands ready to present. Time would, thou hadst never been made wretched by bringing them forth. Oblivion would, in all the graves and sepulchers whose rank jaws thou hast already closed up or shalt yet hereafter burst open, thou couldst likewise bury them forever.

A stiff and freezing horror sucks up the rivers of my blood. My hair stands an end with the panting of my brains. Mine eyeballs are ready to start out, being beaten with the billows of my tears. Out of my weeping pen does the ink mournfully and more bitterly than gall drop on the palefac'd paper, even when I do but think how the bowels of my sick Country have been torn. *Apollo,* therefore, and you bewitching silver-tongued Muses, get you gone. Invocate none of your names. Sorrow and Truth, sit you on each side of me, whilst I am delivered of this deadly burden. Prompt me that I may utter ruthful and passionate condolement. Arm my trembling hand, that it may boldly rip up and Anatomize the ulcerous body of this *Anthropophagized* plague.[26] Lend me Art (without any counterfeit shadowing) to paint and delineate to the life the whole story of this mortal and pestiferous battle, and you the ghosts of those more (by many) than 40,000 that with the virulent poison of infection have been driven out of your earthly dwellings; you desolate hand-wringing widows that beat your bosoms over your departing husbands; you woefully distracted mothers that with disheveled hair fallen into swoons whilst you lie kissing the insensible cold lips of your breathless Infants; you outcast and down-trodden Orphans that shall many a year hence remember more freshly to mourn, when your mourning garments shall look old and be forgotten; and you the *Genii* of all those emptied families, whose habitations are now among the *Antipodes,* join all your hands together, and with your bodies, cast a ring about me. Let me behold your ghastly visages, that my paper may receive their true pictures. *Echo* forth your groans through the hollow trunk of my pen, and rain down your gummy tears into mine Ink, that even marble bosoms may be shaken with terror and hearts of Adamant melt into compassion.

What an unmatchable torment were it for a man to be bard up every night in a vast silent Charnel-house, hung (to make it more hideous) with lamps dimly and slowly burning in hollow and glimmering corners, where all the pavement should instead of green rushes be strewed with blasted Rosemary, withered Hyacinths, fatal Cypress and Yew, thickly mingled with heaps of dead men's bones, the bare ribs of a father that begat him, lying there? Here, the Chapless hollow skull of a mother that bore him. Round about him a thousand Corpses, some standing bolt upright in their knotted winding sheets, others half mouldred in rotten coffins that should suddenly yawn wide open, filling his nostrils with noisome stench and his eyes with the sight of nothing but crawling worms. And to keep such a poor wretch waking, he should hear no noise but of Toads croaking, Screech-Owls howling, Mandrakes shrieking. Were not this an infernal prison? Would not the strongest hearted man (beset with such a ghastly horror) look wild and run mad and die? And even such a formidable shape did the diseased City appear in.

For he that durst (in the dead hour of gloomy midnight) have been so valiant as to have walkt through the still and melancholy streets, what think you should have been his music? Surely the loud groans of raving sick men, the struggling pangs of souls departing. In every house, grief striking up an Alarum, Servants crying out for masters, wives for husbands, parents for children, children for their mothers. Here, he should have met some franticly running to knock up Sextons; there, others fearfully sweating with Coffins to steal forth dead bodies, lest the fatal handwriting of death should seal up their doors. And to make this dismal consort more full, round about him Bells heavily tolling in one place and ringing out in another. The dreadfulness of such an hour is unutterable. Let us go further.

If some poor man, suddenly starting out of a sweet and golden slumber, should behold his house flaming about his ears, all his family destroyed in their sleeps by the merciless fire, himself in the very midst of it, woefully and like a mad man calling for help, would not the misery of such a distressed soul appear the greater if the rich Usurer dwelling next door to him should not stir (though he felt part of the danger) but suffer him to perish, when the thrusting out of an arm might have saved him? O how many thousands of wretched people have acted this poor man's part? How often hath the amazed husband, waking, found the comfort of his bed lying breathless by his side, his children at the same instant gasping for life, and his servants mortally wounded at the heart by sickness! The distracted creature beats at death doors, exclaims at windows. His cries are sharp enough to pierce heaven, but on earth no ear is opened to receive them.

And in this manner do the tedious minutes of the night stretch out the sorrows of ten thousand. It is now day; let us look forth and try what Consolation rises with the Sun. Not any, not any, for before the Jewel of the morning be fully set in silver, hundred hungry graves stand gaping, and every one of them (as at a breakfast) hath swallowed down ten or eleven lifeless carcasses. Before dinner, in the same gulp are twice so many more devoured, and before the sun takes his rest, those numbers are doubled. Threescore, that not many hours before had every one several lodgings very delicately furnisht, are now thrust altogether into one close room, a little noisome room not fully ten foot square. Doth not this strike coldly to the heart of a worldly miser? To some, the very sound of death's name is, instead, of a passing-bell. What shall become of such a coward, being told that the selfsame body of his, which now is so pampered with superfluous fare, so perfumed and bathed in odoriferous waters and so gaily appareled in variety of fashions, must one day be thrown (like stinking carrion) into a rank and rotten grave, where his goodly eyes that did once shoot forth such amorous glances, must be beaten out of his head, his locks that hang wantonly dangling, trodden in dirt under-foot? This, doubtless (like thunder), must needs strike him into the earth. But (wretched man!) when thou shalt see and be assured (by tokens sent thee from heaven) that tomorrow thou must be tumbled into a Muck-pit and suffer thy body to be bruisd and prest with threescore dead men lying slovenly upon thee, and thou to be undermost of all! Yea, and perhaps half of that number were thine enemies! (And see how they may be revenged, for the worms that breed out of their putrefying carcasses shall crawl in huge swarms from them and quite devour thee.) What agonies will this strange news drive thee into? If thou art in love with thyself, this cannot choose but possess thee with frenzy.

But thou art gotten safe (out of the civil city Calamity) to thy Parks and Palaces in the Country, lading thy asses and thy Mules with thy gold (thy god), thy plate, and thy Jewels, and the fruits of thy womb thriftily growing up but in one only son (the young Landlord of all thy careful labors). Him also hast thou rescued from the arrows of infection. Now is thy soul jocund and thy senses merry. But open thine eyes, thou Fool, and behold that darling of thine eye (thy son) turned suddenly into a lump of clay. The hand of pestilence hath smote him even under thy wing. Now doest thou rend thine hair, blaspheme thy Creator, cursest thy creation, and basely descendest into brutish and unmanly passions, threatning in despite of death and his Plague to maintain the memory of thy child in the everlasting breast of Marble. A tomb must now defend him from tempests, and for that purpose, the sweaty hind (that digs the rent he pays thee out of the entrails of the earth) he is sent for, to convey forth that burden of thy sorrow.

But note how thy pride is disdained. That weather-beaten sunburnt drudge that not a month since fawned upon thy worship like a Spaniel and like a bond-slave would have stooped lower than thy feet, does now stop his nose at thy presence and is ready to set his Mastiff as high as thy throat to drive thee from his door. All thy gold and silver cannot hire one of those (whom before thou didst scorn) to carry the dead body to his last home. The Country round about thee shun thee as a Basilisk, and therefore to *London* (from whose arms thou cowardly fledst away) post upon post must be galloping to fetch from thence those that may perform that Funeral Office. But there are they so full of grave-matters of their own that they have no leisure to attend thine. Doth not this cut thy very heart-strings in sunder? If that do not, the shutting up of the Tragical Act, I am sure, will, for thou must be enforced with thine own hands to wind up that blasted flower of youth in the last linen that ever he shall wear. Upon thine own shoulders must thou bear part of him, thy amazed servant the other. With thine own hands must thou dig his grave, not in the Church or common place of burial, thou hast not favor (for all thy riches) to be so happy, but in thine Orchard or in the proud walks of thy Garden. Wringing thy palsy-shaking hands instead of bells (most miserable father) must thou search him out a sepulcher.

My spirit grows faint with rowing in this Stygian Ferry. It can no longer endure the transportation of souls in this doleful manner. Let us therefore shift a point of our Compass and (since there is no remedy, but that we must still be tossed up and down in this *Mare mortuum*) hoist up all our sails and, on the merry wings of a lustier wind, seek to arrive on some prosperous shore.

Imagine then that all this while, Death (like a Spanish Leaguer, or rather like stalking *Tamberlaine*) hath pitcht his tents (being nothing but a heap of winding sheets tackt together) in the sinfully-polluted Suburbs. The Plague is Muster-master and Marshall of the field. Burning Fevers, Boils, Blains, and Carbuncles, the Leaders, Lieutenants, Servants, and Corporals: the main Army consisting (like *Dunkirk*) of a mingle-mangle: *viz*. dumpish Mourners, merry Sextons, hungry Coffin-sellers, scrubbing Bearers, and nasty Grave-makers. But indeed they are the Pioneers of the Camp that are employed only (like Moles) in casting up of earth and digging of trenches. Fear and Trembling (the two Catch polls of Death) arrest every one. No parley will be granted, no composition stood upon, but the Alarum is struck up, the *Toxin* rings out for life, and no voice heard but "*Tue, Tue, Kill, Kill.*" The little Bells only (like small shot) do yet go off and make no great work for worms, a hundred or two lost in every skirmish, or so, but alas, that's nothing. Yet, by those desperate sallies, what by open setting upon them by day and secret Ambuscadoes by night, the skirts of *London* were pitifully pared off, by little and little, which they within the gates perceiving, it was no boot to bid them take their heels, for away they trudge thick and threefold, some riding, some on foot, some without boots, some in their slippers, by water, by land. In shoals swom they Westward. Marry, to *Gravesend* none went unless they be driven, for whosoever landed there never came back again. Hackneys, watermen and Wagons were not so terribly employed many a year, so that within a short time, there was not a good horse in Smithfield nor a Coach to be set eye on. For after the world had once run upon the wheels of the Pest-cart, neither coach nor carriage durst appear in his likeness.

Let us pursue these runaways no longer but leave them in the unmerciful hands of the Country-hard-hearted *Hobinolls* (who are ordained to be their Tormentors) and return back to the stage of the City, for the enemy, taking advantage by their flight, planted his ordnance against the walls. Here the Canons (like their great Bells) roared. The Plague took sore pains for a breach. He laid about him cruelly, ere he could get it, but at length he and his tyrannous band entered. His purple colors were presently (with the sound of Bow-bell instead of a trumpet) advanced and joined to the Standard of the City. He marcht even through Cheapside, and the capital streets of *Troynovant,* the only blot of dishonor that stuck upon this Invader being this, that he played the tyrant not the conqueror, making havoc of all when he had all lying at the foot of his mercy. Men, women, and children dropt down before him; houses were rifled; streets ransackt; beautiful maidens thrown on their beds and ravisht by sickness; rich men's Coffers broken open and shared amongst prodigal heirs and unthrifty servants; poor men used poorly, but not pitifully. He did very much hurt; yet some say he did very much good. Howsoever he behaved himself, this intelligence runs current, that every house lookt like Saint *Bartholomew's* Hospital, and every street like Bucklersbury, for poor *Mithridatum* and *Dragonwater* (being both of them in all the world scarce worth threepence) were boxt in every corner, and yet were both drunk every hour at other men's cost. *Lazarus* lay groaning at every man's door. Marry, no *Dives* was within to send him a crumb (for all your Goldfinches were fled to the woods), nor a dog left to lick up his sores, for they (like Curs) were knockt down like Oxen and fell thicker than Acorns.

I am amazed to remember what dead Marches were made of three thousand trooping together: husbands, wives, and children, being led as ordinarily to one grave as if they had gone to one bed. And those that could shift for a time and shrink their heads out of the collar (as many did) yet went they (most bitterly) miching and muffled up and down with Rue and Wormwood stuft into their ears and nostrils, looking like so many Boarsheads stuck with branches of Rosemary to be served in for Brawne at Christmas.

This was a rare world for the Church, who had wont to complain for want of living and now had more living thrust upon her than she knew how to bestow. To have been Clerk now to a parish Clerk was better than to serve some foolish Justice of Peace or than the year before to have had a Benefice. Sextons gave out, if they might (as they hoped) continue these doings but a twelvemonth longer, they and their posterity would all ride upon footcloths to the end of the world. Amongst which worm-eaten generation, the three bald Sextons of limping Saint *Giles*, Saint *Sepulchres*, and Saint *Olaves*,[27] ruled the roost more hotly than ever did the *Triumvirate of Rome*. *Jehochanan*, *Simeon*, and *Eleazar*,[28] never kept such a plaguey coil in *Jerusalem* among the hunger-starved Jews as these three Sharkers did in their Parishes among naked Christians. Cursed they were, I am sure, by some to the pit of hell for tearing money out of their throats that had not a cross in their purses. But alas! They must have it. It is their Fee, and therefore give the Devil his due. Only Herb-wives and Gardeners (that never prayed before, unless it were for Rain or fair Weather) were now day and night upon their marybones, that God would bless the labors of those molecatchers,[29] because they suck sweetness by this. For the price of flowers, Herbs and garlands, rose wonderfully, in so much that Rosemary, which had wont to be sold for twelve pence an armful, went now for six shillings a handful.

A fourth sharer likewise (these winding-sheet-weavers) deserves to have my pen give his lips a Jew's Letter, but because he worships the Baker's good Lord and Master, charitable Saint *Clement* (whereas none of the other three ever had to do with any Saint), he shall scape the better. Only let him take heed that having all this year buried his prayers in the bellies of Fat ones and plump Capon-eaters (for no worse meat would down this Bly-fox's stomach) let him, I say, take heed lest (his flesh now falling away) his carcass be not plagued with lean ones—of whom (whilst the bill of *Lord have mercy upon us* was to be denied in no place) it was death for him to hear.

In this pitiful (or rather pitiless) perplexity stood *London,* forsaken like a Lover, forlorn like a widow, and disarmed of all comfort—disarmed I may well say, for five Rapiers were not stirring all this time, and those that were worn had never been seen, if any money could have been lent upon them, so hungry is the Estridge disease, that it will devour even Iron.[30] Let us therefore with bag and baggage march away from this dangerous sore City and visit those that are fled into the Country. But alas! *Decidis in Scyllam,*[31] you are peppered if you visit them, for they are visited already. The broad Arrow of Death flies there up and down as swiftly as it doth here. They that rode on the lustiest geldings could not out-gallop the Plague. It over-took them and overturned them too, horse and foot.

You whom the arrows of pestilence have reacht at eighteen and twenty score[32] (though you stood far enough as you thought from the mark), you that sickening in the highway would have been glad of a bed in an Hospital and dying in the open fields have been buried like dogs, how much better had it bin for you to have lyen fuller of biles and Plague-sores than ever did *Job,* so you might in that extremity have received both bodily and spiritual comfort, which there was denied you? For those misbelieving Pagans, the plough-drivers, those worse than Infidels (that like their Swine never look up so high as Heaven) when Citizens boarded [with] them, they wrung their hands and wisht rather they had fallen into the hands of Spaniards, for the sight of a flat-cap was more dreadful to a Lob, than the discharging of a Caliver. A treble-ruff (being but once named "the Merchant's set") had power to cast a whole household into a cold sweat. If one new suit of Sackcloth had been but known to have come out of Burchin Lane (being the common

Wardrobe for all their Clown-ships)[33] it had been enough to make a Market town give up the ghost. A Crow that had been seen in a Sunshine day standing on the top of Paul's would have been better than a Beacon on fire to have raised all the towns within ten miles of *London* for the keeping her out.[34]

Never let any man ask me what became of our Physicians in this Massacre. They hid their Synodical heads as well as the proudest, and I cannot blame them, for their Phlebotomies, Lozenges, and Electuaries, with their Diacatholicons, Diacodium, Amulets, and Antidotes had not so much strength to hold life and soul together as a pot of *Pinder's* Ale and a Nutmeg. Their Drugs turned to dust. Their simples were simple things. *Galen* could do no more good than Sir Giles Goosecap.[35] *Hippocrates, Avicenna, Paracelsus, Rasis, Fernelius,* with all their succeeding rabble of Doctors and Watercasters were at their wits end, or I think rather at the world's end, for not one of them durst peep abroad. Or if any one did take upon him to play the venturous Knight, the Plague put him to his *Nonplus*. In such strange and such changeable shapes did this Chameleon-like sickness appear that they could not (with all the cunning in their budgets) make pursenets to take him napping.

Only a band of Desperviews, some few Empirical madcaps (for they could never be worth velvet caps), turned themselves into Bees (or more properly into Drones) and went humming up and down, with honey-bags in their mouths, sucking the sweetness of Silver (and now and then of *Aurum Potable*) out of the poison of Blains and Carbuncles. And these jolly Mountebanks clapt up their bills upon every post (like a Fencer's Challenge) threatening to canvas the Plague and to fight with him at all his own several weapons. I know not how they sped, but some they sped I am sure, for I have heard them band[36] for the Heavens because they sent those thither that were wisht to tarry longer upon earth.

I could in this place make your cheeks look pale and your hearts shake with telling how some have had eighteen sores at one time running upon them, others ten and twelve, many four and five, and how those that have bin four times wounded by this year's infection have died of the last wound, whilst others (that were hurt as often) go up and down now with sounder limbs than many that come out of *France* and the *Netherlands*. And descending from these, I could draw forth a Catalogue of many poor wretches that in fields, in ditches, in common Cages, and under stalls (being either thrust by cruel masters out of doors or wanting all worldly succor but the common benefit of earth and air) have most miserably perished. But to Chronicle these would weary a second *Fabian*.

We will therefore play the Soldiers who at the end of any notable battle, with a kind of sad delight, rehearse the memorable acts of their friends that lie mangled before them, some showing how bravely they gave the onset, some how politically they retired, others how manfully they gave and received wounds. A fourth steps forth and glories how valiantly he lost an arm, all of them making (by this means) the remembrance even of tragical and mischievous events very delectable. Let us strive to do so, discoursing (as it were at the end of this mortal siege of the Plague) of the several most worthy accidents and strange births which this pestiferous year hath brought forth, some of them yielding Comical and ridiculous stuff; others lamentable; a third kind, upholding rather admiration than laughter or pity.

As first, to relish the palate of lickerish expectation and withal to give an *Item* how sudden a stabber this ruffianly swaggerer (Death) is, you must believe that amongst all the weary number of those that (on their bare feet) have traveled (in this long and heavy vocation) to the Holyland, one (whose name I could for need bestow upon you, but that I know you have no need of it, though many want a good name) lying in that common Inn of sick-men, his bed, and seeing the black and blue stripes of the plague sticking on his flesh, which he received as tokens (from heaven) that he was presently to go dwell in the upper world, most earnestly requested and in a manner conjured his friend (who came to interchange a last farewell) that he would see him go handsomely attired into the wild Irish country of worms, and for that purpose to bestow a Coffin upon him. His friend, loving him (not because he was poor, yet he was poor) but because he was a Scholar—Alack that the West Indies stand so far from Universities and that a mind richly appareled should have a threadbare body!—made faithful promise to him that he should be nailed up; he would board him, and for that purpose went instantly to one of the new-found trade of Coffin-cutters, bespake one, and (like the Surveyor of death's buildings) gave direction how this little Tenement should be framed, paying all the rent for it beforehand. But note upon what slippery ground life goes! Little did he think to dwell in that room himself which he had taken for his friend, yet it seemed the common law of mortality had so decreed, for he was called into the cold company of his grave neighbors an hour before his infected friend and had a long lease (even till doomsday) in the same lodging, which in the strength of health he went to prepare for another. What credit therefore is to be given to breath, which like an harlot will run away with every minute. How nimble is sickness, and what skill hath he in all the weapons he plays withal. The greatest cutter that takes up the Mediterranean Isle in Paul's for his Gallery to walk[37] in cannot ward off his blows. He's the best Fencer in the world. *Vincentio Saviolo* is nobody to him. He has his Mandrittas, Imbroccatas, Stramazons, and Stoccados[38] at his fingers' ends. He'll make you give him ground, though this were never worth foot of land, and beat you out of breath, though *Aeolus* himself play upon your wind-pipe.

To witness which, I will call forth a Dutch-man (yet now he's past calling for has lost his hearing, for his ears by this time are eaten off with worms) who (though he dwelt in Bedlam) was not mad, yet the very looks of the Plague (which indeed are terrible) put him almost out of his wits, for when the snares of this cunning hunter (the Pestilence) were but newly laid, and yet laid (as my Dutchman smelt it out well enough) to entrap poor men's lives that meant him no hurt, away sneaks my clipper of the king's English, and (because Musket-shot should not reach him) to the Low-countries (that are built upon butterfirkins and Holland cheese) sails this plaguey fugitive. But death (who hath more authority there than all the seven Electors[39] and to show him that there were other Low-country besides his own) takes a little Frokin (one of my Dutch runaway's children) and sends her packing; into those Netherlands she departed. O how pitifully looked my Burgomaster, when he understood that the sickness could swim! It was an easy matter to scape the Dunkirks, but Death's Galleys made out after him swifter than the great Turks, which he perceiving, made no more ado, but drunk to the States five or six healths (because he would be sure to live well) and back again comes he, to try the strength of English Beer. His old *Rendezvous* of madmen was the place of meeting, where he was no sooner arrived, but the Plague had him by the back and arrested him upon an *Exeat Regnum*, for running to the enemy, so that for the mad tricks he played to cozen our English worms of his Dutch carcass (which had been fatted here), sickness and death clapped him up in *Bedlam* the second time, and there he lies, and there he shall lie till he rot before I'll meddle any more of with him.

But being gotten out of *Bedlam*, let us make a journey to *Bristol*, taking an honest known Citizen along with us, who with other company traveling thither (only for fear the air of *London* should conspire to poison him) and setting up his rest not to hear the sound of Bow-bell till next Christmas, was notwithstanding in the highway singled out from his company and set upon by the Plague, who had him stand and deliver his life. The rest at that word shifted for themselves and went on. He (amazed to see his friends fly, and being not able to defend himself, for who can defend himself meeting such an enemy?) yielded, and being but about forty miles from *London*, used all the sleights he could to get loose out of the hands of death and so to hide himself in his own house, whereupon, he called for help at the same Inn, where not long before he and his fellow pilgrims obtained for their money (marry yet with more prayers than a beggar makes in three Terms)[40] to stand and drink some thirty foot from the door. To this house of tippling iniquity he repairs again, conjuring the *Lares*[41] or walking Sprites in it if it were Christmas (that it was well put in), and in the name of God to succor and rescue him to their power out of the hands of infection which now assaulted his body. The Devil would have been afraid of this conjuration but[42] they were not; yet afraid they were, it seemed, for presently the doors had their wooden ribs crushed in pieces by being beaten together. The casements were shut more close than an Usurer's greasy velvet pouch. The drawing windows were hanged, drawn, and quartered. Not a crevice but was stopped, not a mouse-hole left open, for all the holes in the house were most wickedly damned up. Mine Host and Hostess ran over one another into the backside, the maids into the Orchard, quivering and quaking, and ready to hang themselves on the innocent Plumb trees (for hanging to them would not be so sore a death as the Plague, and to die maids too! O horrible!). As for the Tapster, he fled into the Cellar, rapping out five or six plain Country oaths that he would drown himself in a most villainous Stand of Ale if the sick Londoner stood at the door any longer. But stand there he must, for to go away (well) he cannot, but continues knocking and calling in a faint voice, which in their ears sounded as if some staring ghost in a Tragedy had exclaimed upon *Rhadamanth*. He might knock till his hands ached and call till his heart ached, for they were in a worse pickle within than he was without, he being in a good way to go to Heaven, they being so frighted that they scarce knew whereabout Heaven stood, only they all cried out, "Lord have mercy upon us," yet, "Lord have mercy upon us" was the only thing they feared. The doleful catastrophe of all is, a bed could not be had for all *Babylon*, not a cup of drink, no, nor cold water be gotten, though it had been for *Alexander* the Great. If a draught of *Aqua vitae* might have saved his soul, the town denied to do God that good service.

What misery continues ever? The poor man standing thus at death's door and looking every minute when he should be let in, behold, another Londoner that had likewise been in the *Frigida zona*[43] of the Country and was returning (like *Aeneas* out of hell) to the heaven of his own home makes a stand at this sight to play the Physician, and seeing, by the complexion of his patient, that he was sick at heart, applies to his soul the best medicines that his comforting speech could make, for there dwelt no Apothecary near enough to help his body. Being therefore driven out of all other shifts, he leads him into a field (a bundle of Straw, which with much ado he bought for money, serving instead of a Pillow). But the Destinies, hearing the diseased party complain and take on, because he lay in a field-bed, when before he would have been glad of a mattress, for very spite cut the thread of his life, the cruelty of which deed made the other that played Charity's part at his wit's end, because he knew not where to purchase ten foot of ground for his grave. The Church nor Churchyard would let none of their lands. Master Vicar was struck dumb and could not give the dead a good word. Neither Clerk nor Sexton could be hired to execute their Office. No, they themselves would first be executed, so that he that never handled shovel before got his implements about him, ripped up the belly of the earth, and made it like a grave, stripped the cold carcass, bound his shirt about his feet, pulled a linen nightcap over his eyes, and so laid him in the rotten bed of the earth, covering him with clothes cut out of the same piece, and learning by his last words his name and habitation. This sad Traveler arrives at *London*, delivering to the amazed widow and children, instead of a father and a husband, only the outside of him, his apparel. But by the way, note one thing: the bringer of these heavy tidings (as if he had lived long enough when so excellent a work of piety and pity was by him finished) the very next day after his coming home, departed out of this world to receive his reward in the Spiritual Court of heaven.

It is plain therefore by the evidence of these two witnesses that death, like a thief, sets upon men in the highway, dogs them into their own houses, breaks into their bed chambers by night, assaults them by day, and yet no law can take hold of him. He devours man and wife, offers violence to their fair daughters, kills their youthful sons, and deceives them of their servants. Yea, so full of treachery is he grown (since this Plague took his part) that no Lovers dare trust him, nor by their good wills would come near him, for he works their downfall, even when their delights are at the highest.

Too ripe a proof have we of this in a pair of Lovers. The maid was in the pride of fresh blood and beauty. She was that which to be now is a wonder: young and yet chaste. The gifts of her mind were great, yet those which fortune bestowed upon her (as being well descended) were not much inferior. On this lovely creature did a young man so steadfastly fix his eye that her looks kindled in his bosom a desire whose flames burnt the more brightly because they were fed with sweet and modest thoughts. *Hymen* was the God to whom he prayed day and night that he might marry her. His prayers were received. At length (after many tempests of her denial and frowns of kinsfolk) the element grew clear, and he saw the happy landing place where he had long sought to arrive. The prize of her youth was made his own, and the solemn day appointed when it should be delivered to him. Glad of which blessedness (for, to a lover, it is a blessedness), he wrought by all the possible art he could use to shorten the expected hour and bring it nearer, for, whether he feared the interception of parents, or that his own soul, with excess of joy, was drowned in strange passions, he would often, with sighs mingled with kisses, and kisses half sinking in tears, prophetically tell her that sure he should never live to enjoy her. To discredit which opinion of his, behold, the sun had made haste and wakened the bridal morning. Now does he call his heart traitor that did so falsely conspire against him. Lively blood leapeth into his cheeks. He's got up and gaily attired to play the bridegroom. She likewise does as cunningly turn herself into a bride. Kindred and friends are met together. Sops and muscadine run sweating up and down till they drop again to comfort their hearts, and because so many coffins pestered London Churches that there was no room left for weddings, Coaches are provided, and away rides all the train into the Country.

On a Monday morning are these lusty Lovers on their journey, and before noon are they alighted, entering (instead of an Inn) for more state into a Church, where they no sooner appeared but the Priest fell to his business, the holy knot was atying. But he that should fasten it, coming to this, *In sickness and in health,* there he stopped, for suddenly the bride took hold of *in sickness,* for *in health* all that stood by were in fear she should never be kept. The maiden-blush into which her cheeks were lately dyed now began to lose color. Her voice (like a coward) would have shrunk away but that her Lover, reaching her a hand, which he brought thither to give her (for he was not yet made a full husband), did with that touch somewhat revive her. On went they again so far till they met with, *For better, for worse.* There was she worse than before, and had not the holy Officer made haste, the ground on which she stood to be married might easily have been broken up for her burial. All ceremonies being finished, she was led between two, not like a Bride but rather like a Corpse, to her bed that must now be the table on which the wedding dinner is to be served up (being at this time, nothing but tears, and sighs, and lamentation), and Death is chief waiter. Yet at length her weak heart wrestling with the pangs gave them a fall, so that up she stood again, and in the fatal funeral Coach that carried her forth, was she brought back (as upon a bier) to the City. But see the malice of her enemy that had her in chase: upon the Wednesday following being overtaken was her life overcome. Death rudely lay with her and spoiled her of a maidenhead in spite of her husband. Oh the sorrow that did round beset him! Now was his divination true. She was a wife, yet continued a maid. He was a husband and a widower, yet never knew his wife. She was his own, yet he had her not. She had him, yet never enjoyed him. Here is a strange alteration, for the rosemary that was washt in sweet water to set out the Bridal is now wet in tears to furnish her burial. The music that was heard to sound forth dances can not now be heard for the ringing of bells. All the comfort that happened to either side being this, that he lost her before she had time to be an ill wife, and she left him ere he was able to be a bad husband.

Better fortune had this Bride to fall into the hands of the Plague than one other of that frail female sex (whose picture is next to be drawn) had so scape out of them. An honest cobbler (if at least cobblers can be honest that live altogether amongst wicked soles) had a wife, who in the time of health treading her shoe often away, determined in the agony of a sickness (which this year had a saying to her) to fall to mending as well as her husband did. The bed that she lay upon, being as she thought or rather feared the last bed that ever should bear her (for many other beds had born her, you must remember), and the worm of sin tickling her conscience, up she calls her very innocent and simple husband out of his virtuous shop, where like Justice he sat distributing amongst the poor, to some halfpenny pieces, penny pieces to some, and two-penny pieces to others, so long as they would last, his provident care being always that every man and woman should go upright. To the bedside of his plaguey wife approacheth Monsieur Cobbler to understand what deadly news she had to tell him and the rest of his kind neighbors that there were assembled. Such thick tears standing in both the gutters of his eyes to see his beloved lie in such a pickle that in their salt water all his utterance was drowned, which she perceiving, wept as fast as he. But by the warm counsel that sat about the bed, the shower ceased, she wiping her cheeks with the corner of one of the sheets and he, his sullied face, with his leather apron. At last, two or three sighs (like a *Chorus* to the tragedy ensuing) stepping out first, wringing her hands (which gave the better action), she told the pitiful *Actaeon*[44] her husband that she had often done him wrong. He only shook his head at this, and cried "humh!" Which "humh," she, taking as the watch-word of his true patience, unraveled the bottom of her frailty at length and concluded that with such a man (and named him, but I hope you would not have me follow her steps and name him too) she practiced the universal and common Art of grafting, and that upon her good man's head, they two had planted a monstrous pair of invisible horns.

At the sound of the horns, my cobbler started up like a march Hare, and began to look wild. His awl never ran through the sides of a boot as that word did through his heart. But being a politic cobbler, and remembering what piece of work he was to underlay, stroking his beard, like some grave headborough of the Parish, and giving a nod, as who should say, "go on," bade her go on indeed, clapping to her sore soul this general salve, that *All are sinners, and we must forgive, etc.*, for he hoped by such wholesome Physic (as Shoemaker's wax being laid to a bile) to draw out all the corruption of her secret villainies. She, good heart, being tickled under gills[45] with the finger of these kind speeches, turns up the white of her eye and fetches out another. Another—O thou that art trained up in nothing but to handle pieces—another hath discharged his Artillery against thy castle of fortification. Here was passion predominant. *Vulcan* struck the cobbler's ghost (for he was now no cobbler) so hardy upon his breast, that he cried "Oh!" His neighbors, taking pity to see what terrible stitches pulled him, rubbed his swelling temples with the juice of patience, which (by virtue of the blackish sweat that stood reeking on his brows and had made them supple) entered very easily into his now-parlous-understanding skull, so that he left wenching and sat quiet as a Lamb, falling to his old vomit of counsel, which he had cast up before, and swearing (because he was in strong hope, this show should wring him no more) to seal her a general acquittance. Prickt forward with this gentle spur, her tongue mends his pace, so that in her confession she overtook others whose boots had been set all night on the Cobbler's last, bestowing upon him the poesy of their names, the time, and place, to the intent it might be put into his next wife's wedding ring. And although she had made all these blots in his tables, yet the bearing of one man false (whom she had not yet discovered) stuck more in her stomach than all the rest. "O valiant Cobbler," cries out one of the Auditors, "how art thou set upon? How are thou tempted? Happy art thou that thou art not in thy shop, for instead of cutting out pieces of leather, thou wouldst doubtless now pare away thy heart. For I see and so do all thy neighbors here (thy wife's ghostly fathers) see that a small matter would now cause thee turn turk and to meddle with no more patches.[46] But to live within the compass of thy wit, lift not up thy collar. Be not horn mad. Thank heaven that the murderer is revealed; *study thou Balthazar's Part in Hieronimo,*[47] for thou hast more cause (though less reason) than he to be glad and sad. Well, I see thou art worthy to have patient *Griseld* to thy wife, for thou bearest more than she. Thou showst thyself to be a right cobbler, and no souter, that canst thus cleanly clout up the seam-rent sides of thy affection."

With this learned Oration, the Cobbler was tutored, laid his finger on his mouth, and cried "*paucos palabros.*" He had sealed her pardon and therefore bid her not fear. Hereupon, he named the malefactor (I could name him too, but that he shall live to give more Cobblers' heads the Bastinado) and told that on such a night when he supped there (for a Lord may sup with a cobbler that hath a pretty wench to his wife) when the cloth, O treacherous linen!, was taken up, and *Menelaus* had for a parting blow given the other his fist, down she lights (this half-sharer) opening the wicket, but not shutting him out of the wicket but conveys him into a by-room (being the wardrobe of old shoes and leather), from whence the unicorn cobbler (that dreamt of no such spirits) being over head and ears in sleep, his snorting giving the sign that he was cock-sure, softly out-steals sir *Paris,* and to *Helen's* teeth[48] proved himself a true Trojan.

This was the cream of her confusion, which being skimmed off from the stomach of her conscience, we looked every minute to go thither, where we should be far enough out of the Cobbler's reach. But the Fates laying their heads together sent a reprieve. The plague that before meant to pepper her, by little and little, left her company, which news being blown abroad, Oh lamentable! Never did the old buskin tragedy begin till now, for the wives of those husbands, with whom she had played at fast and loose came with nails sharpened for the nonce, like cats, and tongues forkedly cut like the stings of adders, first to scratch out false *Cressida's* eyes and then (which was worse) to worry her to death with scolding.

But the matter was took up in a Tavern. The case was altered and brought to a new reckoning (marry, the blood of the *Bordeaux* grape was first shed about it), but in the end, all anger on every side was poured into a pottle pot and there burnt to death. Now whether this Recantation was true, or whether the steam of infection, fuming up (like wine) into her brains, made her talk thus idly, I leave it to the Jury.

And whilst they are canvassing her case, let us see what doings the Sexton of *Stepney* hath, whose warehouses being all full of dead commodities saving one—that one he left open a whole night; yet was it half full too—knowing that thieves this year were too honest to break into such cellars; besides, those that were left there had such plaguey pates that none durst meddle with them for their lives. About twelve of the clock at midnight, when spirits walk and not a mouse dare stir, because cats go a caterwauling, Sin, that all day durst not show his head, came reeling out of an ale-house in the shape of a drunkard, who no sooner smelled the wind but he thought the ground under him danced the Canaries. Houses seemed to turn on the toe, and all things went round insomuch that his legs drew a pair of Indentures between his body and the earth, the principal covenant being that he for his part would stand to nothing whatever he saw. Every tree that came in his way did he jostle and yet challenge it the next day to fight with him. If he had clipt but a quarter so much of the King's silver as he did of the King's English, his carcass had long ere this been carrion for Crows. But he lived by gaming and had excellent casting, yet seldom won, for he drew reasonable good hands but had very bad feet that were not able to carry it away. This setter-up of Malt-men, being troubled with the staggers, fell into the self-same grave that stood gaping wide open for a breakfast next morning, and imagining (when he was in) that he had stumbled into his own house, and that all his bedfellows (as they were indeed) were in their dead sleep, he (never complaining of cold, nor calling for more sheet) soundly takes a nap till he snores again.

In the morning the Sexton comes plodding along and casting upon his fingers' ends what he hopes the dead pay of that day will come to by that which he received the day before (for Sextons now had better doings than either Taverns or bawdy-houses). In that silver contemplation, shrugging his shoulders together, he steps ere he be aware on the brims of that pit, into which this worshipper of *Bacchus* was fallen, where finding some dead men's bones and a skull or two that lay scattered here and there. Before he lookt into this Coffer of worms, those he takes up, and flings them in. One of the skulls battered the sconce of the sleeper, whilst the bones played with his nose, whose blows waking his musty worship, the first word that he cast up was an oath, and thinking the Cans had flyen about, cried, "Zounds! What do you mean to crack my mazer?" The Sexton, smelling a voice (fear being stronger than his heart), believed verily some of the corpses spake to him, upon which, feeling himself in a cold sweat, took his heels, whilst the Goblin scrambled up and ran after him. But it appears the Sexton had the lighter foot, for he ran so fast that he ran out of his wits, which being left behind him, he had like to have died presently after.

A merrier bargain than the poor Sexton's did a Tinker meet withal in a Country Town, through which a Citizen of *London,* being driven (to keep himself under the lee shore in this tempestuous contagion) and casting up his eye for some harbor, spied a bush at the end of a pole, (the ancient badge of a Country Alehouse), into which, as good luck was (without any resistance of the Barbarians that all this year used to keep such landing places), veiling his Bonnet, he struck in. The Host had been a mad Greek (marry, he could now speak nothing but English). A goodly fat Burger he was, with a belly Arching out like a Beer-barrel, which made his legs (that were thick and short, like two piles driven under *London* bridge) to straddle half as wide as the top of Paul's, which upon my knowledge hath been burnt twice or thrice. A leather pouch hung at his side that opened and shut with a Snap-hance and was indeed a flask for gun-powder when King *Henry* went to *Boulogne.*[49] An Antiquary might have pickt rare matter but of his Nose, but that it was worm-eaten (yet that proved it to be an ancient Nose). In some corners of it, there were bluish holes that shone like shells of mother of Pearl, and to do his nose right, Pearls had been gathered out of them. Other were richly garnisht with Rubies, *Chrysolites* and *Carbuncles,* which glistered so oriently that the Hamburgers offered I know not how many Dollars for his company in an East-Indian voyage to have stood a nights in the Poop of their Admiral, only to save the charges of candles. In conclusion, he was an Host to be led before an Emperor, and though he were one of the greatest men in all the shire, his bigness made him not proud but he humbled himself to speak the base language of a Tapster, and upon the Londoner's first arrival, cried, "Welcome! A cloth for this Gentleman." The Linen was spread and furnisht presently with a new Cake and a Can, the room voided, and the Guest left—(like a French Lord) attended by nobody—who, drinking half a Can (in conceit) to the health of his best friend in the City, which lay extreme sick and had never more need of health. I know not what qualms came over his stomach, but immediately he fell down without uttering any more words and never rose again.

Anon (as it was his fashion) enters my puffing Host to relieve with a fresh supply out of his Cellar the shrinking Can, if he perceived it stood in danger to be overthrown. But seeing the chief Leader dropt at his feet, and imagining at first he was but wounded a little in the head, held up his gouty golls and blest himself, that a Londoner (who had wont to be the most valiant rob-pots) should now be struck down only with two hoops,[50] and thereupon jogged him, fumbling out these comfortable words of a soldier, "If thou be a man, stand a thy legs." He stirred not for all this, whereupon the Maids being raised (as it had been with a hue and cry) came hobbling into the room, like a flock of Geese, and having upon search of the body given up this verdict, that the man was dead and murdered by the Plague. Oh, daggers to all their hearts that heard it! Away trudge the wenches, and one of them having had a freckled face all her lifetime was persuaded presently that now they were the tokens and had liked to have turned up her heels upon it. My gorbelly Host, that in many a year could not without grunting crawl over a threshold but two foot broad, leapt half a yard from the corpse (It was measured by a Carpenter's rule) as nimbly as if his guts had been taken out by the hangman. Out of the house, he wallowed presently, being followed with two or three dozen of napkins to dry up the lard that ran so fast down his heels that all the way he went was more greasy than a kitchen-stuff-wife's basket. You would have sworn it had been a barrel of Pitch on fire if you had looked upon him, for such a smoky cloud (by reason of his own fatty hot steam) compassed him round, that but for his voice, he had quite been lost in that stinking mist. Hanged himself, he had, without all question (in this pitiful taking), but that he feared the weight of his intolerable paunch would have burst the Rope, and so he should be put to a double death. At length the Town was raised. The Country came down upon him, and yet not upon him neither, for after they understood the Tragedy, every man gave ground, knowing my pursy Ale-conner could not follow them.

What is to be done in this strange Alarum? The whole Village is in danger to lie at the mercy of God and shall be bound to curse none but him for it. They should do well therefore to set fire on his house before the Plague scape out of it, least it forage higher into the Country and knock them down, man, woman, and child, like Oxen, whose blood (they all swear) shall be required at his hands. At these speeches, my tender-hearted Host fell down on his marybones, meaning indeed to entreat his audience to be good to him, but they, fearing he had been peppered too, as well as the Londoner, tumbled one upon another and were ready to break their necks for haste to be gone. Yet some of them (being more valiant than the rest, because they heard him roar out for some help) very desperately stept back, and with rakes and pitch-forks lifted the gulch from the ground, concluding (after they had laid their hogsheads together, to draw out some wholesome counsel) that whosoever would venture upon the dead man and bury him should have forty shillings (out of the common town-purse, though it would be a great cut to it) with the love of the Churchwardens and Sidesmen, during the term of life. This was proclaimed, but none durst appear to undertake the dreadful execution. They loved money well. Marry, the plague hanging over any man's head that should meddle with it in that sort, they all vowed to die beggars before it should be Chronicled they killed themselves for forty shillings, and in that brave resolution, every one with bag and baggage marcht home, barricading their doors and windows with firbushes, fern, and bundles of straw to keep out the pestilence at the staves end.

At last a Tinker came sounding through the Town, mine Host's house being the ancient watering place where he did use to cast Anchor. You must understand, he was none of those base rascally Tinkers that with a ban-dog and a drab at their tails and a pikestaff on their necks, will take a purse sooner than stop a kettle. No, this was a devout Tinker. He did honor God *Pan*—a Musical Tinker that upon his kettle-drum could play any Country dance you called for, and upon Holidays had earned money by it when no Fiddler could be heard of. He was only feared when he stalkt through some towns where Bees were, for he struck so sweetly on the bottom of his Copper instrument that he would empty whole Hives and lead the swarms after him only by the sound.

This excellent, egregious Tinker calls for his draught (being a double Jug). It was filled for him, but before it came to his nose, the lamentable tale of the Londoner was told, the Chamber-door (where he lay) being thrust open with a long pole (because none durst touch it with their hands) and the Tinker bidden (if he had the heart) to go in and see if he knew him. The Tinker, being not to learn what virtue the medicine had which he held at his lips, poured it down his throat merrily, and crying "trillill," he "fears no plagues," in he stept, tossing the dead body to and fro, and was sorry he knew him not. Mine Host that with grief began to fall away villainously, looking very ruthfully on the Tinker and thinking him a fit instrument to be played upon, offered a crown out of his own purse if he would bury the party. A crown was a shrewd temptation to a Tinker. Many a hole might he stop before he could pick a crown of it, yet being a subtle Tinker (and to make all Sextons pray for him, because he would raise their fees), an Angel he wanted to be his guide, and under ten shillings (by his ten bones) he would not put his finger into the fire. The whole parish had warning of this presently. Thirty shillings was saved by the bargain, and the Town like to be saved too; therefore, ten shillings was levied out of hand, put into a rag, which was tied to the end of a long pole and delivered (in sight of all the Parish, who stood aloof, stopping their noses) by the Headborough's own self in proper person to the Tinker, who with one hand received the money and with the other struck the board, crying "Hey, a fresh double pot," which armor of proof being fitted to his body, up he hoists the Londoner on his back (like a Schoolboy), a Shovel and Pick-axe standing ready for him. And thus furnished, into a field some good distance from the Town, he bears his deadly load, and there throws it down, falling roundly to his tools, upon which the strong beer having set an edge, they quickly cut out a lodging in the earth for the Citizen. But the Tinker, knowing that worms needed no apparel saving only sheets, stript him stark naked, but first dived nimbly into his pocket to see what livings they had, assuring himself that a Londoner would not wander so far without silver. His hopes were of the right stamp, for from out of his pockets he drew a leather bag with seven pounds in it. This music made the Tinker's heart dance. He quickly tumbled his man into the grave, hid him over head and ears in dust, bound up his clothes in a bundle, and carrying that at the end of his staff on his shoulder, with the purse of seven pounds in his hand, back again comes he through the town, crying aloud, "Have ye any more Londoners to bury? Hey down a down derry. Have ye any more Londoners to bury?"—the Hobinolls running away from him, as if he had been the dead Citizen's ghost, and he marching away from them in all the haste he could, with that song still in his mouth.

You see therefore how dreadful a fellow Death is, making fools even of wise men and cowards of the most valiant. Yea, in such a base slavery hath it bound men's senses that they have no power to look higher than their own roofs, but seem by their Turkish and barbarous actions to believe that there is no felicity after this life, and that (like beasts) their souls shall perish with their bodies. How many upon sight only of a Letter (sent from *London*) have started back and durst have laid their salvation upon it that the plague might be folded in that empty paper, believing verily that the arm of Omnipotence could never reach them unless it were with some weapon drawn out of the infected City, in so much that even the Western Pugs[51] receiving money there have tied it in a bag at the end of their barge and so trailed it through the Thames, lest plague-sores sticking upon shillings, they should be nailed up for counterfeits[52] when they were brought home.

More venturous than these block-heads was a certain Justice of peace to whose gate being shut (for you must know that now there is no open house kept), a company of wild fellows being led for robbing an Orchard, the stouthearted Constable rapt most courageously and would have about with none but the Justice himself, who at last appeared in his likeness above at a window, inquiring why they summoned a parley. It was delivered why. The case was opened to his examining wisdom and that the evil doers were onely Londoners. At the name of Londoners, the Justice, clapping his hand on his breast (as who should say, "Lord have mercy upon us"), started back, and being wise enough to save one, held his nose hard between his fore-finger and his thumb, and speaking in that wise (like the fellow that described the villainous motion of *Julius Caesar* and the Duke of *Guise*, who, as he gave it out, fought a combat together)[53] pulling the casement close to him, cried out in that quail-pipe voice, that "if they were Londoners, away with them to *Limbo*, take only their names," they were "sore fellows," and he would "deal with them when time should serve" (meaning, when the plague and they should not be so great together) and so they departed, the very name of Londoners being worse than ten whetstones to sharpen the sword of Justice against them.

I could fill a large volume and call it "the second part of the hundred merry tales" only with such ridiculous stuff as this of the Justice, but *Dii meliora*,[54] I have better matters to set my wits about. Neither shall you wring out of my pen (though you lay it on the rack) the villainies of that damned Keeper who killed all she kept. It had been good to have made her keeper of the common

Jail and the holes of both Counters,[55] for a number lie there that wish to be rid out of this motley world. She would have tickled them and turned them over the thumbs.[56] I will likewise let the Churchwarden in Thames street sleep (for he's now past waking) who being requested by one of his neighbors to suffer his wife or child (that was then dead) to lie in the Churchyard, answered in a mocking sort, he kept that lodging for himself and his household, and within three days after was driven to hide his head in a hole himself. Neither will I speak a word of a poor boy (servant to a Chandler) dwelling thereabouts, who, being struck to the heart by sickness, was first carried away by water to be left anywhere, but landing, being denied by an army of brownbillmen that kept the shore, back again was he brought and left in an out-cellar, where lying, groveling and groaning on his face (amongst fagots but not one of them set on fire to comfort him), there continued all night and died miserably for want of succor. Nor of another poor wretch in the Parish of *Saint Mary Overy,*[57] who being in the morning thrown, as the fashion is, into a grave upon a heap of carcasses that stayed for their complement,[58] was found in the afternoon gasping and gaping for life. But by these tricks, imagining that many a thousand have been turned wrongfully off the ladder of life, and praying that *Derrick* or his executors may live to do those a good turn that have done so to others, *Hic finis Priami,*[59] here's an end of an old Song.

Et iam tempus Equum fumantia solver colla.[60]

Finis.

Notes

Notes to Chapter 1.

1. *Freres Preachers.* Principle part of the Order of Saint Dominic.

2. *even Christian.* Fellow Christian.

3. *or.* Before. (After this note, "or" is retained without a note of explanation.)

4. *speculo historiali.* Mirror of History, part of Vincent's *Speculum Maius* (the Great Mirror), his famous compendium of knowledge.

5. *With Christ . . . sins.* Future editions for Protestant readers replace these words with "and amending their life."

6. *privates.* Secrets; God's hidden or mysterious ways.

7. *De cura februm.* Avicenna, the fourth book of his *Canon,* dedicated to pestilent fevers. All following references to Avicenna are to this source, demonstrating its popularity and the variation in citation formats.

8. *Libro interpretationem.* This is most likely the book of astrology and astronomy by Masha'allah ibn Atharī (in early modern England known as Mashalla, Massahalla, and Messahallek). See Glossary of Names.

9. *fenors.* Later editions record this term as *fevores* (feverous).

10. *Letwares.* Obsolete term. Its context suggests it is the equivalent of a cordial. Also spelled *letwers, letewaris,* and *lectewaris.*

11. *Perial rial.* This is likely pennyroyal, which is a mint plant. See Medical and Herbal Glossary.

Notes to Chapter 2.

1. *hymwarde.* To himself; in this case, to David.

2. *Paralipomenon.* Two books of the Bible containing a summary of sacred history from Adam to the end of the Captivity. The title meaning "things passed over," these books are found in the Vulgate and in Protestant Bibles.

3. *The first and second tomes.* These refer to *Certain sermons, or homilies, appointed by the King's Majestie, to be declared and read, by*

all persons, vicars, or curates, every Sunday in their churches where they have cure (1547) and *The second tome of homilies of such matters as were promised and intitled in the former part of Homilies set out by the authority of the Queen's Majesty, and to be read in every parish church agreebly* (1563).

4. [Marginal note] 2 Paralipomenon 20; Jonas 3.

5. [Marginal note] Gen. 12; Job 36a; Ps. 7, 12, 119; Isa. 26c; Jer. 30b; Job 5c; Tob.3c; 2 Pet. 3b. The letters and all following letters in the biblical references in this document correspond to those in The Great Bible (1539), also found in The Bishop's Bible (1568).

6. [Marginal note] Jer. 20f and 5a.

7. [Marginal note] Isa. 3c; Matt. 24; Mark 13.

8. [Marginal note] Goths.

9. [Marginal note] 2 Paralipomenon 28a; Jer. 2f and 5a; Ezek. 24; Haggai 2; Zeph. 3; Prov. 1d and 29a; Isa. 30c.

10. [Marginal note] Lev. 26f, 30g; Deut. 8b; Ps. 118; Jth. 8d; Job 5c.

11. *roundeth... ears.* To cut off part of the ears of a dog so as to prevent their being torn by the briars and thorns or to prevent disease; here used figuratively.

12. *Lean off.* To cease to lean on.

13. [Marginal note] Tob. 3c.

14. [Marginal note] Hosea 6a; Isa. 29.

15. [Marginal note] Heb. 12b.

16. [Marginal note] Rom. 8g; 1 Cor. 11g.

17. [Marginal note] 3 Kings 8d.

18. [Marginal note] Jer. 28a, 19c, 31d.

19. [Marginal note] Ezek. 18e.

20. [Marginal note] Joel 2c; Ps. 81b.

21. [Marginal note] Jer. 24a, 16a; 1 Cor. 1a; Matt. 11d.

22. [Marginal note] Ps. 4a, 31c, 34a, d, 77a, 86b, 118b, 141a, 143c; Ps. 8a, 116a; 2 Kings 20a.

23. [Marginal note] Eccles. 48d; Jon. 2.

24. [Marginal note] Gen. 21c; 2 Paralipomenon 33c; Dan. 4; Luke 15; Rom. 10.

25. [Marginal note] 1Cor. 11.

26. [Marginal note] Deut. 4e, 30a; Ps. 125d; Isa. 58a; Jer. 29c; Eccles. 2c; Luke 1g.

27. [Marginal note] Ps. 105d; Rom. 5a; 2 Cori. 1b; Jacob 1a; 2 Cor. 4d.

28. [Marginal note] Jacob 4; Job.

29. [Marginal note] Isa. 58d; Dan. 4c.

30. [Marginal note] Job 13c; Deut. 31f; Wis. 16; Rom. 14; John 18d.

Notes to Chapter 3.

1. *Nullus...viderit.* No mortal man ever declares his good fortune before it has rightly come to him.

2. *De Produndis.* Out of the depths. The first words of Psalm 129, used in services for the dead and as part of the Catholic Office of Vespers.

3. *Withie of a Cowtail.* A cow tail made into a noose.

4. *felon, sharp man on my hands.* Fierce and keen.

5. *no man...fell.* No man could master me, even when I was lukewarm (lacking passion, not angry), because I was so fierce.

6. *buke farles.* Packs of bookish debates.

7. *Damask...store.* Gown of rich Damascan fabric still in possession.

8. *Flagon-chain...angels.* A chain-bracelet to which a flask (F. *flacon*) could be attached, here made of or full of angels, or English coins.

9. *Honor...king.* Sirach 38:1. Though not included in the Hebrew Bible after the first century A.D., nor accepted by Protestants, the Book of Sirach has been recognized by the Catholic Church as canonical. It was included in Cranmer's Great Bible, first published in 1539.

10. [Marginal note] Ps. 15.

11. *Qui...deus.* This is Psalm 14:1: The fool hath said in his heart, there is no God.

12. *Quantum...sacer.* Mount Parnassus, mythological home of the muses, had two peaks, one dedicated to Bacchus (Bromio) and one to Apollo (Phoebo). See Lucan's *Pharsalia* 5.71–74.

13. *parvum literatus.* The small intellectual.

14. *Habitare...thing.* The opening line of Vulgate Psalm 132 (in English translation, Psalm 133): Behold, how good and joyful a thing it is: brethren to dwell together in unity.

15. *Sicut...principio.* As it was in the beginning.

16. *Saecula saeculorum.* Forever and ever.

17. *lay a straw.* Pause.

18. *αντιβαλλόμενα. Αντιβαλλό* (antiballo) means to throw away from. *Μενα* (mena) is less clear in this context, but the entire term *αντιβαλλόμενα* is intended to mean roughly, something for something, this for that.

19. *Quid...Intelligis?* Turn the tables, and use your skill to make do. Understand?

20. *Etiam domine.* Yea, Lord. This is John 21:15, the first of Simon Peter's responses to Jesus' thrice repeated question, "Do you love me."

21. *Move...agas.* Whatever you do, do it with prudence.

22. [Marginal note] A black sanctus. [A kind of burlesque hymn.]

23. *Drawn and engrossed his books.* Collected and written out financial portfolio.

24. *Be... banning.* Be that as it may, it is not prohibited.

25. *pad in the straw.* A lurking or hidden danger.

26. *Dives* and *Pauper.* Latin words for rich and poor. See Proverbs 28:6 and *Dives and Pauper* (ca.1405–11), a prose commentary on the ten commandments.

27. [Marginal note] A crafty villain.

28. *Only... stay.* Only to lend her support.

29. [Marginal note] Pettifoggers fit for the pillory. [Hereafter marginal notes will be limited to those that introduce new content, as opposed to those such as this one that announce the same content to be found within the dialogue proper.]

30. *Gospeling Preachers.* Puritan preachers who proselytized in the highly trafficked location of Smithfield.

31. *Roast these fellows.* Roast: a form of torture.

32. *De vera obedientia.* By Stephen Gardinar (c.1493–1555), Bishop of Winchester. Bonner wrote the prologue to it; put to their hands. Make use of their hands.

33. *Prudenter agere.* To act with prudence.

34. *Quasi Leo... devoret.* This is 1 Pet. 5:8: Be sober and watch: for your adversary the devil as a roaring lion walketh about, seeking whom he may devour.

35. *Montpellier.* The Dominican university in Montpellier was famed for its teaching of rhetoric; hence, the terms that follow, although Ambodexter's flawed terminology shows his lack of knowledge in this area.

36. *Rapax, capax, tenax.* Rapacious, capacious, and tenacious.

37. *Surgeon.* Here is a new character, who appears in the 1573 and 1578 editions with the name M. Wise. In those editions, he is given Crispine's next two lines. In this edition he is only mentioned here and is the only character that does not figure in the list at the head of the narrative.

38. *Medium... mundi.* Middle earth, middle world.

39. *Axis coeli.* Axis of the heavens.

40. *Unam aerem... paratos.* This is a restatement of the preceding section, roughly that putrid air and putrid humors from bad food are causes of the fever. [Marginal note] *Hippocrates, De Flatibus; Galen, libri 1, De differentiis Febrium, chapter 5.*

41. *Avicenna... chapter 1.* Avicenna, the fourth tract (or, book) of his *Canon,* dedicated to pestilential fevers, poisons, etc.

42. [Marginal note] *Actius, de remedica, libri 5; Paulus, libri. 2.* [Actius, possibly his *libri medicinales;* Paulus, *The Seven Books of Medicine.*]

43. [Marginal note] *Rasis in libri de pest; Galen, libri 1, De diffentiis Febrium, chapter 4.* [Rasis, perhaps *De variolis et morbillis liber.*]

44. *her poison.* This is a rare, and perhaps unique, personification of the plague as female; plague in almost every other early modern context is personified as male.

45. [Marginal note] *Hippocrates, Aphorisms 19.*

46. *Et communicat multitudine hominem, etc.* And it is imparted by the multitude of people, etc.

47. [Marginal note] *Rufus, avicto fatetur; Actius, chapter 95, libri 5, 8; Paulus Libri.1, chapter 35.*

48. *Libri 3. De presage... almansorem.* Galen, *Presages of the Pulse,* book 3; Rasis, *Ad Almonsorem,* the chapter on the plague.

49. *ex pul. qua propter... erit.* A restatement of the preceding section, roughly that on account of these things there shall be no hope of cure.

50. [Marginal note] Good air. *Galen, de ter. ad Piso, chapter 16* [Galen, *De theriaca ad Pisonem*]; *Paulus, libri 1, chapter 36; Avicenna, de preser. a peste. fen 2, tract 4; Rasis, ad almonsorem, libri de pest., chapter 2.*

51. [Marginal note] Note also that clysters are good, before opening of veins.

52. [Marginal note] *Libri Epid. Sect. 2, Apho. 4.* [Likely a cross-reference to Hippocrates *Epidemia* and *Aphorisms.*]

53. [Marginal note] *Avicenna, Curati. febri Pesti, libri 4, fen 1, tract. 4.*

54. [Marginal note] *Leo. Actus de medend, mor., libri 4.* [Possibly Galen's *Methodus medendi, vel de morbis curandis.*]

55. [Marginal note] *Rufus, contra pest; Avicenna, libri 4, fen. 1, tract 4; Paulus, Libri 2, Chapter 36.*

56. [Marginal note] *Galen, libri 9, de simplic.* [Galen, *de simplic. medic. temper. ac facult.*].

57. [Marginal note] *Fuch. de medendi morbis, libri. 4.* [Perhaps another reference possibly to Galen's *Methodus medendi, vel de morbis curandis.*]

58. [Marginal note] *Avicenna libri 4, fen 1, tract 4; Rasis.*

59. [Marginal note] The best remedy, the worst mean.

60. [Marginal note] *Fuch. libri. 4, de morb.*

61. *the very Dictamnus.* This is an effort to emphasize that one should purchase the leaves from a true (the very) *Dictamus* plant, as opposed to something similar, like *Marrubium pseudodictamnus,* known as *bastard dittany.*

62. *earth of Limodes.* One might consider this a part of a lemon—perhaps the seed or skin, but it may be that what is intended here is *earth of Lemnos* (see *terra sigillata* in Medical and Herbal Glossary), which is more fitting given its context with *Bole Armeniac.*

63. *of Carbo a Cole.* The etymological background of carbuncle, originally "small coal," suggesting it looked fiery red like a hot, small coal.

64. *Book... king.* Rasis, *Ad Almonsorem.*

65. [Marginal note] *Galen attributus alter dimidis.* [The second part attriubuted to Galen.]

66. *crevishels.* Obsolete term, appears in context to be a type of shell.
67. [Marginal note] An epicure's talk.
68. [Marginal note] A nice gentleman.
69. [Marginal note] No wind but it doth turn some men to good.
70. *blue cross.* A cross affixed to homes and shops as a warning that those within have been quarantined.
71. [Marginal note] James 3. [This is a variation on James 4:13–15.]
72. [Marginal note] Eph. 5.
73. [Marginal note] Gen. 22. [See for Jacob and Esau, Gen. 27; for Saul and David 1 Sam. 19; for Elias and Jezebel 1 Kings 19.]
74. *nursed.* Wetnursed.
75. [Marginal note] A wise cockney.
76. *Palm Sunday battle... Warwick.* Also known as the battle of Towton, the single bloodiest battle in the War of the Roses, this was not in fact the place where Warwick (Richard Neville, Earl of Warwick [1428–71]) died, but rather where he won a decisive victory for Edward IV. This error points up Roger's consistent misreading of texts.
77. *Upon our Saint George's.* On the feast day of Saint George.
78. *fair... fain.* Proverbial, flattery makes fools glad.
79. [Marginal note] Merry when friends do meet.
80. *quarterstaff... bless-beggar.* A pole serving as a weapon that he calls, in jest, a thing with which to bless a beggar.
81. *Foolosophers' stone.* A play on the philosophers' stone, a mythical panacea able also to turn any metal to gold.
82. *Latro.* Highwayman or robber.
83. [Marginal note] What wisemen should do to preserve health.
84. *Roger.* In the 1564 edition this reads Uxor, but *Uxor*'s line is amended to *Roger* in all future editions.
85. *cast of legerdemain.* Slight of hand.
86. *bottles.* Bundles.
87. *O mulier... calamitas.* Roughly, "Oh woman, she has dared [to commit] every [evil deed], but nothing is worse nor ever will be than a woman among the calamities of men."
88. [Marginal note] The Lord Crumwell, a play on Thomas Cromwell.
89. *Mourn of the chine.* A horse disease; figuratively, to be sullen.
90. [Marginal note] Children sick of the mother: remedy is the gallows.
91. *person.* A man of high rank or distinction.
92. [Marginal note] One pure well giveth but clean water.
93. [Marginal note] Note also that virtue and gentleness maketh a gentleman. Even so, ancient blood wrapped in vice is but gross gentleness.
94. *the great Uncle.* Satan.
95. *store.* Stock.
96. [Marginal note] Ludgate.
97. [Marginal note] A lesson for a lubber. [See Prov. 6:6–8.]

98. [Marginal note] Well fished.

99. *Trenchmore* and *Hey de Gie*. Country dances considered wild, as opposed to restrained or mannered, and having an Irish origin.

100. [Marginal note] Well taken.

101. [Marginal note] A good wife.

102. [Marginal note] A ruffian.

103. *The black ox... day.* Mendax combines two proverbs: to have the black ox trod on your foot is to know sorrow, so the combination means essentially, I have not known sorrow, but I will one day.

104. [Marginal note] Irony.

105. *Porto Santo... Ferro, etc.* All but Eractelentiae and Magnefortis are identifiable islands of Portugal or of the Canaries, and they may be variations of early names for the other islands of the Canaries, part of what Mendax calls Fortunata, the Fortunate Isles of Greek mythology.

106. [Marginal note] No lie, no lie.

107. *Scorea.* This may be Socotra, an island off the tip of Somalia, which Marco Polo named as being just north of Madagascar. See also the following note that supports Bullein's knowledge of Polo's account.

108. *Maabar.* An Indian province so named in Marco Polo's *Travels.*

109. *Isle... land.* The lands of Marco Polo's "Great Khan"; Mongolia. The "Isle of *Ruc*" is more difficult to trace, "Ruc" in Polo appearing only as the name for a large, Griffin-like bird that Polo sees on Madagascar.

110. [Marginal note] The best meat and the worst meat.

111. *tick tack, Irish on the tables.* Board games like backgammon.

112. [Marginal note] A great loss, it have undone all England.

113. *Non finis... vidi.* Words are not enough to describe everything that is in detail: rivers and caves, sea or open space, woods and ponds and hills and sunshine.

114. *venture the best joint.* Take a great risk.

115. [Marginal note] Pirates, heirs of Wapping for their snapping. [*Wapping.* Where pirates were hung; *snapping.* The share of stolen goods.]

116. [Marginal note] Well rid of evil store.

117. [Marginal note] Witchcraft.

118. *Saint George to borrow.* A prayer: Saint George, be our pledge or security.

119. *En adsum... rearum.* Death is the limit of everything.

120. [Marginal note] A friend at need.

121. *Deprivation in materia.* Material deprivation, one of four causes of plague Mors says are false.

122. *by setting... Death.* By flight.

123. [Marginal note] Ezek. 9; Job 14.

124. [Marginal note] Ps. 138.

125. [Marginal note] 2 Cor. 15; Ps. 51 and 119.

126. [Marginal note] The best way.

127. [Marginal note] Past remedy.
128. [Marginal note] A wiseman.
129. [Marginal note] Tob. 12.
130. *places.* Passages.
131. [Marginal note] Matt. 10.
132. [Marginal note] Ps. 90; John 11; Rom. 8.
133. [Marginal note] Matt. 10; Luke 15.
134. [Marginal note] 1 Cor. 13; Ps. 14; Ps. 4.
135. [Marginal note] Ps. 2.
136. [Marginal note] 2 Cor. 15.
137. [Marginal note] Matt. 27.
138. [Marginal note] Matt. 13; Isa. 58; Dan. 12; Matt. 25; Job 14.
139. [Marginal note] An exhortation to death.
140. *Who... death.* This is Ps. 89:48.
141. *This... lived.* See Aelian's *Various History,* book 3, chapter 2.
142. [Marginal note] 2 Macc. 7.
143. [Marginal note] *De vani. huius mundi* [the vanity of this world]. The greatest of the dead.
144. [Maringal note] Spend all succeeding Gathrall. (This is a reference to Roger's recitation of the usurer's epitaph. See p. 122.)
145. [Marginal note] A prayer in trouble or death.
146. [Marginal note] Heb. 11; The best medicine.
147. [Marginal note] A blessed end.
148. [Marginal note] A prayer in the time of death.
149. [Marginal note] Through the holy Trinity is creation and salvation.
150. [Marginal note] A prayer.
151. [Marginal note] Vanity, plain vanity in this world.
152. *How can... worm.* This is a variation on Job 25.
153. [Marginal note] Gen. 2; Wisd. 10.
154. [Marginal note] Tob. 13; Matt. 25.
155. [Marginal note] Job 14.
156. [Marginal note] Lam. 4; Matt. 18; Luke 19.
157. [Marginal note] Eccles. 11.
158. [Marginal note Luke 12; Matt. 5.
159. [Marginal note] God's messenger. Mal. 1; John 10.
160. [Marginal note] Augustine, *De natura et origine animae,* chapter 43, etc.
161. [Marginal note] Ps. 124.
162. *Anima cum ratione sua.* The soul with its reason. See chapter 11 of *The Second Helvetica Confession* (the second of two documents codifying the beliefs of the Reformation church in Switzerland).
163. [Marginal note] Matt. 12.
164. [Marginal note] Matt. 15; James 5.
165. *Inter mortals... fratrem.* Among mortals none are more beloved to me than you; you are more, who in truth value and love are as a brother.

166. The following letter to Richard Turner was translated by Teresa Hooper with guidance from Maura K. Lafferty and final editing by Rebecca Totaro.

William Bullein sends many greetings to his most worshipful brother in Christ, the Master of Divinity Richard Turner.

Most reverend and respected brother, I suppose that you have received my letter in which I wrote a regimen for you against the plague [*pestem*], and for that reason I will not be overly wordy about the pestilential fever [*febre pestilenti*]. For every fever which we call "pestilental" [*pestilentem*] proceeds from the kind of putrefaction which occurs from excess moisture. In fact, it should be acknowledged that this fever, as Galen says, doubtlessly proceeds from the rotting of overabundant moisture rather than by an increase of heat. The humidity arises from material festering in the veins, from which heat naturally arises greatly and, within the space of a day, all bodily powers fail, the urine is malodorous, and so forth. Galen, Avicenna, Rasis, Trallianus, and the rest affirm that there are a great number of obstructions in a pestilential fever, especially when that material pushes into the skin and head. The large amount of both this material and undigested food is responsible.

The remedy is to curb this putrefaction. Obstructions must therefore be unblocked. But if [the obstruction] goes away on its own, then nothing should be done. Moreover, here is a remedy, as the Veronese Johannes Baptista Montanus says: prescription: 1/2 ounce chicory and rhubarb syrup; 3 ounces borage-water, acidified; let a citron be placed and cooked down in this. Next, a chest ointment against the plague: prescription: 1 ounce Mesua's strengthening rose-salve; 1 ounce cordial spices; 1 scruple white sandalwood; 1/2 ounces dried roses. Mix this together carefully and use it as a liniment for the heart and for the entire abdomen. This is a remarkable remedy against the poison of the plague.

In regards to restriction of nourishment, in cases where the putrefaction is greatest (as Hippocrates, *Aphorisms* 17 says), where the humors are corrupt and putrid, nothing is more ruinous than to administer a thin diet, because you should consider chicken broth and always put it in your food along with acidic citron juice. Concerning the rest, I would urge you to do as you have read in Galen and the others. Farewell and farewell again, most learned sir, and may you be in good spirits. I am drawing this letter to a close, for I have no need to write much more, lest I hinder inconveniently your greatest more important efforts in the vineyard of the Lord.

March, in the 1564th year of the Incarnation

Yours in all things, William Bullein

167. [Marginal note] *Causa pestis. Signa pestis.* Causes of plague. Signs of plague.

168. [Marginal note] *Curatio in quam considerandum.* The cure to be considered closely.

169. *Rx*. Recipe.

170. ℥ 1 ß = One ounce, halved. ℥ = Ounce; ß = half.

171. *unguenti... mesues*. An ointment of roses and lard, the name referring to medieval medical authority Mesua (Yahya ibn Masawaihi). This ointment appears in Thomas Gale's book.

172. ℈ = Scruple.

173. [Marginal note] *Dieta in temporac pestis*. Diet in time of plague.

174. This letter to Thomas Gale was translated by Teresa Hooper with guidance from Maura K. Lafferty and final editing by Rebecca Totaro.

William Bullein sends many greetings to the most beloved and respectable Sir, Master Thomas Gale, surgeon.

Most noble Sir, I pray to God, most powerful and great, for your health both in body and spirit. There is nothing in this time which I will write to you other than that I have read and reread the book which you have given me, for which I thank you, and I shall regard it as the greatest possible gift. For I have also understood from this the love and feeling you have for me, and I have judged that your work will be useful to not only to myself but to all English people everywhere. In fact, all of us can be regarded as lovers and supporters of your most distinguished book. For this reason, how could this gift be more gratifying to me, especially since it was given to me by so great a surgeon? I will never forget this matter, but as much as I can, let me show my gratitude with a willing spirit. Farewell to you sir, and in the meantime I bid you farewell, and I commend myself to you; I wish that you [also] give my thanks to that most learned man, Master Baxter, in my words and wish to commend myself greatly [to him.]

March 28th, in the 1564th year of the Incarnation
Your most obedient servant,
William Bullein

175. *Bactero*. Translated as Baxter. Unidentified individual.

176. The folio numbers here are those listed in the original text. Alteration was made only when it was difficult to make out the number, and then the corresponding page was located and its folio number recorded. In general, this index is a useful overview of predominant issues and themes within the dialogue, identified for the use of its original readers.

Notes to Chapter 4.

1. [Marginal note] Preservatives.

2. *Arras root*. Unidentified. This may be a root from Arras, capital of Artois in the French Netherlands, or it may be a more common root with a variant spelling.

3. [Marginal note] Curatives.

Notes to Chapter 5.

1. *Andrew Eastcheap.* This is another name for Saint Andrew Hubbard, in Eastcheap.
2. *Anne at Aldersgate.* This is another name for Saint Ann in the Willows as well as for the Saint Ann and Saint Agnes Church.
3. *Antholin at Budge Row.* This is now called Saint Anthony's.
4. *Benet Paul's Wharf.* This is another name for Benet Woodwhorf.
5. *George by Pudding Lane.* This is another name for Saint George Botolph Lane and Saint George Eastcheap.
6. *Mary Botolph.* This is another name for Saint Mary Bothaw.
7. *Michael in the Royal.* This is another name for Saint Michael Paternoster Royal.
8. *Nicholas Golden Abbey.* This is another name for what was also called Nicholas Cole Abbey or Nicholas Cold Abbey.
9. *Nicholas Willows.* This is perhaps Saint Nicholas Olave.
10. *Peter in Cheap.* This is another name for Saint Peter Woodstreet.

Notes to Chapter 6.

1. *French Post.* A person who travels express with letters to or from France.
2. *Amphitruo.* A mythological burlesque written by Plautus (254–184 BC).
3. *Hinc... Dolor!* Here is shame, or rather, here is suffering!
4. *Nam... ampliüs.* For of such a kind, these great ones are nowhere.
5. *like... away.* It has been related that dogs drink at the river Nile running along, that they may not be seized by the crocodiles (one of Aesop's fables).
6. *Banks his Curtal.* Reference to a famous performing horse of London, owned by Banks and possibly also mentioned by Shakespeare in *Loves Labor's Lost* act 1, scene 2.
7. *Goths and Geats.* Tribes posing a threat to Rome but here used generally as synonyms for barbarians.
8. *Haec... facis.* These are bad, but the verses that you write are no better.
9. [Marginal note] Upon the 23 of March the Spring begins by reason of the Sun's entrance into Aries. [*And instead... rays.* At this wedding celebration, the doubly gilded horns of the sun in Aries replace the traditional gilded rosemary sprigs as gifts, marking the beginning of spring.]
10. *Not... Arms.* Because of his injury, physically unable to show his heraldic armor that distinguishes him as a gentleman.
11. *Signior Soldado.* This refers to the soldier Dekker describes above.

12. All verse in *The Wonderful Year* is italicized the original. I have dropped the italics for all verse in order to call attention to the words within the verse that are set in regular typeface amidst the italicization; in this case those emphasized words appear in italics.

13. *make legs.* To bow.

14. *Rank... dams.* Misers scurry on bent legs to save their hoards.

15. *Born upon... departed from it.* She was born on the eve of the Nativity of the Virgin and died on the eve of the Annunciation. The mayors mentioned are Sir Thomas Leigh (1558–59) and Robert Lee (1602–03).

16. *Sibil's... annus.* A prophecy made in 1475 by Regionmontanus (German astronomer and mathematician Johann Müller [1436–76]), predicting that 1588 would be a bad year, full of disasters for the entire world.

17. *Armado.* An alternative spelling for Armada, a fleet of ships of war, in this case referring to the Spanish Armada, which threatened England and was defeated in 1588.

18. *some English great ones.* Perhaps Sir Walter Raleigh, Lord Grey of Wilton, and Henry Brooke, Lord Cobham who were imprisoned for involvement in a plot to remove King James I and VI from power and, with Spain's aid, replace him with Arabella Stuart.

19. *Stow's... Holinshed.* John Stow published abridged versions (released in *octavo* and *decimo sexto* formats of the much larger and more expensive *folio* editions of Raphael Holinshed's *Chronicles* of England, Scotland, and Ireland (1577, 1587).

20. *Set-card.* This is likely a sea-card. See *sea-card* in the General Glossary.

21. *Pro Troia stabat Apollo.* "Apollo stood for Troy," proverbial from Ovid's *Tristia*: "Mulciber in Troiam, pro Troia stabat Apollo" (1.2).

22. *Vintners... before.* Wine sellers stopped advertising with their usual flags and bushes and instead put out Jew bushes, known for their purgative quality; this said for humor.

23. *Lincoln... shall be.* Proverbial: Lincoln was the best city, London is, and York shall be.

24. *Theobalds.* The home of the Cecils in Hertfordshire.

25. *Hinc illae lachrimae.* A quotation from *The Lady of Andros* by Roman playwright Terence, literally meaning "hence those tears."

26. [Marginal note] Anthropophagi are Scythians that feed on men's flesh.

27. *Saint Giles, Saint Sepulchres, and Saint Olaves.* Churches of London. Saint Giles is patron saint of cripples; hence "limping."

28. *Jehochanan, Simeon,* and *Eleazar.* See 2 Chron. 23; Luke 2; and Exod. 3; Numb. 19–20.

29. *those molecatchers.* The three bald sextons; commonly, people employed to catch moles, also used as a slang term for a lecher, as "mole" was a slang word for vagina.

30. *Disarmed, I say... Iron.* Plague disarmed the city, with evidence being that no one displayed or carried swords, and this suggested that the plague was like the ostrich of fables, able to eat iron.

31. *Decidis in Scyllam.* You fall upon Scylla (in trying to avoid Charybdis).

32. *at eighteen and twenty score.* At 18 and 20 times 20 paces; far from home.

33. *Birchin Lane... Clown-ships.* A London street known for its second-hand clothing shops. The joke is that this is where some bought metaphorical "clown-suits" or clothing above their status to impress others.

34. *For those... ghost.* Each of these scenarios illustrates the fear that the country dwellers (here called pagans and plough-drivers, some of whom live in market towns and not cities) have of all Londoners, with their many tells, like the flat-cap or treble-ruff. Ironically with hindsight, a crow from London is said to be feared worse than threat of a fire.

35. *Sir Giles Goosecap.* A simpleton; *Sir Giles Goosecap* was the name of a farcical play popular at the time (entered into the Stationer's Register in 1606).

36. *band.* Form a company; unite.

37. *The greatest... walk.* The greatest tailor or person concerned with clothes who shows off his fashions by strutting down the middle aisle of St. Paul's.

38. *Mandrittas, Imbroccatas, Stramazons,* and *Stoccados.* Fencing moves.

39. *seven Electors.* After a series of continuing conflicts with the papacy over the choice of emperor, the imperial electors decided in 1338 that henceforth, the candidate receiving the majority of votes would be king of the Germans. The king would also automatically become the Holy Roman emperor without being crowned by the pope. This continued until 1438.

40. *than a beggar... terms.* Than a beggar makes during the three active sessions of court, when he may face prosecution; many.

41. *Lares.* The guiding spirits of the house; here also a play on the alcoholic spirits in the tippling house, where such beverages are sold.

42. *but.* If.

43. *frigida zona.* Each of the two regions of the globe which lie within the north and south polar circles respectively. Here used metaphorically to mean parts of England that were inhospitable to Londoners.

44. *Actaeon.* The mythological hunter turned into a stag by Diana, with a play upon his becoming "horned," a sign of being cuckolded.

45. *tickled under the gills.* Proverbial: a trout being thus tickled became docile and easy to catch.

46. *turn...patches.* Change your ways, no longer working as a tailor or suffering fools.

47. *Study...Hieronimo.* This is a reference to Balthazar, a character in Thomas Kid's revenge play *Spanish Tragedy,* whose son is murdered.

48. *to Helen's teeth.* A playful version of "to the teeth"; so as to be utterly committed. This extends the comparison between Menelaus and the Cobbler, Paris and the Lord, and Helen and the Cobbler's wife.

49. *when...Boulogne.* King Henry VIII took this French town in 1544.

50. *Struck...hoops.* Drunk after two rounds.

51. *Western pugs.* Men who navigated barges down the Thames to London.

52. *nailed...counterfeits.* Referring to the ale-house practice of nailing counterfeit bills up on the walls.

53. *like that...together.* Sources suggest that the "motion" here is a reference to a popular puppet show called Julius Caesar. In Christopher Marlowe's play *Massacre at Paris* (c.1590), the Duke of Guise (Henry I, Prince of Joinville, Duke of Guise [1550–58]) compares himself to Caesar as he is murdered.

54. *Dii meliora.* The gods forbid.

55. *holes of both Counters.* The worst of cells in the debtors' prisons.

56. *Turn...thumbs.* To get or have under one's control.

57. *Saint Mary Overy.* A church in Southwark near the cathedral of St. Saviour.

58. *Stayed...complement.* To be compelled to wait for their full number.

59. *Hic finis Priami.* Literally, "Here is the end of Priam" from Virgil's *Aeneid* (2.554), a statement on the abrupt end to human greatness in the death of the beloved king Priam.

60. *Et...colla.* But we have covered an enormous distance and it is now time to loose the smoking necks of the horses from the yoke.

Medical and Herbal Glossary

acanthus. A genus of herbaceous, spiny-leaved Mediterranean plants with hooded purple and white flowers.

agallicum. An odoriferous Indian and Arabian wood. Also called *agallochum* and *agalloch.*

ague. An acute or violent fever.

aleberry. Ale boiled with spice and sugar and sops of bread.

alembic. A gourd-shaped distilling apparatus with a head or cap and a beak to remove condensed liquid.

aloe. A genus of succulent plants with fleshy leaves and tubular, clustered, yellow or red flowers. Also, the juice of this herb. Distinct from *lignum aloes.*

alum. A whitish transparent mineral salt used in dying, tanning, and medicine.

amber. Yellowish translucent fossil resin, burns with an agreeable odor.

ammoniac. A salt and a gum, both obtained from the Libyan region of Ammonia near the shrine of Jupiter Ammon. Also a corrupted form of armeniac, as in *bole armeniac.*

ana. Each an amount of the same.

angelica. *Angelica archangelica:* a common perennial herb with large compound umbels of white or greenish-white flowers.

anthrax. A *carbuncle.*

apostemation. The formation of an abscess or tumor; festering.

aqua caelestis. "Celestial water": rectified alcohol.

aqua vitae. An inflammable, combustible, potable liquid; unrectified alcohol, such as brandy.

aristolochia. One of many a tuberous perennial herbs in the *Aristolochia* genus, the most common being *A. rotunda* and *A. longa.*

ash. *Franxinus excelsior:* a well-known forest tree noted for its silver bark, winged seeds, and close-grained wood.

aurum potable. Drinkable gold: gold held in a state of minute subdivision in some volatile oil; used as a cordial.

balm. An aromatic ointment, often that exuded from trees of the genus *Balsamodendron.*

barberry. *Berberis vulgaris:* a shrub with spiny shoots, small yellow flowers, oblong, red, acidic berries.
barley. *Hordeum vulgare:* a common grain.
basilica. The large vein of the arm from the elbow to armpit; *basilic* means royal, indicating the importance of this vein.
bay. *Laurus nobilis:* the bay laurel, a tree with dark green leaves and a profusion of dark purple berries.
bayberries. The fruit of the *bay* tree.
benedicta laxativa. A mild laxative medicine.
benjamin. Popular name for gum benzoin, the fragrant resin of the tree, *Styrax benzoin.*
betony. *Stachys betonica:* a plant with spiked purple flowers and egg-shaped, scalloped leaves.
bile. See *boil.* Also, a substance secreted by the liver, associated with ill temper.
bitumen. A kind of mineral pitch.
blain. An inflammatory swelling or sore on the surface of the body.
boil. A hard, inflamed, suppurating tumor.
bole armeniac. A soft friable fatty earth of a pale red color, native to Armenia and used as an astringent. See also *ammoniac.*
bole oriental. An earthy red clay from the orient.
borage. *Borago officinalis:* a plant with bright blue flowers, the stem and leaves covered with prickly hairs.
botch. Bubo, a swollen lymph node in the armpit, neck, or groin; the defining symptom of bubonic plague.
bought. Bend or curve; esp. a hollow angle or bend in the animal body.
bray. To beat small.
bruise. To beat small, pound, or crush.
bugloss. A name applied to several boraginaceous plants, closely related to *borage;* family *Boraginaeae.*
buphthalmos. See *cotula foetida.*
bur. Any rough or prickly seed-vessel or flower-head of a plant.
bushel. A measure of capacity used for corn, fruit, etc., containing four pecks or eight gallons.
butterbur. *Petasites vulgaris:* a plant with large soft leaves, growing in wet land. Also called pestilent wort.
calamint. A genus of aromatic herbs, *Calamintha* (family *Labiatæ*), including the Common Calamint (*C. officinalis*).
camomile. *Anthemis nobilis:* an aromatic creeping herb, with downy leaves and flowers with white rays and yellow disks.
camphor. A whitish crystalline volatile substance issued from camphor-producing trees. Also the tree that yields it (*Cinnamomum camphora, Dryobalanops camphora,* etc.).
canel. Cinnamon; perhaps including the similar but inferior Cassia bark.

capon. A castrated cock.

carbuncle. A blackish pustule, a telling symptom of plague that forms at the site of a flea-bite. It differs from a boil in having no central core. Also called an anthrax.

cardiacle. A vein associated with the heart; often the median vein in the arm.

caudle. A warm drink consisting of thin gruel mixed with wine or ale, sweetened and spiced.

celandine. Two yellow-flowered plants: the common or greater (*Chelidonium majus*) and the small or lesser (*Ranunculus ficaria*).

cephalica. The common carotid artery on either side of the neck.

cerate. A kind of stiff ointment composed of wax together with lard or oil and other ingredients.

ceruse. A name for white lead, a mixture or compound of carbonate and hydrate of lead.

chafin dish. A vessel to hold burning charcoal or other fuel.

chalcanthum. An old name for blue vitriol (sulphate of copper).

choleric. A body full of choler (yellow bile), associated with a hot, angry disposition.

cicatrix. The scar or seam remaining after a wound, sore, or ulcer is healed.

cinnamon. Dried and rolled bark from the east Indian tree *Cinnamomum zeylanicum.*

clyster. A medicine injected into the rectum to empty the bowels.

cold seeds. Seeds of cucumber, melons, goards.

coleworts. Originally, a general name for any plant of the cabbage kind, genus *Brassica.*

comfrey. *Symphytum officinale:* a tall common plant with rough leaves and drooping clusters of yellowish or reddish bell-shaped flowers.

complexion. The combination of the four humors of the body in a certain proportion. Also called temperament. See *humors.*

confection. A sweetened medicinal compound. Also called an *electuary.*

confection of Hamech. A mixture of herbs made into a paste.

conserve. A preserving agent.

cordial. A medicine to comfort or invigorate the heart.

corn. Grain or kernel.

costive. Constipated.

cotula foetida. *Anthemis cotula* of the family Compositæ, allied to *camomile* and in appearance to the daisy with white petals and yellow disc. Also called ox-eye and buphthalmos.

crown. A silver coin the value of five shillings, the equivalent of 48 pence or 1/4 pound.

cubeb. The berry of a climbing shrub of the Javanese islands, *Piper cubeba* or *Cubeba officinalis.*

danewort. *Sambucus ebulus:* resembles the elder, with white flowers and soft, white internal fiber.

darnel. *Lolium temulentum:* a deleterious grass, which in some countries grows as a weed among corn.

delayed. Diluted.

diacatholicon. A laxative electuary, its name suggesting its purpose as a universal remedy.

diachylon. A kind of ointment composed of vegetable juices.

diacodium. A syrup prepared from poppy-heads.

diatessaron (adj.). Through or composed of four.

dictamnus. One of the perennial herbs of the genus *Dictamnus,* especially *Dictamnus albus* (known as white dittany) or the shrub *Origanum dictamnus* (dittany of Crete).

dittany. See *dictamnus.*

dolor. Physical suffering.

dragons. *Dracunculus vulgaris:* a perrenial plant with a distinctive purple-black spike enfolded in a similarly colored sheathing leaf.

dragonwater. A medicinal preparation, possibly consisting of water infused with dragons.

dram. A weight named after the ancient Greek drachma. In Apothecaries' weight, a weight of 60 grains or 1/8 of an ounce. Abbreviated *d.* and roughly the weight of one British penny. The penny is also abbreviated *d.*, making for their comfortable interchange when determining approximate weights.

electuary. A medicinal conserve or paste, consisting of a powder or other ingredient mixed with honey, preserve, or syrup of some kind.

elixir. A preparation by the use of which it was sought to change metals into gold.

endive. *Cichorium endivia:* a leaf vegetable belonging to the daisy family.

enula campana. *Inula helenium:* a perennial composite plant with very large yellow radiate flowers and bitter aromatic leaves and root.

feverfew. *Pyrethrum parthenium:* a perennial herbaceous plant also called Wild Camomile for its resemblance to *camomile.*

fennel. *Foeniculum vulgare:* a fragrant perennial umbellifer with yellow flowers.

flux. A morbid bodily discharge; an early name for dysentery.

frankincense. An aromatic gum resin yielded by trees of the genus *Boswellia,* or a resin resembling this.

French crown. The English name for the French coin called *edu,* commonly regarded as equivalent to the English *crown.*

frontary. A medicine applied to the forehead.

fume. Vapor or steam given out by bodies and substances when heated.

fumosity. See fume.

fundament. The excretory opening or anus.

galbanum. A gum resin obtained from certain Persian species of *Ferula.*

gall. An excrescence produced on trees, especially the oak, by the action of insects. Also, the secretion of the liver, bile.

Gallia muscata. French wine made from muscat or similar grapes.

gentian. A genus of flowering plants often with leaves in rosette and trumpet-shaped flowers.

God's marks. *A botch or carbuncle.* Also called tokens.

gout. A disease occurring in episodes of increased acuteness, characterized by painful inflammation of the joints and organs.

groat. A coin equal to four pence in value and in weight, or 1/8 of an ounce of silver.

grain. The smallest British weight equivalent to 1/24 *pennyweight.*

guaiacum. A genus of trees and shrubs native to the West Indies and South America. Also called *lignum sanctum.*

gum. A viscid secretion of certain trees and shrubs, which hardens but is soluble in water.

hart's horn. The horn or antler of a male deer.

hepatica. Early spring-flowering plant, the three-lobed leaves of which were thought to resemble the liver.

herb of grace. See *rue.*

hops. *Humulus lupulus.* A climbing perennial plant with rough lobed leaves shaped like those of the vine.

houseleek. *Sempervivum tectorum:* a succulent herb with pink flowers and thick stem and leaves that form a dense rosette near the root.

humors. Four chief bodily fluids body (blood, phlegm, yellow bile or choler, and black bile or black choler), often associated with personality types: *sanguine, phlegmatic, choleric,* and *melancholic.*

hyssop. A small bushy aromatic herb of the genus *Hyssopus.*

ignem persicum. Fire peach.

jecorary. Associated with the liver; hepatic.

Jew bush. A plant known for its milky juice and quality as a purgative, genus *Pedilanthus.*

julep. A medicated, sweetened drink used as a comforting, or gently stimulating mixture.

juniper. *Juniperus communis:* a hardy spreading shrub or low tree with prickly leaves and bluish-black berries, yielding a volatile oil.

ladanum. A gum resin which exudes from *Cistus incanus creticus.*

laurel. See bay.

laserpitium. *Laserpitium latifolium:* an umbelliferous, white-flowered plant from which the gum resin, laser, comes.

lavender. *Lavandula vera:* a small shrub with small pale lilac-colored flowers, and narrow oblong leaves.

leprous. Afflicted with or causing leprosy, depending on the context.

lignum aloes. The resinous wood of *Aquilaria agallocha,* a large Malaysian tree. Also called wood aloes. Distinct from the *aloe.*

limond. Lemon.

linseed. The seed of flax (*Linum usitatissimum*), well known as the source of linseed oil.

lint. A soft material for dressing wounds, prepared by scraping linen cloth.

lipothymion. Fainting.

litharge of gold. Litharge when colored red by mixture of red lead.

litharge of silver. *A* by-product in the separation of silver from lead.

lovage. *Levisticum officinale:* a flowering herb resembling the *angelica* and daisy.

lozenge. A small flavored cake or tablet to be held and dissolved in the mouth.

maces. An aromatic spice consisting of the fleshy covering surrounding the seed in the fruit of the nutmeg tree, *Myristica fragrans.*

malleola. Of or pertaining to the malleolus; in the region of the malleoli, the ankle joint.

mallow. *Malva sylvestris:* common plant with purple flowers found in waste areas.

mandrake. *Mandragora officinaru:* a poisonous, narcotic Mediterranean plant reputed to shriek and cause death to those who uproot it.

manus Christi. A kind of restorative confection or cordial drink.

marigold. A plant of the genus *Calendula* with golden or bright yellow flowers.

mastic. An aromatic gum or resin which exudes from the bark of the mastic tree, *Pistacia lentiscus.*

mediana. A vein occupying a middle or midline position, specifically in the forearm.

melancholic. A body full of black bile, associated with a brooding, unsociable disposition.

mithridatum. Any of various medicinal preparations, usually electuaries compounded of many ingredients.

morsus diaboli. *Scabiosa succisa:* a common meadow plant with blue flowers, it gets its name from a legend that the devil bit out of anger at its usefulness as a medicine to humans.

myrrh. A bitter, aromatic gum resin from various Arabian and African trees (genus *Commiphora*), especially. *C. abyssinica* and *C. myrrha.*

nux vomica. The highly poisonous seeds of a the South Asian tree *Strychnos nux-vomica.*

oil de bay. Oil of bay (obtained from the *bay laurel*). See *bay.*

olibanum. See *frankincense.*

ox-eye. See *cotula foetida.* Also called *buphthalmos.*

peck. A unit of capacity for dry goods equal to a quarter of a *bushel.*

pence. Plural for *penny.*

penny. The smallest form of British coin used also as a weight in recipes and abbreviated *d.* for *denarius,* the Greek coin considered to be roughly of the same weight both of the penny and of the drachma, the basis for the dram. See *pennyweight* and *dram.*

pennyroyal. *Mentha pulegium:* a small-leaved, creeping mint.

pennyweight. A unit of weight equal to 24 grains (1/20 troy ounce), and formerly to 1/240 Tower pound, i.e. 22 1/2 grains, which was the actual weight of a silver penny. Abbreviated *dwt* because the British penny is abbreviated *d.* and weight is *wt.*

pestilent wort. See *butterbur.*

petimorel. Any of several kinds of nightshade with black or deep purple berries; the fruit of the plant.

phlebotomer. One who performs bloodletting or ventosing.

phlegmatic. A body full of phlegm, associated with a sluggish, apathetic disposition.

pills of Rufus. A combination of aloes and myrrh, as stimulant cathartic in debility and constipation.

pimpernel. Any of several flowering herbaceous plants with opposing, feather-shaped leaves, of the genus *Pimpinella.*

pinder's ale. Pinders were employed to impound stray animals, a base job, and likely a base ale.

pith. The soft internal tissue of a plant part.

plaster. A solid medicinal or emollient substance spread on a bandage and applied to the skin to speed healing.

pomander. A mixture of aromatic substances, usually made into a ball, and carried in a small box or bag.

posset ale. A drink made from hot milk curdled with ale, flavored with sugar, spices, etc.

pottage. A thick soup or stew.

poultice. A moist, heated substance with a soft, pasty consistency, applied to a bandage to speed healing.

purgative. Causing evacuation of the bowels; cathartic.

purple. A purple or livid spot, botch, or pustule; another name for the bubo of the plague. See *botch.*

purslane. *Portulaca oleracea:* a low, succulent garden herb.

push. Pustule; boil.

quince. The hard, acid, yellowish, pear-shaped fruit of a small tree (*Pyrus cydonia,* now called *Cydonia oblanga*) belonging to the pear family.

receipt. A recipe or statement of the ingredients and mode of procedure for cookery or medicine.

red sanders. Wood of the east Indian tree red sandalwood, *Pterocarpus santalinus.*

resin. An organic substance formed by secretion in special canals in almost all trees and plants.

rock alum. See *alum.*

rosemary. *Rosmarinus officinalis:* an evergreen shrub with spiny, fragrant leaves.

rosewater. Water distilled from roses.
rue. *Ruta graveolens:* a perennial evergreen shrub having bitter, strong-scented leaves; also called *herb of grace.*
sallow. One of many species of willow, of the genus *Salix.*
saffron. *Crocus sativus:* a flowering plant of the iris family with purple flowers and orange stigmas.
sage. *Salvia officinalis:* a small evergreen shrub with woody stems, grayish leaves, and blue to purplish flowers.
sallatte. Salad; a dish of cold herbs or vegetables.
salve. An ointment for healing, applied to open wounds and sores.
Sandalorum alborum. White sandalwood. See *sanders.*
sanders. Fragrant woods and their essential oils, mostly derived from trees of the *Santalaceae* family. Also called *sandalwood.*
sanguine. A body full of blood, associated with a courageous, hopeful, or amorous disposition.
saphena. The name of two veins in the leg, the internal and the external.
savor. Taste; usually related to a quality, as sweetness, bitterness, etc. Sometimes includes the odor that influences taste.
scabious. Herbaceous plants, genus *Scabiosa,* with many small flowers of lavender blue, lilac or creamy white in a single head on a tall stalk.
scruple. A unit of weight equal to 20 grains (1.295 grams), 1/3 of a dram, 1/24 ounce, apothecaries' weight. Abbreviated *s.*
searsed. Sifted.
second bread. A bread made from flour that is less refined.
sengrene. See *houseleek.*
setwall. The root of the East Indian plant *Curcuma zedoaria.*
share. The fork of the body; groin.
shilling. A silver coin the equivalent in value and weight of 12 pence.
shrift. Auricular confession.
simphatum. See *simple.*
simple. Consisting or composed of one substance, ingredient, or element.
smallage. One or other of several varieties of celery or parsley, especially the wild celery or water parsley, genus *Apium.*
solanum. A plant of the nightshade family (*Solanaceae*), or the genus of plants the petals of which are fused.
solutive. Laxative.
sorrel. *Rumex acetosa:* a short, perennial plant with oblong leaves.
spikenard. An aromatic substance obtained from the Northern Indian *Nardostachys jatamansi* plant, of the family *Valerianaceae.*
spirit. The animating or vital principle in animate beings the gives life to the physical body; the breath of life.
stilled. Distilled. A substance that has been heated to vaporous form and then condensed, a process thought to purify substances.

storax. A fragrant gum resin.
sweating sickness. A fatal epidemic causing high fevers and death in the sixteenth century.
tallow. A substance of somewhat hard animal fat separated by melting and clarifying from the membranes naturally mixed with it.
terra lemnia. An astringent bole, of fatty consistence and reddish color, obtained from the Greek island of Lemnos. Also called *terra sigillata.*
terra sigillata. See *terra lemnia.*
tisane. A medicinal tea or infusion made from herbs.
theriac. See *treacle.*
threepence. Three pennies; a coin of this value, originally of silver (a three-penny piece).
treacle. A medicinal salve composed of many ingredients, formerly in repute as an antidote to poisons. Also called *theriac.*
turpentine. The semifluid resin of the terebinth tree, *Pistacia terebinthus.*
unicorn horn. A horn, often in powdered form, alleged to be obtained from the legendary unicorn.
valerian. *Valeriana officinalis:* a hardy perennial flowering plant, with heads of sweetly scented pink or white flowers.
vapor. Matter in the form of a steamy or imperceptible exhalation.
ventose. Cupping glass: a warmed vessel used as a suction on the skin for the purpose of drawing humors to the surface.
vervain. *Verbena officinalis:* an herbaceous or semi-woody perennial plant with small mauve flowers. Also called herb of the cross.
virgin wax. Unused or purified bees wax.
vittal. Victual: whatever is normally required for consumption in order to support life.
wambling. Squeamish.
wormwood. *Artemisia absinthium:* a herbaceous perennial plant, with a woody horizontal stem and spirally greenish-gray, hairy leaves. Also called absinth, which usually refers to the essence of wormwood.

Glossary of Names

Acheron. The mythical river of the Lower World; hence, the infernal regions.

Actius. Actius of Amida (502–75), an early Christian physician in a city of Mesopotamia.

Aelian. Claudius Aelianus (c. 175–235), Roman author and teacher of rhetoric.

Aeolus. The mythic god of the winds.

Aganippe. A fountain on Mount Helicon, sacred to the Muses and giving poetic inspiration.

Aileward, William. William Aylward (fl. 1560), Minister and member of London's protestant elite, about whom little is known but that he had some association with Edmund Grindal, Bishop of London.

Aristophanes (448–380 BCE). Athenian comic dramatist, author of *The Frogs* and *Lysistrata,* among other comedies.

Augenius. Orazio Augenio (1527–1603), Italian physician.

Avicenna. Abū Alī al-Husayn ibn Abd Allāh ibn Sīnā (980–1037), Arabian physician and philosopher who codified western medical knowledge in his famous *Canon of Medicine.*

Bales, Peter (d. 1610?). English writing master and calligrapher famed for his gift to Queen Elizabeth I of a ring inscribed with the Ten Commandments, the Credo, and other devotional texts.

Barker, Christopher (1528/9–99). Royal printer from 1577 to 1594.

Barlow, Frances. Unidentified. (This is perhaps Frances Parker, *née* Barlow [1550/51–1629], the fourth daughter of William Barlow [d. 1568], bishop of Chichester.)

Barnes, Ambrose. Unidentified.

Barrett, Edward, esquire (1581–1644/5). Lord Barrett of Newburgh. William Bullein dedicated *A Dialogue both pleasant and pietyful* to him but given the dates of the *Dialogue* and of Edward's birth, it is more likely that Bullein knew his father, Charles Barrett (1555/6–1584), who in 1578 entertained Queen Elizabeth I at Bellhouse.

Bartley. Alexander Barclay (c. 1484–1552), poet, clergyman, and translator of Brandt's *Ship of Fools.*

Benedictus, Alexander. Alessandro Benedetti (d. 1525), Paduan author of *De Observatione in pestilentia.*

Boner, Bishop. Edmund Bonner (d. 1569), Bishop of London (1539–49, 1553–59), chief prosecutor of heretics under Queen Mary I.

Brigham, Nicholas (d. 1558). English scholar and antiquarian who wrote the inscription for Chaucer's tomb in Westminster Abbey.

Cawood, John (1513/14–72). Royal printer under Mary Tudor, Cawood joined Richard Jugge in this capacity in 1558, printing *A Form to be used in Common prayer* (1563), among other things.

Charlewood, John (d. 1593). London printer with a continuous printing record from 1562 to 1593, he printed *The Number of all those that hath died* (c. 1583).

Charon. In Greek and Latin mythology the name of the ferryman who conveyed the shades of the departed across the river Styx.

Conscience, William. See *William Aileward.*

Creede, Thomas (c. 1554–1616). London printer from 1593 to 1617, he printed a number of Shakespeare's plays as well as Dekker's *The Wonderful Year* (1603).

Cressida. By legend, a self-proclaimed "false" (unconstant) woman, depicted in many medieval and Renaissance retellings of the story of the Trojan War, especially *Troilus and Cressida.*

Cromwell, Thomas (c. 1485–1540). Earl of Essex; chief minister to King Henry VIII from 1532 to 1540.

Darbel. Nicholas de Orbellis (1400–75), Franciscan theologian and philosopher.

Derrick. The most famous hangman at Tyburn, he decapitated the Earl of Essex in 1601.

Dioscorides, Pedanius (c. 40–90). A Greek physician, pharmacologist and botanist.

Duns. John Duns Scotus (1266–1308), English philosopher and theologian.

Ennius. Quintus Ennius (239–169 BCE) was a writer during the period of the Roman Republic, often considered the father of Roman poetry.

Erra Pater. Fictitious author of *Prognosticacton for ever of Erra Pater: A Jew born in Jewry, a Doctor in Astronomy, and Physic,* first published in 1540.

Euripides (480–08 BCE). Tragedian of classical Athens; author of *Alcestis, Medea, Electra,* and *The Bacchae.*

Eusebius (d. 341). Bishop of Nicomedia and Constantinople.

Fabian. *Robert Fabian* (d. 1513), a draper, London alderman, and author of *New Chronicles of England and France* (c. 1504), also known as *Fabian's Chronicle.*

Fernelius. Jean Francois Fernel (1497–1558), French physician and author of *On the Natural Part of Medicine* (1542).

Flora. Mythological goddess of flowers.

Gale, Thomas (d. 1567). London barber-surgeon and author.

Galen. The celebrated physician born at Pergamus in Asia Minor in the second century CE.

Gower, John (d. 1408). English poet, a contemporary of William Langland; author of the lengthy English poem *Confessio amantis.*

Griseld. The stereotype of the patient wife, mentioned by Boccaccio and Chaucer.

Helen. See *Menelaus.*

Helicon. A mythological mountain sacred to the Muses, from which issue the fountains of Aganippe and Hippocrene, sources of inspiration.

Hermes. Messenger of the gods.

Hesiod. Greek poet of about the eighth century BCE; author of *Theogeny* and *Works and Days.*

Hippocrates. Famous ancient Greek physician born about 460 BCE.

Holinshed, Raphahel (d. 1580?). Primary editor and major compiler of the exhaustive history of England, Scotland, and Ireland known as Holinshed's *Chronicles* (1577; expanded and reprinted, 1578).

Hymen. Greek and Roman god of marriage.

Jovis. Jupiter.

Jugge, Richard (c. 1514–77). Bookseller and printer who printed with Cawood *A Form to be used in Common prayer* (1563).

Kingston, John (1553–c. 1584). London printer who printed all three editions of Bullein's *A Dialogue both pleasant and pietyful.*

Linse, Davie. Sir David Lindsey (c. 1490–c. 1555), author of the oldest armorial register in Scotland and member of the royal house of Scotland.

Lucan (39–65 AD). Roman poet and author of the *Pharsalia.*

Lydgate, John (c. 1370–1449/50?). Prior of Hatfield Regis and prolific English poet, known for these early fifteenth century poems: *The Troy Book, The Siege of Theibes,* and *The Fall of Princes.*

Masha'allah ibn Atharī (c. 740–d. 815 AD). Persian Jewish astrologer and astronomer from Basra and author of many influential astrological texts.

Menelaus. In Greek mythology, Spartan husband of Helen; central figure in the Trojan War.

Midas. Mythological king who could turn into gold all that he touched.

Montanus, Johannes Baptista (1498–1551). Italian humanist physician, author, and teacher to famous English physician John Cauis (1510–73).

Paris. Mythological son of Priam, king of Troy, whose affair with Helen, wife of Menelaus, started the Trojan War.

Parnassus. Mount Parnassus, in mythology regarded as the source of poetic inspiration.

Paulus. Paul of Aegina, a seventh century Byzantine Greek physician and author of an influential seven-book medical encyclopedia.

Phlegethon. The name of a mythological river of fire, one of the five rivers of Hades.

Phoebus. Apollo as the god of light or of the sun; the sun personified.

Plato (c. 427–347 BCE). Famous Greek mathematician, philosopher, and founder of the Academy of Athens.

Rasis. Abū Bakr Muhammad ibn Zakarīya Rāzi, a tenth century Persian alchemist, physician, and philosopher.

Rufus of Ephesus (fl. Late first century). Greek physician, anatomist, and prolific author of medical texts, for whom the Pills of Rufus are named.

Saviolo, Vincentio (fl. 1595). Italian swordsman; author of the first English fencing manual.

Skelton. John Skelton (c. 1460–1529), English poet, tutor to the young King Henry VIII, and in 1512, self-appointed *orator regius,* speaker for the king.

Stow, John (1524/25–1605). English historian and author of the *Survey of London* (1598).

Tagus. The longest river on the Iberian peninsula, emptying into the ocean at Lisbon, and mythologically known for golden sands.

Tamburlaine. Tyrant and conqueror in Christopher Marlowe's sixteenth century two-play hit, *Tamburlaine the Great.*

Thuresby, M. Cuthbert. Thomas Dekker dedicated *The Wonderful Year* to this man he calls a "Water bailiff," but there is no record for him, and this has led some to conclude that Dekker made him up, an extension of his satire.

Trallianus. Alexander of Tralles (c. 525–605 BCE), Greek physician; author of *The Twelve Books of Medicine.*

Troynovant. New Troy, an early name for London.

Turnero, Richardo. Richard Turner (d. 1565?), zealous Church of England reformer.

Vincent. Vincent of Beauvais (c. 1190–1264), Dominican friar and author of the encyclopedic *Speculum Maius.*

Wyre, Robert (fl. 1524–56). London printer; he printed a number of the earliest editions of *The Mirror or Glass of health,* in which Moulton's plague remedy figures as the first chapter.

Wolsey, Cardinal (1470/71–1530). Thomas Wolsey, royal minister, archbishop of York, and Cardinal; tried for treason and executed by Henry VIII.

Zoilist. One who follows the Greek critic Zoilus (fourth century BCE), famous for criticism of works attributed to Homer.

General Glossary

a. Expressing position within, situation, etc.: in, with, of.
accompt. Account.
aconited. Poisonous.
ale-conner. Inspector of ale.
almer. Almoner: an official distributor of the alms of another.
ambuscadoes. Ambushes.
angel. An English gold coin, the new issue of the Noble, showing the image of St. Michael the archangel piercing a dragon.
applesquier. A harlot's servant or personal attendant.
auld. Old.
baily. Bailiff: the steward of a landholder, who manages his estate.
bale of dice. Set of dice, usually three.
bairn. A child; a son or daughter.
bait. To feed, especially at a stage of a journey.
ban-dog. Guard dog.
Barnard's blow. Using a decoy to swindle.
basilisk. A reptile of legend, said to be hatched by a serpent from a cock's egg, its look and breath deadly to humans.
Bastinado. A punishment, beating the soles of feet.
baston. A staff or stick used as a weapon or a staff of office.
beadle. One who carries out the mandates of an authority.
bergomaster. Mayor or head of a German town.
blackbill. A military spear.
bly-fox. One like a fox; cunning.
bolt. Projectile; arrow.
bonnet. Cap.
bow-bells. The bells of Bow Church (St. Mary Bow in Cheapside).
brawne. A boar (or swine) as fattened for consumption.
broker. Seller of second-hand goods.
brownbillmen. Watchmen armed with brownbills, a combination spear and battle-axe painted brown.
bull. Bubble.
bumbaste. To beat on the posteriors, to thrash.

bush. A branch or bunch of ivy (perhaps to recall Bacchus), hung up as a vintner's sign.
buskin tragedy. Tragedy signified by the high thick-soled boot worn by actors in ancient Athenian tragedy.
buskins. Half-boots.
butt. Large cask for transporting goods.
butterfirskin. Small casks for containing butter.
byre. A cow-house.
cadente. Falling.
caliver. A light, portable firearm.
canaries. Spanish dance.
canicular days. See *dog days.*
cannon royal. A large gun of a size that requires it to be mounted for firing.
capon-eaters. Eaters of dainty meats, like the capon, which is a castrated cock.
carbuncle. A name applied to precious stones of a red or fiery color. For this reason, a name given to red plague sores.
cart. Vehicle delivering criminals to the gallows.
casement. Window.
cast. Chaste. This may also mean cast-off, depending on the context.
Castalian. Of Castalia, the name of a spring on Mount Parnassus, home of the Muses.
catchpole. A tax-collector; warrant officer who arrests for debt.
caterwauling. Making the sound of cats in heat; howling.
cavil. To raise captious and frivolous objections.
chamber of presence. A place prepared for ceremonial attendance.
chandler. Retail dealer in supplies, once specifically in candles.
chapless. Missing the chap (lower jaw).
charnel-house. A house for dead bodies.
chrysolite. A name formerly given to several different gems of a green color, such as zircon, tourmaline, topaz.
churl. Countryman. Also used as a term of disparagement or contempt; base fellow, villain.
churlish. Intentionally boorish or rude in behavior.
clerk. Churchman of any distinction except the highest.
clout. To patch.
cock-horse. Mounted (as on a horse).
cock-sure. Absolutely secure.
cockney. A derisive name for a townsman or a Londoner.
codware. A pillow case.
cogging. Deceiving.
coil. Disturbance.
common. To make common to others with oneself; to communicate.
compt. To state, to say.

controller. One who takes to task, calls in question, reproves, or censures.
costs. Habits of living; necessities and customs of life.
cousin germane. A near relative.
cozen. To cheat.
crown. See the Medical and Herbal Glossary.
cub. An undeveloped, uncouth, unpolished youth.
curate. A clergyman who has the spiritual charge of a parish (or parochial district); a pastor.
curtal. A horse with its tail cut short or docked.
damosel. A young unmarried lady. Also called *damsel.*
dawpatus. A daw-pate; a bird-head or bird-brain.
deaurate. To gild.
decimo sexto. The smallest size for a book, in which each leaf is one-sixteenth of a full sheet; properly *sexto-decimo* (usually abbreviated 16 mo.).
descant. Melodious accompaniment to a simple musical theme, the *plain-song.*
ding ding. A term of affection.
discumbent. One who reclines at table; a guest at a feast.
distichons. Couplets.
dog days. The days about the time of the rising of the Dog-star, the hottest and least wholesome part of the year. Also called *canicular days.*
dole. Guile, deceit, fraud.
donative. A benefice bestowed freely by a patron.
drab. Dirty and untidy woman; a slut, slattern.
dryads. Wood-nymphs.
dumbshow. Part of a play represented by action without speech.
ecleped. Called.
eftsoons. Soon afterwards.
element. The sky.
esquire. A man belonging to the higher order of English gentry, ranking immediately below a knight.
factor. Benefactor.
fat. Nickname for the well-to-do.
ferme. Food, provision; hence, a banquet, feast.
fold. An enclosed piece of ground forming part of a farm, as a farmyard.
folio. A volume made up of sheets of paper folded once; a volume of the largest size.
footcloth. A richly ornamented cloth laid over the back of a horse or mule, a sign of status.
foisting. Cheating.
fresh-water. Unpracticed; unskilled.
fry. Newly spawned fish.
furlong. The length of a common field, estimated also as the length of a Roman stadium or one-eighth a Roman mile, now roughly 220 acres; a short distance.

gage. Wager.
gall. The secretion of the liver; bile. Also, an excrescence produced on trees, especially the oak, by the action of insects.
genii. Plural of the "genius" of classical pagan belief, the attendant spirit allotted to people at birth to govern fortunes and to conduct them out of the world.
gloss. To comment upon, explain, interpret, especially with respect to a text.
gittern. An old instrument similar to the guitar, strung with a wire; a cithern.
gnato. Latin word for parasite.
goldfinches. Slang for people with plenty of gold.
goll. Hand.
gorbelly. A protuberant belly.
gulch. A glutton or drunkard.
hackneys. Horses kept for hire or servile work, as opposed to war horses.
hail-shot. Small shot which scatters like hail when fired.
hand and seal. Signature and personal seal.
hared. Harried; harassed.
harnessed. Defended; fortified.
harott. Herald.
headborough. A parish officer identical in functions with the petty constable.
hind. Household servant or slave. A *hind* in other contexts more often means a female deer.
hobinolls. A negative term for country folks.
hogsheads. Casks for storing large quantities of liquid.
holpe. Helped.
horn-book. An elementary school book for teaching children to read; a primer.
horse-bread. Bread made of beans, bran, etc. for horses.
hosteler. One who receives, lodges, or entertains guests and strangers.
hothouse. A bathhouse; a brothel. Also called a *stew.*
hundred. A subdivision of a county or shire having its own court.
hamadryads. A wood-nymph fabled to live and die with the tree which she inhabited.
imp. Sapling; figuratively, a child.
imprimis. In the first place.
in fine. In the end.
indeed-la. Stereotypical exclamation of Puritans.
indentures. Agreements.
indue. To invest or endow.
ingram. Ignorant.
inhigh. To elevate.

item. Likewise, also; used to announce each new article in a series.
Jack-sauce. A saucy or impudent fellow.
keeper. Appointed guardian of the quarantined plague-sick.
ken. Know.
kine. Cattle.
kitchen-stuff-wife. Woman whose job it is to collect refuse or waste products of the kitchen.
knot. A flower-bed laid out in a fanciful or intricate design.
lading. Loading.
last. A wooden model of the foot, on which shoemakers shape boots and shoes.
lee shore. A shore that affords shelter from the wind.
letted. Hindered; impeded.
leuer. Rather.
Levant Taffaty. Silky fabric from the Levant.
liberties. Districts within the limits of a county but outside the city walls, having separate legal jurisdiction.
lickerish. Greedy.
limmer. Knavish, scoundrelly.
lob. Country bumpkin.
longanimity. Long-suffering.
lubber. A big, clumsy, stupid fellow, especially one who lives in idleness.
lucrify. To make gain of or by; to turn to account.
lust. To desire.
mantle. Blanket.
mare mortuum. Sea of death.
mark. A measure of weight for gold and silver, roughly eight ounces.
Marie. See *Marry.*
Marry. Variant of Mary: expressing surprise, outrage, etc., or otherwise used to give emphasis.
marybones. The shins: used humorously especially when referring to prayers on one's knees.
mazer. Head.
medin-hills. Dunghills.
merchant's set. See *treble-ruff.*
meritrix. Having the nature of a prostitute.
miching. Lurking.
mickle. Much; great.
middes. The middle part or point; the midst.
middest. Most central; situated in the middle.
minion. Lover.
Morians. Moors.
mouldred. Turned to dust; crumbled; decayed.
mousing. To handle as a cat or bird does a mouse; to claw at and bite.

muckle. Much; great.
muster-book. A register of military personnel.
muster-master. Keeper of the roll-call.
nicebecetur. A fine, dainty, or fashionable girl or woman.
nullafidian. An person of no faith.
octavo. The size of a small book in which a standard printing sheet is folded three times to form a section of eight leaves.
onely. Singly; uniquely. This is an early version of only, which often carries a slightly different connotation than our use of "only" implies.
onset. Began the attack.
or. Ere: before.
ordure. Dung.
orison. Prayer.
out-parish. A parish lying outside the walls or municipal boundaries of a city or town, but for some purpose regarded as belonging to it.
overthwart. Opposed; thwarted.
paucos palabros. Few words.
parable. Able to be readily prepared or procured.
pared. The outer surface sheared off.
pate. Head.
pelf. Possessions.
pence. See *penny* in the Medical and Herbal Glossary.
penny-father. Miser.
perfume. To fumigate.
petty constable. A town or parish officer charges with keeping the peace.
pettifogger. An inferior legal practitioner who dealt with petty cases.
plainsong. A principle melody accompanied by a running melody or *descant.*
plaudite. An appeal for applause at the end of a play.
pikestaff. Walking stick.
pinder's ale. Pinders were employed to impound stray animals, a base job, and likely a base ale.
portas. Porteous: a portable breviary.
pottle pot. A half-gallon pot or tankard.
prave. Corrupt, depraved.
prefidence. Overconfidence.
prelate. A church official of high rank.
pricksong. Written or printed vocal music, as opposed to that sung from memory.
privy council. A body of advisers selected by the sovereign.
provender. Dry food, as hay, oats, for horses.
proviso. Condition.
pursenets. Bag-shaped nets, the mouth of which can be drawn together with cords, used for hunting small animals.
pursey. Fat; short of breath.

quail-pipe. A pipe or whistle for imitating the call of the quail.
rank-riders. Reckless riders.
raze. Wear off; scrape off.
resets. Receipts; recipes.
rochets. Vestments.
rogue. One of various kinds of beggars and vagabonds.
rooks. Crows. Often applied to persons as an abusive or disparaging term.
rowfooted. Rough footed.
ruthful. Full of compassion or pity.
sallet. In medieval armor, a light, globular headpiece.
satingull. A simpleton dressed in finery.
scapes. Children born out of wedlock.
scrubbing. Beggarly.
scud. To hustle.
sea-card. Chart of the sea.
sellers. Storehouses or cellars where wine or ale is kept.
sepulture. Burial.
sexton. A church officer with oversight of material affairs: ringing the bells, digging graves.
sharkers. Cheaters.
shift themselves. Change.
shilling. See the Medical and Herbal Glossary.
sidesmen. Persons elected as assistants to the churchwardens of a parish.
single sole. Having a single thickness of material in the sole; poor.
sithen(ce). Since.
skill. To avail, help.
sluttish. Untidy.
snaffle. Bridle bit.
snap-hance. A spring catch or fastening.
soothly. Truthful.
sop. A piece of bread or the like dipped or steeped in water, wine, etc., before being eaten or cooked.
sops and muscadine. Bread soaked in spiced wine, a traditional item at weddings.
sounding lead. Lead attached to a line to determine the depth of water.
souter. A slang word for a shoemaker, employed as a term of abuse.
spar. To fasten (a door or gate) with a bar or bold; to close firmly or securely.
spurgalled. Spurred to injury; vexed.
stamell. Course wool cloth.
standish. A stand containing ink, pens and other writing materials and accessories.
starting hole. A hole in which a hunted animal (or person) takes refuge (from the law).
states. A legislative assembly representing the three estates (clergy, nobles, commons); persons of note.

staves end. At a distance, away from close quarters or familiarity.
stay. The action of stopping or bringing to a stand or pause.
stew. A heated room for baths or *hothouse;* a brothel.
stoned. Castrated.
stripe. Lash or beating; stroke of divine judgment.
stripling. A youth, one just passing from boyhood to manhood.
Swizzer. A Swiss.
tablemen. Pieces used in a board game.
tallow. A substance of somewhat hard animal fat separated by melting and clarifying from the membranes naturally mixed with it.
tapster. A man or woman employed to draw the beer for ale-house customers.
thatcher. One whose job it is to thatch houses, corn, or haystacks, for protection.
tinker. A craftsman (usually itinerant) who mends metal household utensils.
tippling. The drinking of intoxicating beverages.
torrid zona. Torrid zone; the region of the earth between the tropics.
tosspots. Heavy drinkers.
treble-ruff. A starched linen or muslin triple ruffle about the neck; an article of high cost and fashion.
treetrip. A game (otherwise unidentified).
triplicity. A combination of three of the twelve signs of the zodiac, each distant 120 degrees or the third part of a circle from the other two.
troth. Truth, faithfulness.
trowe. Trust.
tue. A hunting cry.
ve ve ve. An expression of woe.
Venus. The desire for sexual intercourse; indulgence of sexual desire.
vintner. Wine merchant or seller.
viz. Namely; short for *videlicet.*
vowson. Patronage for.
wallet. Knapsack.
wambling. Rolling; wriggling.
wicket. Any small gate for foot passengers.
winching. Recoiling or resisting.
wight. A living being; a person.
wist / wit. To know.
wonted. Accustomed.
worm. To extract the "worm" from the tongue of a dog; a practice used to prevent madness; often applied figuratively to humans.
writhen. Twisted.

Suggestions for Further Reading

Berry, Herbert. "A London Plague Bill for 1592, Crich, and Goodwyffe Hurde." *English Literary Renaissance* 25, no. 1 (1995): 3–25.

Bower, Rick. "Antidote to the Plague: Thomas Dekker's Storytelling in *The Wonderfull Yeare* (1603)." *English Studies* 73, no. 3 (1992): 229–39.

Bullen, Mark W., and A. H. Bullen, eds. *A Dialogue Against the Fever Pestilence by William Bullein.* Early English Text Society 52. New York: Trubner, 1888.

Carmichael, Ann G. "Universal and Particular: The Language of Plague, 1348–1500." In *Pestilential Complexities: Understanding Medieval Plague,* edited by Vivian Nutton, 17–52. Medical History 27. London: The Wellcome Trust Centre for the History of Medicine at UCL, 2008.

Creighton, Charles. *A History of Epidemics in Britain.* 2 vols. Cambridge: The University Press, 1891–94.

Dobson, Mary J. *Contours of Death and Disease in Early Modern England.* Cambridge Studies in Population, Economy and Society in Past Time 29. New York: Cambridge University Press, 1997.

———. *Contours of Death and Disease in Early Modern England.* Cambridge: Cambridge University Press, 2006.

Dyer, Alan. "The Influence of Bubonic Plague in England 1500–1667." *Medical History* 22 (1978): 308–26.

Fissell, Mary E. "The Marketplace of Print." In *Medicine and the Market in England and Its Colonies, c. 1450–1850,* edited by Mark S. J. Jenner and Patrick Wallis, 108–32. New York: Palgrave Macmillan, 2007.

Gilman, Ernest B. *Plague Writing in Early Modern England.* Chicago: University of Chicago Press, 2009.

Gottfried, R. S. *Epidemic Disease in Fifteenth Century England.* New Brunswick, N.J.: Rutgers University Press, 1978.

Greenberg, Stephen. "Plague, the Printing Press, and Public Health in Seventeenth-Century London." *Huntington Library Quarterly* 67, no. 4 (2004): 508–27.

Grigsby, Byron Lee. *Pestilence in Medieval and Early Modern English Literature.* New York: Routledge, 2004.

Grindal, Edmund. *The Remains of Edmund Grindal, Successively Bishop of London and Archbishop of York and Canterbury*. Edited by William Nicholson. Parker Society Publications 19. Cambridge: Cambridge University Press, 1968.

Harding, Vanessa. "Burial of the Plague Dead in Early Modern London." In *Epidemic Disease in London*, edited by J. A. I. Champion, Center for Metropolitan History, Working Paper Series 1 (1993): 53–64. Accessible online: http://www.history.ac.uk/cmh/epiharding.html. Accessed May 25, 2009.

Harris, Jonathan Gil. *Sick Economies: Drama, Mercantilism, and Disease in Shakespeare's England*. Philadelphia: University of Pennsylvania Press, 2004.

Hawkins, Ann Hunsaker, and Marilyn Chandler McEntyre. *Teaching Literature and Medicine*. New York: Modern Language Association, 2000.

Healy, Margaret. "Anxious and Fatal Contacts: Taming the Contagious Touch." In *Sensible Flesh: On Touch in Early Modern Culture*, edited by Elizabeth D. Harvey, 222–38. Philadelphia: University of Pennsylvania Press, 2000.

———. "Discourses of the plague in early modern London." *Epidemic Disease in London*, edited by J. A. I. Champion, Center for Metropolitan History, Working Paper Series 1 (1993): 53–64. Accessible online: http://www.history.ac.uk/cmh/epiheal.html.

———. *Fictions of Disease in Early Modern England: Bodies, Plagues and Politics*. New York: Palgrave MacMillan, 2001.

Hibbard, G. R., ed. *Three Elizabethan Pamphlets*. London: George G. Harrap and Company, 1951.

Hobby, Elaine, ed. *The Midwives Book; or, The Whole Art of Midwifry Discovered: Jane Sharp*. Women Writers in English, 1350–1850. Oxford: Oxford University Press, 1999.

Horrox, Rosemary, trans. and ed. *The Black Death*. Manchester Medieval Sources Series. Manchester: Manchester University Press, 1994.

Houlbrooke, Ralph. *Death, Religion, and the Family in England, 1480–1750*. Oxford Studies in Social History. New York: Oxford University Press, 1998.

Keiser, George R. "Two Medieval Plague Treatises and Their Afterlife in Early Modern England." *Journal of the History of Medicine and Allied Sciences* 58, no. 3 (2003): 292–324.

Mack, Arien, ed. *In Time of Plague: The History and Social Consequences of Lethal Epidemic Disease*. New York: New York University Press, 1991.

Manley, Lawrence. *Literature and Culture in Early Modern England*. Cambridge: Cambridge University Press, 1995.

Martin, A. Lynn. *Plague? Jesuit Accounts of Epidemic Disease in the Sixteenth Century.* Sixteenth Century Studies 28. Missouri: Sixteenth Century Journal, 1996.

Maslen, R. W. "The Healing Dialogues of Doctor Bullein." *Yearbook of English Studies* 38, no. 1 (2008): 119–35.

———. Introduction to *News from Gravesend: Sent to Nobody,* by Thomas Dekker and Thomas Middleton. In *Thomas Middleton: The Collected Works,* edited by Gary Taylor and John Lavagnino, 128–31. Oxford: Oxford University Press, 2008.

McConchie, R. W. *Lexicography and Physicke: The Record of Sixteenth-Century English Medical Terminology.* Oxford: Clarendon Press, 1997.

McCutcheon, Elizabeth. "William Bullein's *Dialogue Against the Fever Pestilence:* A Sixteenth-Century Anatomy." In *Miscellanea Moreana: Essays for Germain Marc'hadour,* edited by Clare M. Murphy, Henri Gibaud, and Mario A. Di Cesare, 342–59. Binghamton, N.Y.: Medieval & Renaissance Texts & Studies, 1989.

McKeithen, Anne. "Dating the First English Plague Orders: 1578?" In *The Plague Book.* University of Virginia Historical Collections at the Claude Moore Health Sciences Library. Available online at http://historical.hsl.virginia/plague/mckeithen.cfm. Accessed September 20, 2009.

McKerrow, R. B., ed. *A Dictionary of Printers and Booksellers in England, Scotland and Ireland, and of Foreign Printers of English Books 1557–1640.* London: Blades, East & Blades, 1910.

Mullett, Charles F. *The Bubonic Plague and England.* Lexington: University of Kentucky Press, 1956.

Munkhoff, Richelle. "Searchers of the Dead: Authority, Marginality, and the Interpretation of Plague in England, 1574–1665." *Gender & History* 11, no. 1 (1999): 1–29.

———. "God's Arithmetick: Women and the Reckoning of Plague in Early Modern London." In *Rhetorics of Bodily Disease and Health in Medieval and Early Modern England,* edited by Jennifer Vaught. Ashgate Press, forthcoming.

Neill, Michael. *Issues of Death: Mortality and Identity in English Renaissance Tragedy.* New York: Oxford University Press, 1997.

Pelling, Margaret. *The Common Lot: Sickness, Medical Occupations, and the Urban Poor in Early Modern England,* London: Longman, 1998.

———. *Medical Conflicts in Early Modern London: Patronage, Physicians, and Irregular Practitioners, 1550–1640.* Oxford: Oxford University Press, 2003.

Pendry E. D., ed. *Thomas Dekker: Selected Prose Writings.* Cambridge, Mass.: Harvard University Press, 1968.

Plomer, Henry R. *A Dictionary of the Booksellers and Printers Who Were at Work in England, Scotland, and Ireland, from 1641 to 1667.* London: The Bibliographical Society, 1968.

Rappaport, Steve. *Worlds within Worlds: Structures of Life in Sixteenth-Century London.* Cambridge Studies in Population, Economy, and Society in Past Time. Cambridge: Cambridge University Press, 1989.

Robertson, J. C. "Reckoning with London: Interpreting the *Bills of Mortality* before John Graunt." *Urban History* 23 (1996): 325–50.

Shrewsbury, J. F. D. *A History of the Bubonic Plague in the British Isles.* Cambridge: Cambridge University Press, 1970.

Singer, Dorothea Waley, and Annie Anderson. *Catalog of Latin and Vernacular Plague Tracts in Great Britain and Eire in Manuscripts Written before the Sixteenth Century.* Collection de Travaux de L'Académie Internationale d'Histoire des Sciences, no. 5. London: Heineman, 1950.

Slack, Paul. *The Impact of Plague in Tudor and Stuart England.* Oxford: Oxford University Press, 1985.

Steel, David. "Plague Writing from Boccaccio to Camus." *Journal of European Studies* 11, no. 2 (1981): 88–110.

Sutherland, Ian. "When Was the Great Plague? Mortality in London, 1563 to 1665." *Population and Social Change,* edited by D. V. Glass and Roger Revelle, 289–89. London: Edward Arnold, 1972.

Totaro, Rebecca. *Suffering in Paradise: The Bubonic Plague in English Literature from More to Milton.* Pittsburgh: Duquesne University Press, 2005.

———. "Chicken Soup (and Orange Juice) for the Plague-Time Soul? Francis Bacon's Utopian Prescription." *English Language Notes* 47 (Spring 2010).

———. "Plague's Messengers: Communicating Hope and Despair in England 1500–1700." *Journal of the Washington Academy of Science* 89, no. 1–2 (2003): 87–94.

Totaro, Rebecca, and Ernest B. Gilman, eds. *Representing the Plague in Early Modern England.* New York: Routledge, 2010.

Twigg, Graham. "Plague in London: Spatial and Temporal Aspects of Mortality." In *Epidemic Disease in London,* edited by J. A. I. Champion, Center for Metropolitan History, Working Paper Series 1 (1993): 1–17. Accessible online: http://www.history.ac.uk/cmh/epitwig.html. Accessed May 25, 2009.

University of Virginia. *The Plague Book.* Historical Collections at the Claude Moore Health Sciences Library. Available online at http://historical.hsl.virginia.edu/plague/cfm. Accessed September 20, 2009.

Waage, Frederick. *Thomas Dekker's Pamphlets, 1603–1609, and Jacobean Popular Literature.* Salzburg: Institut für Englische Sprache und Literatur, 1977.

Wear, Andrew. "Fear, Anxiety, and the Plague in Early Modern England: Religious and Medical Responses." In *Religion, Health, and Suffering,* edited by J. Hinnels and Roy Porter, 339–63. London: Routledge and Kegan Paul, 1999.

———. *Knowledge and Practice in Early Modern English Medicine, 1550–1680.* New York: Cambridge University Press, 2000.

Webster, Charles, ed. *Health, Medicine, and Mortality in the Sixteenth Century.* Cambridge: Cambridge University Press, 1979.

Wilson, F. P., ed. *The Plague Pamphlets of Thomas Dekker.* Oxford: Clarendon Press, 1925.

———. *The Plague in Shakespeare's London.* Oxford: Oxford University Press, 1927.

Yachnin, Paul. Introduction to *The Meeting of Gallants at an Ordinary; or, The Walks in Paul's,* by Thomas Middleton and Thomas Dekker. In *Thomas Middleton: The Collected Works,* edited by Gary Taylor and John Lavagnino, 183–85. Oxford: Oxford University Press, 2008.

Index

www.ingramcontent.com/pod-product-compliance
Lightning Source LLC
Chambersburg PA
CBHW020923110726
47900CB00001B/279
9780271087283